THE HUMAN BODY

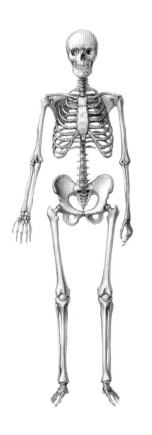
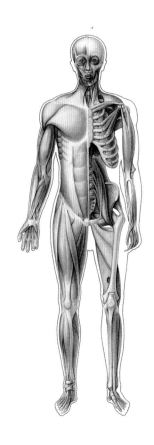
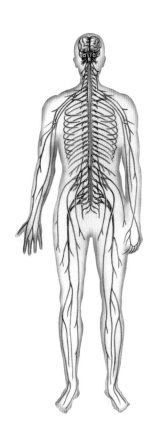

Derek Hall

Grange
BOOKS

This edition published in 2005 by Grange Books
an imprint of Grange Books Plc
The Grange
Kingsnorth Industrial Estate
Hoo, Near Rochester
Kent ME3 9ND
www.Grangebooks.co.uk

© 2005 The Brown Reference Group plc

ISBN: 1-84013-810-6 (paperback)
ISBN: 1-84013-791-6 (hardback)

Printed in China

Editorial and design:
The Brown Reference Group plc
8 Chapel Place
Rivington Street
London
EC2A 3DQ
UK
www.brownreference.com

PHOTOGRAPHIC CREDITS
Brindo Books: 63; **The Brown Reference Group
plc:** 13, 58; **Derek Hall and Associates:** 141 (top),
191, 194, 195; **Eddison Sadd Editions:** 159; **Frank
Spooner Pictures:** Roger Job/Gamma 114 (left), Mike
Persson/Gamma 90; **Image Select International (ISI):**
117, 181, Chris Fairclough 46, 52, 54, 72-73, 77, 91,
95, 96, 99, 105, 107 (top), 122, 123 (top left), 123
(bottom right), 124, 129 (bottom), 142-143, 144,
145, 157, 164-165, 192; **ISI/Allsport:** 181; **ISI/Alton
Towers:** 117; **Richard Greenhill:** 70, 87, 98-99, 131,
139, 143; **Sally Greenhill:** 53, 56, 60, 80, 83, 86, 97,
104, 110, 111, 125 (top left), 132, 137 (top), 138,
149, 156, 183; **Sally and Richard Greenhill:** 73,
82 (bottom), 84, 88, 101, 125 (top right), 127,
137 (center), 137 (bottom), 160 (right), 187; **Philip
Raby/911 and Porsche World:** 50; **Robert Harding
Picture Library:** 48, 75, 78-79, 129 (top), 134, 150,
151, 162, 196, International Stock/Scott Barrow 128,
Mark Bolster 85 (top), 85 (bottom) 178, C. Bowman
160 (left) 160, Martyn F. Chillmaid 112, Robert Francis
62, William Maughan 118, The Picture Book Ltd 93,
Silvestris/Siegried Kerscher 107 (bottom), Charlie
Westerman 82 (top), Adam Woolfitt 135, 182;
Science Photo Library: Simon Fraser/NCCT, Freeman
Trust, Newcastle-upon-Tyne 175, Petit Format/Nestle
146; **St. John Ambulance:** 180; **The Stock Market:**
47, 66, 71, 74, 79, 81, 92-93, 94, 100, 108, 113,
114-115, 140, 141 (bottom), 167, 186, Richard Abarno
188, John Feingersh 31, Elizabeth Hathon 126, Michael
Heron 197, Ronnie Kaufman 184, 190, Tom and Deeann
McCarthy 133, Gabe Palmer 130, Pete Saloutos 120,
Norbert Schafer 102, Ariel Skelley 109.

CONTENTS

INTRODUCTION

THE HUMAN BODY can be thought of as a complicated living machine. It needs energy in the form of food to make it work, it has its own in-built monitoring systems, and it can usually be repaired when it fails. The result of millions of years of gradual modification and improvement, the human body is versatile and adaptable and is capable of performing remarkable physical and mental feats.

This chapter deals with the structure and functions of our key body systems. We look at all the major types of cells, tissues, and organs. The brain and the senses are considered in *The Brain and Senses* (pages 38–71).

How Cells Are Arranged

The basic "building unit" of all living things is the cell. The human body is made up of billions of cells. Some of these cells are put together in the body to form tissues. Among the most common tissues are muscles and bones. In certain parts of the body, different tissues are combined to form organs. Organs do specific jobs. For example, the heart is an organ whose task is to pump blood around the body.

The body is further organized into a series of systems. Systems are groups of organs and tissues that together are responsible for carrying out all the major body functions. For our bodies to remain healthy, all the systems need to be working efficiently and with each other. The systems described below are dealt with later in the chapter.

Body Systems

The **skeletal system** provides a bony framework and support for other parts of the body. The bones also play a major role in the production of blood cells and minerals. The **muscular system** enables movement to occur. The **nervous system**— the brain, spinal cord, and nerves—controls our thoughts and actions and helps monitor the other systems. The heart and blood vessels make up the **cardiovascular system**, whose prime function is to pump blood around the body. Cardiac (heart) muscle beats continuously throughout our lives without getting tired. Closely associated with the cardiovascular system is the **respiratory system**. This allows oxygen from the air to enter the bloodstream via the blood vessels that surround the lungs and for waste carbon dioxide to be expelled.

The **digestive system's** main function is the digestion and absorption of food and the elimination of waste products. The **urinary system** removes soluble waste and helps maintain the body's salts and water balance. The female and male **reproductive systems** are responsible for the creation of new individuals. The **endocrine system** consists of a series of glands that secrete chemicals known as hormones into the bloodstream and other body fluids to help maintain the body's internal equilibrium. Finally, there is the **immune system** (see *Health and Illness*, pages 154–155) whose task is to help defend against infectious diseases and foreign bodies.

fact file

Elements that make up the human body are: oxygen (65%), carbon (18.5%), hydrogen (9.5%), nitrogen (3.2%), calcium (1.5%), phosphorus (1%), other elements (1.3%).

Our bodies contain nearly 200 different types of cells.

Nearly 70% of the body is made up of water.

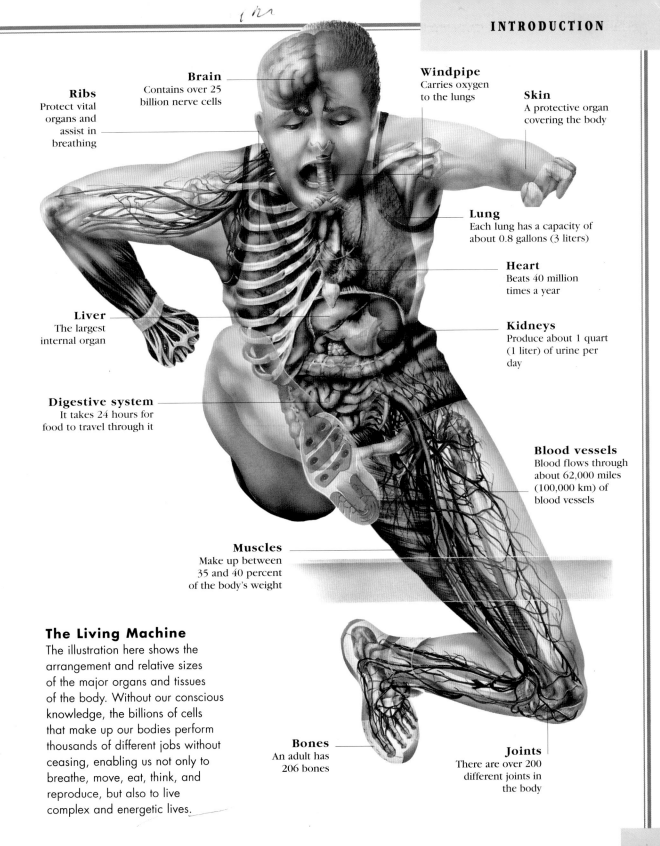

Brain
Contains over 25
billion nerve cells

Windpipe
Carries oxygen
to the lungs

Skin
A protective organ
covering the body

Ribs
Protect vital
organs and
assist in
breathing

Lung
Each lung has a capacity of
about 0.8 gallons (3 liters)

Heart
Beats 40 million
times a year

Liver
The largest
internal organ

Kidneys
Produce about 1 quart
(1 liter) of urine per
day

Digestive system
It takes 24 hours for
food to travel through it

Blood vessels
Blood flows through
about 62,000 miles
(100,000 km) of
blood vessels

Muscles
Make up between
35 and 40 percent
of the body's weight

The Living Machine

The illustration here shows the
arrangement and relative sizes
of the major organs and tissues
of the body. Without our conscious
knowledge, the billions of cells
that make up our bodies perform
thousands of different jobs without
ceasing, enabling us not only to
breathe, move, eat, think, and
reproduce, but also to live
complex and energetic lives.

Bones
An adult has
206 bones

Joints
There are over 200
different joints in
the body

CELLS

THE HUMAN BODY is made up of more than 50 billion cells, and there are more than 200 different kinds of varying sizes and shapes. These tiny but vital structures were first given the name "cell" by the 17th-century scientist Robert Hooke, who thought that the internal structure of the plant tissue cork looked similar to the cells used by monks in monasteries.

Most of the cells in the human body are so small that they are invisible to the naked eye. Even the largest cell in the body, the female egg or ovum, is no bigger than a small dot. Yet these tiny structures carry out all the processes of life. They can move, breathe, reproduce, respond to stimuli, and generate energy. They also collectively form all the components of the body.

When viewed under a microscope, a cell appears as a bag-like structure surrounded by a double-layered coating, called the cell membrane. The cell membrane encloses a jellylike substance, the cytosol, in which are embedded tiny structures called organelles. Organelles carry out the cell's activities. The organelles and cytosol are together called cytoplasm.

Organelles

The largest organelle is usually the **nucleus**. It is the control center and contains the hereditary material that ensures the cell will reproduce itself correctly. **Mitochondria** are the site of both respiration and energy production. **Lysosomes** break down harmful substances and remove waste. **Ribosomes** assist in the production of proteins. The **centrioles** play an important part in cell division. **Endoplasmic reticulum** acts

Types of Cell

Cells in the human body (left) are modified for different tasks. Thus sperm cells have a tail for swimming; red blood cells are packed with hemoglobin; epithelial cells of the stomach have brushlike borders to increase the surface area for absorption; muscle cells form elongated bundles of tissue.

Cell Structure

The illustration (right) shows a typical human cell as seen from the outside and in cross-section. Most human cells are too small to see without high magnification.

as a pathway for materials through the cell and for making protein. The **golgi apparatus** processes proteins before release at the cell membrane. **Microtubules** provide a frame-work for the cell and assist in the movement of materials.

DNA

The cell nucleus contains the material that is necessary for cell division and duplication. It is a molecule called DNA (deoxyribonucleic acid). Cells duplicate by dividing (see pages 36–37). During this process the nucleus breaks down, and DNA forms paired, threadlike struc-tures called chromosomes. Each chromosome is made up of a series of genes. Genes carry codes that the cell can read so it can manufacture the chemi-cals that form the cell and control its activities.

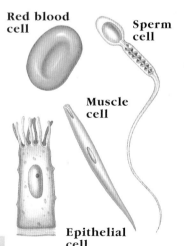

Red blood cell

Sperm cell

Muscle cell

Epithelial cell

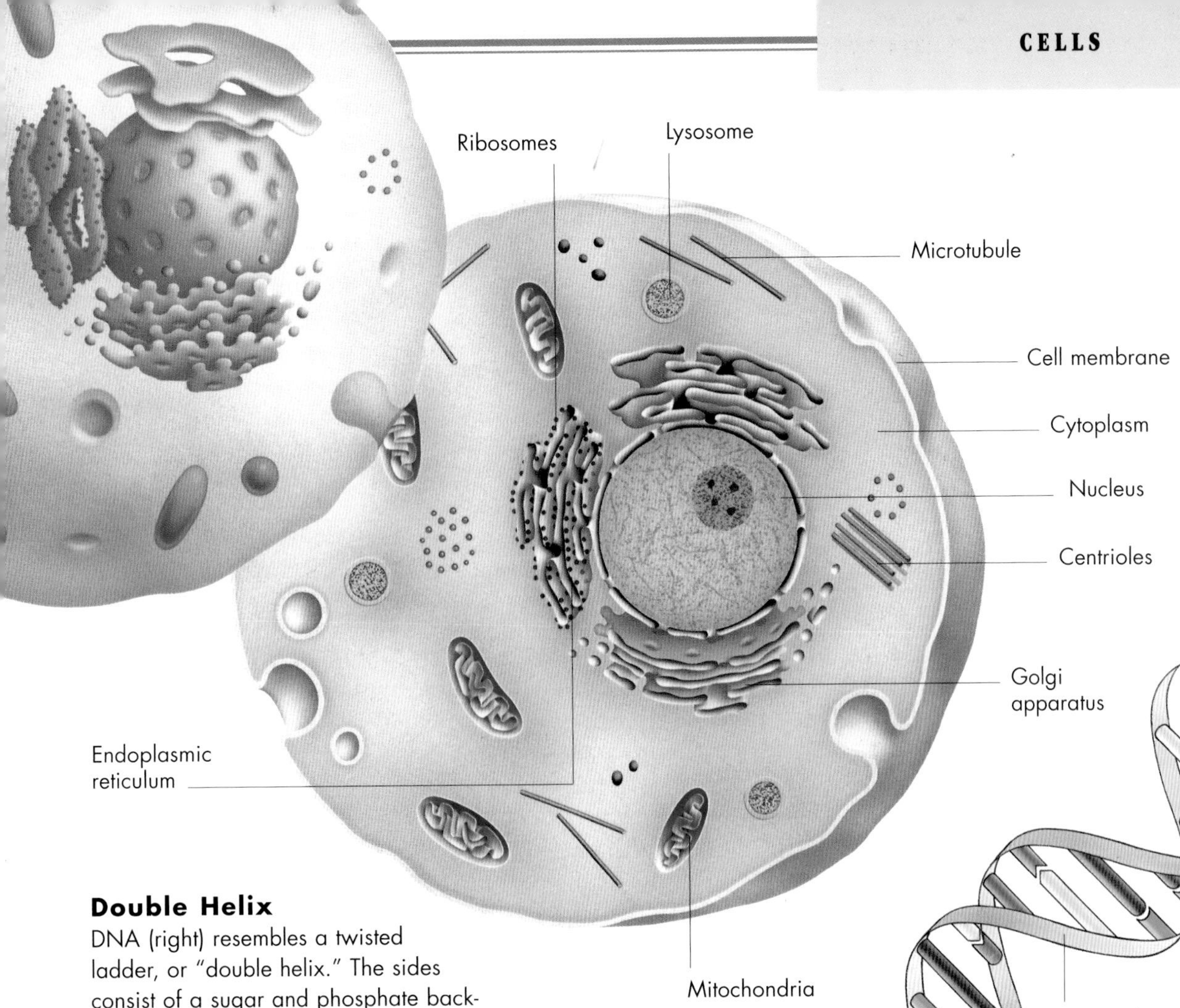

Ribosomes

Lysosome

Microtubule

Cell membrane

Cytoplasm

Nucleus

Centrioles

Golgi
apparatus

Endoplasmic
reticulum

Mitochondria

Double Helix

DNA (right) resembles a twisted ladder, or "double helix." The sides consist of a sugar and phosphate backbone, with pairs of chemicals called bases forming the rungs. The bases are cytosine, guanine, thymine, and adenine. Cytosine links only with guanine, and thymine links only with adenine. When a DNA molecule splits, it "unzips," breaking the base links and leaving one of each base pair attached to one or the other side of the original DNA ladder. These single strands now act as a template for making new strands with matching bases. The original molecule thus produces a matching pair of molecules, each of which has one original strand and one new strand.

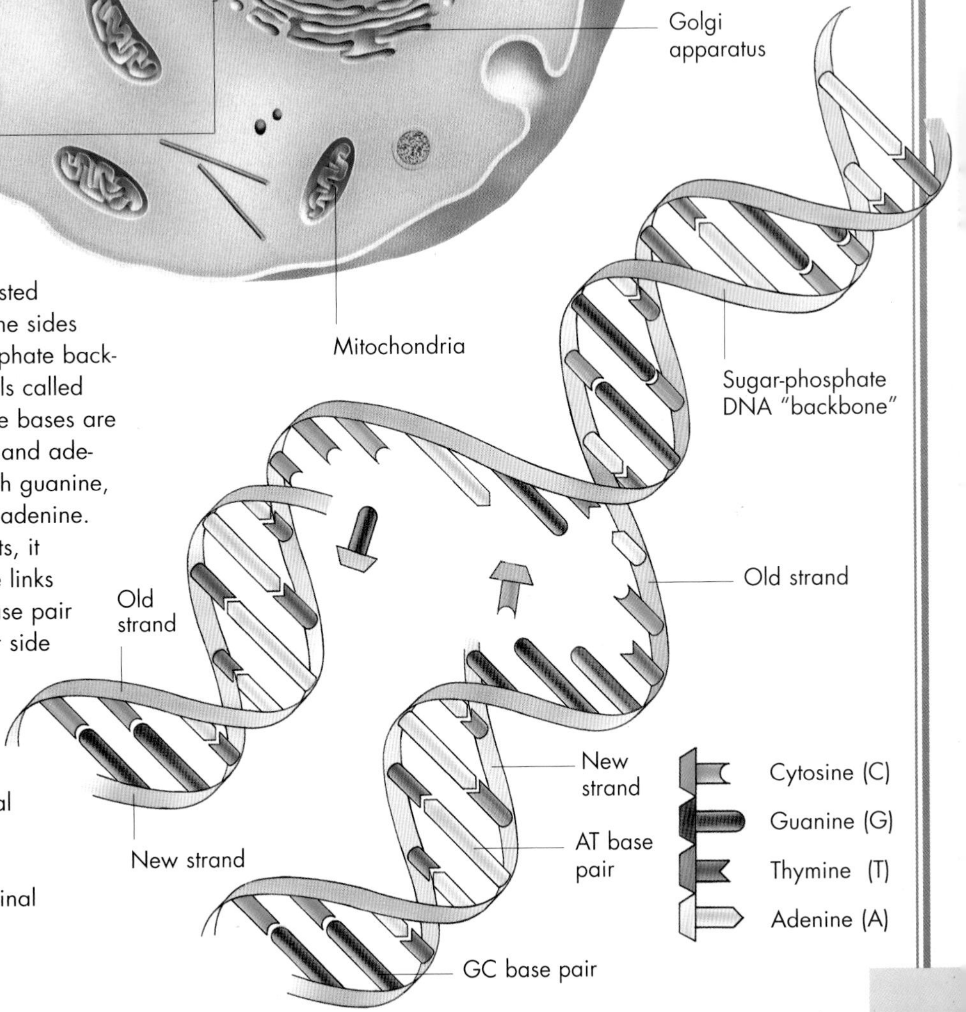

Sugar-phosphate
DNA "backbone"

Old strand

Old
strand

New
strand

AT base
pair

New strand

GC base pair

Cytosine (C)

Guanine (G)

Thymine (T)

Adenine (A)

TISSUES AND ORGANS

TISSUES ARE GROUPS of similar cells that form the main fabric of not only the human body but also the bodies of nearly all plants and animals. Some tissues are soft, like the inner layers of the skin, the tissues of the liver, and muscle tissue, and others are hard, such as bone and fingernails. Organs combine tissues of more than one kind and do specific tasks to help the body work.

Tissues are grouped together according to the role they play in the body. In this section we look at all the major kinds of tissues and also at some of the different tissues and their functions.

We also see how different sorts of tissues combine to form organs. (Many of the body's major organs—such as the **heart, lungs, stomach, liver, sex organs**, and **kidneys**—and the part they play in the working of the body are also discussed later in this chapter.)

Types of Tissue

Epithelial tissue covers the internal and external surfaces of the body. It usually lies over connective tissue and consists of layers of cells packed closely together. The simplest type of epithelial cells are found lining blood vessels, the lungs, the eardrum, and the heart cavity. They consist of a single layer of flattened cells. The epithelial cells of the digestive system are much thicker and secrete enzymes and mucus. The epithelial cells that line the

respiratory passages have tiny beating hairs that keep mucus flowing. The bladder is lined with transitional epithelial cells. These can stretch as the bladder fills with urine.

The outer parts of the body, such as the skin, are composed of a tough, multilayered epithelium, the outermost layers of which have a horny substance called keratin in them. Finally, some epithelial cells form glands. The contents of these cells empty into a central cavity or diffuse into the blood.

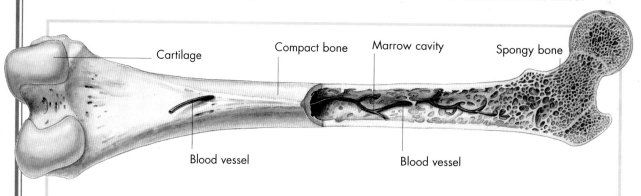

Cartilage — Compact bone — Marrow cavity — Spongy bone

Blood vessel — Blood vessel

Bone

Bone is a specialized connective tissue. Bones are not solid but have a hollow marrow cavity. Within the marrow, millions of

new red blood cells are produced daily. The outer layer of a bone, such as the femur shown here, consists of hard, compact bone

cells surrounding lighter, spongy bone. Blood vessels and nerves run in channels through the outer layers to the hollow center.

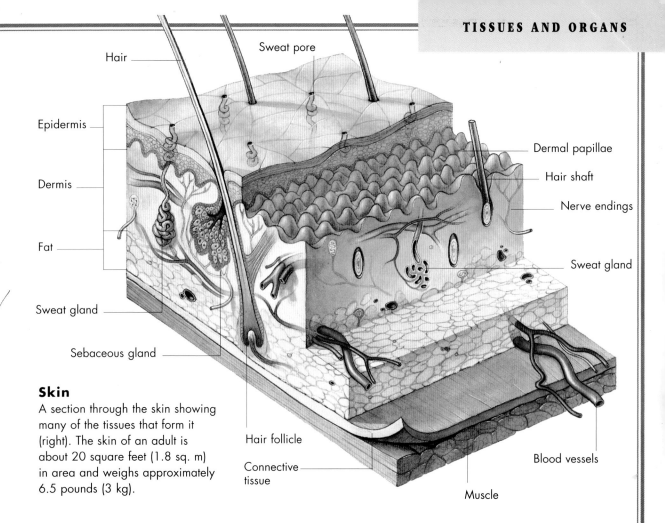

Hair

Sweat pore

Epidermis

Dermis

Fat

Sweat gland

Sebaceous gland

Dermal papillae

Hair shaft

Nerve endings

Sweat gland

Hair follicle

Connective tissue

Blood vessels

Muscle

Skin

A section through the skin showing many of the tissues that form it (right). The skin of an adult is about 20 square feet (1.8 sq. m) in area and weighs approximately 6.5 pounds (3 kg).

Connective tissue consists of cells surrounded by fibers and other materials. Elastic cartilage contains stretchy fibers. It allows, for example, the epiglottis to vibrate when we speak. Some types of connective tissue are associated with bone: fibrocartilage is found between the vertebral disks; hyaline cartilage caps the ends of bones; dense connective tissue forms ligaments and tendons (see pages 10–11). Loose connective tissue packs and binds organs and carries nerves and blood vessels. Fat is stored in adipose tissue.

Blood (see pages 18–19) is a fluid tissue. The fluid, known as serum, contains three main types of cells—red cells, white cells, and platelets.

Nervous tissue (see pages 14–15) forms a network of nerve cells in the body and also forms the brain and spinal cord.

Lymphatic tissue (see *Health and Illness*, page 155) consists of vessels that extend throughout the body. Embedded in it are white blood cells known as lymphocytes. Lymphocytes can enter the blood system to fight foreign bodies. They are responsible for immune reactions and produce antibodies to neutralize invasive organisms.

Muscle tissue (see pages 12–13) forms the bulk of the soft tissues in a healthy body.

Organs

Organs are structures made up of various types of tissues. Important organs within the body include the brain, heart, liver, eyes, and lungs. The skin is one of the largest organs in the body. It consists of muscle, fat, nerve, blood, and connective tissues, over which are layers of epithelial tissue.

THE SKELETON

THE SKELETON IS the rigid framework of bones inside our bodies. It protects delicate organs such as the brain, heart, and liver, and it enables us to maintain our posture and—by means of attached muscles—to move our limbs and turn our heads. Movements of the rib cage help us to breathe by inflating our lungs, while movements of some of the bones of the skull enable us to eat

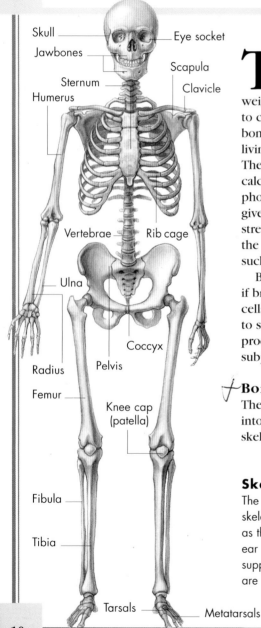

Skull
Jawbones
Sternum
Humerus
Eye socket
Scapula
Clavicle
Vertebrae
Rib cage
Ulna
Coccyx
Radius
Pelvis
Femur
Knee cap (patella)
Fibula
Tibia
Tarsals
Metatarsals

The skeleton is a remarkable structure. It is strong enough to support our weight, yet light enough for us to carry around and move. The bones of the skeleton are vital, living factories within the body. They contain large amounts of calcium, potassium, and phosphorus. These minerals not only give bone its hardness and strength but are also needed by the body for other processes, such as the workings of nerves.

Bones can repair themselves if broken by forming new bone cells. They also have the ability to strengthen themselves by producing extra calcium when subjected to great stresses.

Bones of the Skeleton

The skeleton can be divided into two main parts: the axial skeleton includes the skull, ribs,

Skeletal System

The main bones which make up the skeleton are shown left. Some, such as the three bones of the middle ear and the hyoid bone that supports the muscles of the tongue, are too small to illustrate here.

and bones of the vertebral column and sternum; while the arms, legs, clavicle, scapula, and pelvis together make up the appendicular skeleton.

The skull is made up of 22 bones. The eight bones protecting the brain are called cranial bones. The skull also protects the eyes and ears. The jawbones enable us to eat. The spine, or vertebral column, consists of 26 bones: seven neck bones, 12 thoracic bones, five lumbar bones, and the sacrum and coccyx. Each arm and hand has 32 bones, and

fact file

Babies have about 350 bones, but an adult has 206. As the skeleton grows, some of the smaller bones fuse to form larger ones.

The hands and feet together consist of over 120 bones.

Bones are one of the most durable parts of the body, occasionally lasting for over a million years.

each leg and foot has 31 bones. Most people have 12 pairs of ribs, although a few people are born with one or more additional ribs. Each rib is roughly semicircular and is attached to the sternum at the front and to the thoracic vertebrae at the back. Thus the ribs form a rigid cage around organs such as the heart, the lungs, the stomach, the liver, and the kidneys.

The largest bones are the femurs, accounting for about a quarter of the skeleton's weight. The smallest bone is the stirrup bone in the middle ear (see *The Brain and Senses*, pages 66–67). This bone is only 0.1 inch (3 mm) long.

Attachment for Muscles

It is the action of muscles (see pages 12–13) pulling on bones that allows us to move, and many bones have special surfaces to enable muscles to attach securely. For example, the scapula, or shoulder blade, is a large, flat bone that provides anchorage points for the muscles that together move the bones of the shoulder and arm. Muscles are connected to bones by means of connective tissues called tendons.

Joints

Bones are rigid structures, but they form joints where they meet so that bending, twisting, and turning movements are possible. There are over 200 different joints in the body.

Some joints, like the ones between the skull bones, do not allow movement. In a movable joint, such as the knee (where the femur meets the tibia), the cartilaginous ends of the bones are lubricated by a fluid called synovial fluid. This is secreted by the synovial membrane that encloses the joint. Ligaments surround the joint and help keep it stable during movement.

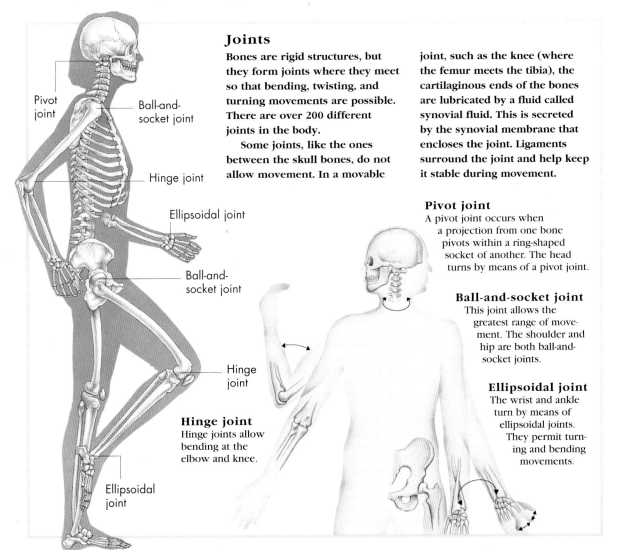

Pivot joint

Ball-and-socket joint

Hinge joint

Ellipsoidal joint

Ball-and-socket joint

Hinge joint

Ellipsoidal joint

Hinge joint
Hinge joints allow bending at the elbow and knee.

Pivot joint
A pivot joint occurs when a projection from one bone pivots within a ring-shaped socket of another. The head turns by means of a pivot joint.

Ball-and-socket joint
This joint allows the greatest range of movement. The shoulder and hip are both ball-and-socket joints.

Ellipsoidal joint
The wrist and ankle turn by means of ellipsoidal joints. They permit turning and bending movements.

MUSCLES AND MOVEMENT

MUSCLES ACCOUNT FOR nearly half the body's total weight and form the bulk of the soft tissue. They provide the forces necessary to move our limbs, keep our heart beating regularly, and control the actions of many of the body's systems.

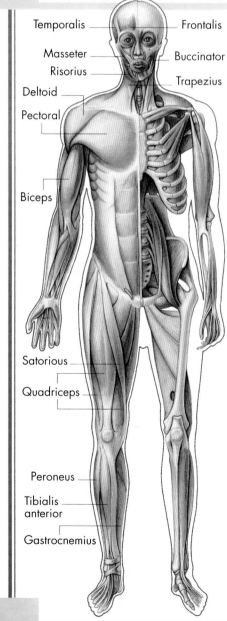

Temporalis
Masseter
Risorius
Deltoid
Pectoral
Biceps
Frontalis
Buccinator
Trapezius
Satorious
Quadriceps
Peroneus
Tibialis anterior
Gastrocnemius

There are three different kinds of muscles in the human body: skeletal, or voluntary, muscle; smooth, or involuntary, muscle; and cardiac, or heart, muscle. They share the ability to contract (shorten) in response to a stimulus, to stretch, and to return to their original shape. Muscles are always arranged in pairs. Since muscles can only pull, it needs an opposite muscle to reverse the movement.

Muscle Structure and Function

Skeletal muscle is made up of tightly packed groups of muscle cells known as fibers, held together by connective tissue. It is richly supplied with blood vessels and nerves. Blood provides the oxygen and glucose that are necessary to generate

Arrangement of Muscles

The illustration (left) shows many of the skeletal muscles. Even when the muscles are not actively moving a limb, they may still be contracting. The contraction, or "tone," gives the body its shape.

the energy for muscle contraction, and the nerves carry the impulses from the brain that initiate the contraction. Skeletal muscle is also called voluntary muscle because its actions are under our conscious control. Skeletal muscles are attached, in pairs, to all the skeletal bones in the body and, by moving our joints, allow us to move our limbs, bend our back, make facial expressions, turn our head, and breathe in and out.

When movements like these are made, several groups of muscles act together under the control of the brain. For instance, raising the leg involves not just the leg muscles but also muscles in the back and hips that adjust the balance and position of the rest of the body.

Smooth muscle is so called because under the microscope its fibers lack the fine cross-markings that are visible on skeletal muscle. Its contractions are also slower than those of skeletal muscle. Smooth muscle encases the digestive system, the uterus, the bladder, and blood vessels. Smooth muscle is also called involuntary muscle because its actions are controlled by the brain without our conscious knowledge. We do not have to think about focusing our eyes or making our stomach churn up food, for example.

Cardiac muscle is found only in the heart. It has the unique property of never getting tired. Cardiac muscle is made of branches of interconnecting fibers that allow nerve impulses to spread rapidly so that it can contract quickly and powerfully. Its activity is also controlled unconsciously by the brain.

How Muscles Contract

Each muscle fiber is made up of millions of tiny filaments. There are two kinds of filaments: short, thick filaments made from a protein called myosin and thin ones made from the protein actin. When muscle fibers contract, the start of the

Muscle Contraction

The action of moving a limb, such as bending the arm shown here, involves sets of muscles working in pairs. First, the biceps muscle contracts, pulling the lower arm bones upward. In order for the arm to straighten, the triceps muscle now contracts, pulling the arm bone down. The movement takes place at a joint, in this case the elbow joint. Sets of muscles that work together like this are called antagonistic muscles.

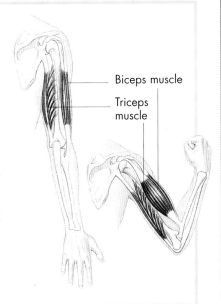

Biceps muscle

Triceps muscle

process is a signal from the brain that travels along a nerve to the muscle. The nerve endings release a chemical, acetylcholine, that makes the actin filaments slide between the myosin filaments. This pulls the ends of the muscle toward the

middle, shortening it. A chemical called ATP produced during respiration (see pages 22–23) provides the energy. During contraction ATP's chemical energy is converted into the mechanical energy needed to slide the molecules together.

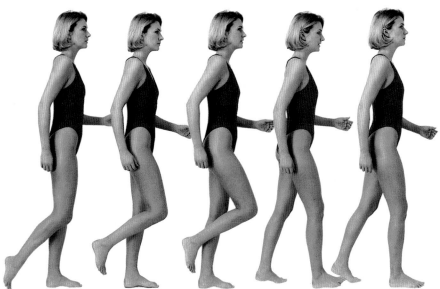

Walking Along

The human body is adapted for a two-legged walking action, or gait, and a complicated movement such as this requires the coordinated activity of many sets of muscles. Not only must each leg be raised and moved forward in turn, but the body must also maintain its balance and rhythm during this process. Notice how the arms are used to help do this (left).

THE NERVOUS SYSTEM

THE NERVOUS SYSTEM is designed to pass messages from one part of the body to another, sometimes at speeds of up to 390 feet (120 m) per second. Nerve endings reach into all parts of the body, from the organs to the skin. Masterminding this remarkable network is the brain, a control center that is capable of coordinating and directing the activities of hundreds of millions of signal pathways.

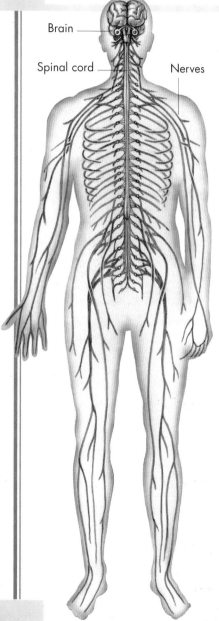

Brain

Spinal cord

Nerves

The nervous system in humans can be divided into two parts. The brain and the spinal cord together are known as the **central nervous system.** The highly complex, delicate brain is protected inside a bony case, the skull.

The spinal cord is a thick bundle of nerve cells that extends from the base of the brain down through the center of the bones of the vertebral column. The spinal cord acts as a pathway, carrying millions of nerve impulses between the brain and the limbs and the trunk.

In cross-section the spinal cord has a gray central part and a white outer part. The white matter is composed of nerve cells that relay impulses up and down the spinal cord. The gray matter controls the transfer of messages from nerve cell to nerve cell.

Passing through spaces between the spinal vertebrae, pairs of spinal nerves radiate from the brain and spinal cord. These nerves branch and extend into all parts of the body and form the second part of the nervous system, namely, the **peripheral nervous system.** The many branching nerve endings of the peripheral nervous system report constantly on events both inside and outside the body. Connections between the nerves of the peripheral nervous system and muscles allow the muscles to be stimulated so that contractions, and hence movements, can occur.

Nervous System

The brain and spinal cord make up the central nervous system. The peripheral nervous system extends into all the organs and tissues of the body. It is formed by the cranial nerves, which branch from the brain, and the spinal nerves, which branch from the spinal cord (left).

Nerve Structure

Individual nerve cells are called neurons. They carry tiny electrical impulses that make up a nerve message. Impulses are relayed to the brain by sensory neurons, and motor neurons carry them away. There are many different kinds of

Nucleus

Cell body

Dendrite

Myelin sheath

Schwann cell

Axon

neurons, varying in size as well as shape. Each type of neuron has a cell body with a nucleus, and radiating from the cell are fine filaments. Most neurons have several short filaments called dendrites and one long filament called an axon. Dendrites receive messages in the form of electrical impulses and pass them to the center of the neuron, and axons carry messages to the dendrites of the next nerve cell. The body's main nerves are composed of bundles of axons.

Surrounding the axon there is often a myelin sheath—a fatty layer that insulates and protects the axon and speeds up impulses.

Transmission of Impulses

When a neuron is stimulated, the impulse travels along it due to minute temporary changes in the electrical charge of the cell membrane. For the impulse to pass along the nerve, it must now bridge the tiny gap (called the synapse) that exists between the ends of all axons and dendrites. As the impulse arrives at the synapse, it causes the release of a chemical called a neurotransmitter. The chemical passes across the gap and activates the next neuron so that the message can continue its journey.

Neurons of the voluntary nervous system carry out the instructions of our conscious thought—for example, walking, talking, or writing. The neurons of the autonomic nervous system carry out activities that occur unconsciously—such as altering the heart rate and controlling the speed at which food is digested.

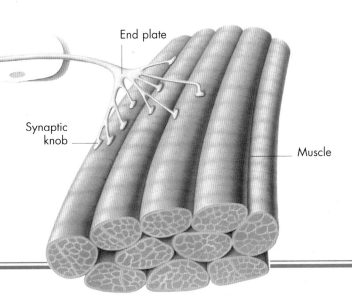

End plate

Synaptic knob

Muscle

Peripheral Nerve

A typical neuron in the peripheral nervous system (above). The neuron divides into many branches before it reaches a muscle. Impulses from the nerve, sent by the brain (or the spinal cord in a reflex reaction), make the muscle fibers contract, resulting in movement.

THE HEART

THE HEART IS the organ responsible for pumping life-giving blood around the body, circulating the entire contents of the blood system approximately once a minute. As it does so, it carries nutrients and oxygen to organs and tissues, and at the same time takes away harmful wastes. Without ceasing or tiring, it beats, on average, 40 million times each year—an incredible three billion times in an average person's lifetime.

The human heart is an organ about the size of a clenched fist. It lies in the chest cavity between the two lungs, but slightly to the left. The heart is made up of a special kind of involuntary muscle called cardiac muscle that does not get tired and can therefore contract (beat) rhythmically and continuously. This is vital, since organs and tissues must be constantly supplied with fresh blood. For example, if the brain is deprived of oxygen for more than a few minutes, brain cells begin to die, and then serious brain damage will occur as a result.

fact file

The heart of a 75-year-old will have pumped enough blood to fill Central Park, New York, to a depth of 50 feet (15 m).

Blood travels through the arteries at about 3.3 feet (1 m) per second.

The human heart beat rate varies between about 30 and 200 beats per minute.

The heart is made up of four separate chambers. These form two separate pumps, lying side by side and separated from each other by a wall of muscle called the septum. The septum prevents the blood from one

Parts of the Heart

A section through the human heart (left). The atria pump blood to the ventricles. The ventricles have much thicker, more muscular walls, since they pump blood to all the other parts of the body.

Superior vena cava

Ascending aorta

Right pulmonary artery

Right pulmonary veins

Right atrium

Right ventricle

Inferior vena cava

Descending aorta

Left pulmonary artery

Left atrium

Left pulmonary veins

Pulmonary valve

Papillary muscles

Left ventricle

Septum

One Complete Heart Beat

1. Deoxygenated blood enters the right atrium, and oxygenated blood enters the left atrium.

2. The atria contract, forcing blood into the ventricles.

3. The ventricles contract, forcing blood out of the heart and into the main arteries—the pulmonary artery leads to the lungs, and the aorta leads to the body's arteries.

The sequence of events that occurs during a single heart beat is called the cardiac cycle. In normal resting adults this cycle takes place about 70 times a minute, but this can double during vigorous exercise.

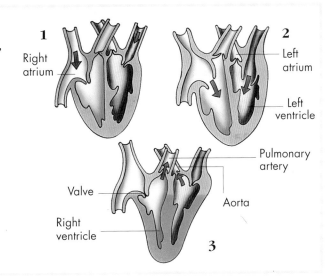

side of the heart mixing with the blood from the other side of the heart. The upper chamber of each side of the heart is called the atrium (plural: atria). The larger, and more powerful, lower chamber of each side is called the ventricle.

The flow of blood between the atrium and the ventricle of each side is controlled by valves made up of fibrous tissue. Valves prevent blood from flowing backward by forming a blood-tight seal and operate by blood pressure. There are also valves at the exit of each of the ventricles.

Because it requires a rich oxygen supply, the heart has its own blood supply, called the coronary system. This envelops the heart but is prevented from mixing with blood being pumped through the heart.

Muscular Contractions

When the muscular walls of the heart contract, the chambers become smaller, forcing blood first out of the atria into the ventricles and then out of the ventricles and into blood vessels known as arteries. The two sides of the heart work together; the right side pumps blood to the lungs to receive oxygen, and the left side pumps oxygenated blood to the body.

The rate at which the heart beats is regulated by the brain stem. Nerve signals can make the heart beat faster or slower. When we are afraid or become excited, hormones released into the bloodstream can also make the rate increase. A special group of heart muscle cells called the pacemaker controls the pace of each heart beat.

check your pulse rate

The left ventricle pumps blood into the arteries in squirts. These squirts make the slight throbbing called a pulse that can be felt in some arteries just beneath the skin. A person's normal resting pulse rate is about 70 beats per minute. Place your first and second finger as shown, and count how many pulses you feel in a minute. After some vigorous exercise quickly check your pulse again. It will have increased but should return to its resting rate within two or three minutes.

THE CARDIOVASCULAR SYSTEM

A VAST NETWORK of large vessels and smaller capillaries forms a complex transportation system 62,000 miles (100,000 km) long that carries life-giving blood to every part of the body through the pumping action of the heart.

Jugular vein

Heart

Aorta

Pulmonary artery

Femoral artery

Femoral vein

Great saphenous vein

The efficient transport of blood is vital for maintaining a healthy body. Blood carries oxygen and food substances and also removes waste products, such as the gas carbon dioxide, made by the cells. The blood also maintains the water content of the body and its chemical balance, or pH, and regulates the body temperature.

There are between 1 and 1.3 gallons (4–5 liters) of blood in a grown woman and 1.3 and 1.6 gallons (5–6 liters) in a man, making up one-sixteenth of the total body weight. Approximately 50 percent of the blood is plasma (water containing proteins and salts), and the rest is composed of red blood cells, white blood cells, and clotting agents.

Blood Cells

Red blood cells, also known as erythrocytes, are flattened, disklike structures without a nucleus. There are about 5 million per 0.06 cubic inch (1 milliliter) of blood, and they are produced, in the bone marrow, at the rate of 2 million every second. The red color of red blood cells comes from the iron in hemoglobin—the chemical that is responsible for carrying oxygen in the blood.

White blood cells, or leukocytes, are larger than red blood cells, and they contain a nucleus. There are about 5,000 per 0.06 cubic inch (1 milliliter) of blood. Some white blood cells (called macrophages) engulf and consume foreign bodies such as bacteria, and others are involved in fighting infections and producing immunity to diseases.

Platelets are small cells that form blood clots on the surface of damaged blood vessels and prevent blood loss.

Circulatory System

Veins—which carry blood to the heart—are shown blue, and arteries—which carry blood away from the heart—are shown red (left). All arteries carry oxygenated blood, except for the pulmonary artery which runs from heart to lungs.

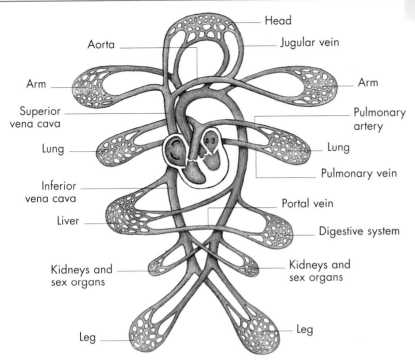

Head
Aorta
Jugular vein
Arm
Arm
Superior vena cava
Pulmonary artery
Lung
Lung
Inferior vena cava
Pulmonary vein
Liver
Portal vein
Digestive system
Kidneys and sex organs
Kidneys and sex organs
Leg
Leg

Vital Transport

Arteries, like the one below, are made up of layers of epithelial cells, connective tissue, and muscle layers. Veins have valves that prevent blood from flowing the wrong way. Within the vessels blood flows throughout the body. There are five main types of white blood cells, making up 10 percent of the total blood volume. Red blood cells are approximately one thousand times more numerous than white blood cells.

Circulation of Blood

Blood is carried by the pulmonary artery to the lungs. Here it receives oxygen before returning to the left side of the heart, where it is pumped to the organs and tissues. After delivering its supply of oxygen, it returns through the veins to the heart. Before blood from the digestive system reaches the heart, it first flows through the liver, where nutrients are deposited (above).

branch to form tiny capillaries. Capillaries carry blood right into the body's tissues. Food and oxygen are transferred across the thin walls of the capillaries and into the cells. Waste products such as carbon dioxide are carried away. Capillaries join again, forming thicker venules. These join with the veins and return blood to the heart.

Blood Vessels

The human body's network of blood vessels extends throughout every part of it, with minute branches reaching all the cells in the body. The strongest vessels are the arteries, whose walls must withstand the high pressure of blood as it is pumped from the heart. Arteries branch into smaller vessels called arterioles, which also

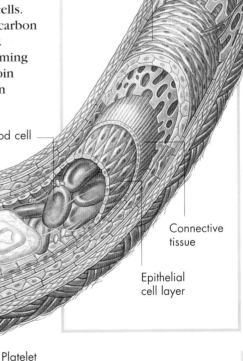

Outer sheath
Elastic layer
Muscle and fibrous tissue
White blood cell
Red blood cell
Plasma
Connective tissue
Epithelial cell layer
Platelet

LUNGS AND BREATHING

WE BREATHE AIR into our lungs so that our bodies can extract vital oxygen from it. Oxygen is needed to drive the process of respiration and thus provide the body's cells with energy. As we breathe out, we expel carbon dioxide, a waste product, from the body. We cannot store oxygen, and so we must breathe constantly throughout our lives. Although we can control our breathing rate, we also breathe unconsciously.

The nose, throat, windpipe, lungs, and certain muscles of the chest form what is called the respiratory system. Working together, they bring air into the body and remove carbon dioxide through the action of breathing in and breathing out. The frequency of breathing varies according to what our bodies are required to do. We normally breathe in about ten times each minute, but during strenuous exercise or if we are frightened, our breathing rate may increase to about 80 times a minute. Normally our breathing occurs automatically, but we can also control our breathing rate when we are awake.

Structure of the Respiratory System

Air, drawn into the nose or mouth through the action of breathing, is warmed before

Lung Structure

The air passages of the lungs end in air sacs called alveoli (singular: alveolus). They are surrounded by a network of blood vessels (below) through which gaseous exchange occurs.

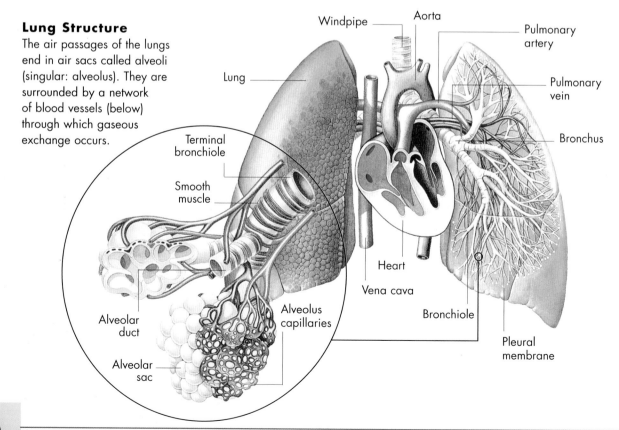

Windpipe

Aorta

Pulmonary artery

Lung

Pulmonary vein

Bronchus

Terminal bronchiole

Smooth muscle

Heart

Vena cava

Bronchiole

Alveolar duct

Alveolus capillaries

Pleural membrane

Alveolar sac

Breathing In and Out

The action of breathing in makes the rib cage lift up and the diaphragm (a sheet of muscle separating the chest cavity from the abdominal cavity) flatten, as shown on the far right. This increases the size of the chest cavity and reduces pressure within the lungs. Air moves from areas of high pressure to areas of low pressure and is thus automatically sucked into the lungs. Usually only about 30 cubic inches (500 cc) of air are drawn in with each breath.

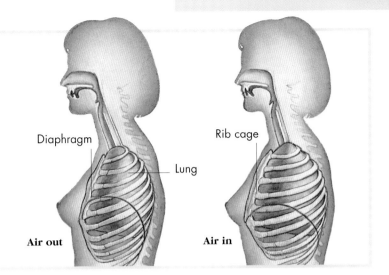

Diaphragm

Lung

Air out

Rib cage

Air in

passing down the throat and into the windpipe. Tiny hairs in the nose act as a filter, trapping particles of dust on mucus to prevent them from entering the lungs. The bottom of the windpipe divides into two further pipes called bronchi, one bronchus leading to each lung. The lungs themselves occupy the thoracic (chest) cavity and lie on either side of the heart. They are surrounded by a thin sheet of tissue called the pleural membrane. Below the lungs is the muscular diaphragm.

Within the lungs the bronchi divide again many times into smaller and smaller tubes called bronchioles. Each bronchiole ends in a small sac known as an alveolus. There are about 300 million alveoli in the lungs. If flattened out, they would cover an area about the size of a tennis court.

How Breathing Is Controlled

The breathing response is initiated not by levels of oxygen in the bloodstream but by carbon dioxide levels. Cells in the brain stem react quickly to tiny changes in the gas concentration and alter the breathing rate of the lungs to correct it.

Gaseous Exchange

The alveoli are surrounded by tiny blood capillaries. These are the fine, branched endings of the pulmonary arteries—which carry deoxygenated blood to the lungs (shown in blue on the opposite page) and the pulmonary veins—which carry oxygenated blood back to the heart (shown in red). Oxygen

Voice Box

The voice box, or larynx, lies at the top of the windpipe (right). Our ability to speak is brought about by the action of air passing through the larynx, making the vocal cords inside vibrate. By moving the muscles of our tongue, lips, and face, we can turn this vibrating note into the variety of tones we call speech.

in the lungs diffuses through the thin walls of the alveoli into the capillaries and enters the bloodstream. From here it is carried by the blood, via the heart, to the body's tissues and organs. At the same time, waste carbon dioxide diffuses into the alveoli. It is then breathed out.

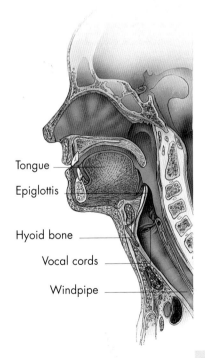

Tongue

Epiglottis

Hyoid bone

Vocal cords

Windpipe

THE CHEMISTRY OF RESPIRATION

IN ADDITION TO the physical stage of respiration, during which oxygen is passed into the bloodstream and carbon dioxide is removed, there are also complex chemical reactions in the cells during which energy is produced to power the workings of the body.

The key component in the process by which oxygen in the air reaches the cells of our bodies is a substance called hemoglobin. Hemoglobin is an iron-containing protein. There may be as many as 280 million molecules of hemoglobin in every red blood cell. The reason that mature red blood cells do not have a nucleus is to allow more vital hemoglobin molecules to be packed in.

Hemoglobin acts as a ferrying system, picking up oxygen from the lungs and transporting it to the cells before returning to pick up more oxygen. When oxygen has combined in the blood capillaries of the lungs with hemoglobin, it forms a bright red substance called oxyhemoglobin. After it has shed its load of oxygen, hemoglobin turns a dark blue-red color and is called deoxyhemoglobin. Every molecule of hemoglobin can pick up, ferry, and deliver four atoms of oxygen. During a single minute, the body transports 56,000 million million million atoms of oxygen. When our bodies are faced with a scarcity of oxygen, for example at high altitudes, they automatically produce even more red blood cells and thus more oxygen-carrying hemoglobin.

Mitochondria

Mitochondria (below) are found in all cells. Within them a series of chemical reactions occurs, breaking down glucose and producing energy for the cell. The energy is stored in the form of the chemical compound ATP.

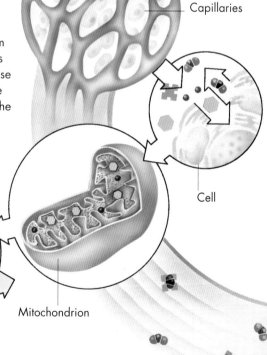

Capillaries

Cell

Mitochondrion

Waste

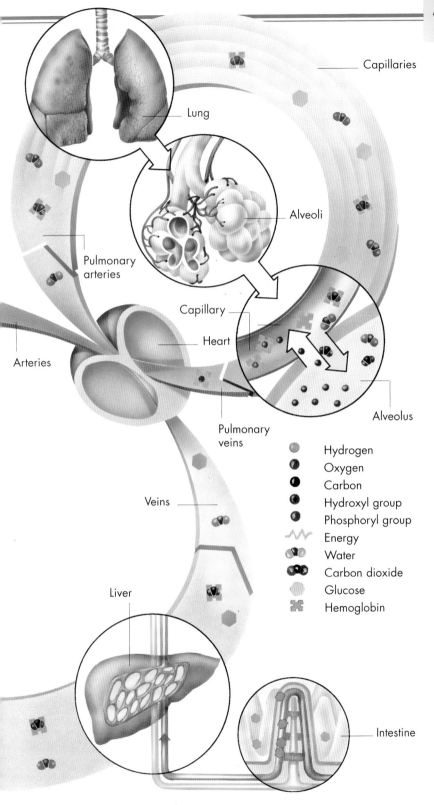

Capillaries

Lung

Alveoli

Pulmonary
arteries

Capillary

Heart

Arteries

Alveolus

Pulmonary
veins

Veins

Hydrogen
Oxygen
Carbon
Hydroxyl group
Phosphoryl group
Energy
Water
Carbon dioxide
Glucose
Hemoglobin

Liver

Intestine

Hemoglobin

The alveoli of the lungs (left) are the sites at which oxygen diffuses into the blood capillaries, and carbon dioxide leaves the blood and enters the lungs. Within the capillaries the oxygen combines with hemoglobin—a special kind of protein that is carried in the red blood cells. Hemoglobin forms a chemical bond with oxygen and in this way carries the vital element from the lungs to all the cells of the body.

How Energy Is Produced

As it reaches the cells, oxygen leaves the bloodstream and enters the cell through the cell membrane. Once inside the cell the oxygen then combines with glucose, which is carried to the cells from the digestive system by the blood (see page 27), in a series of chemical reactions. The reactions release energy locked in the glucose molecules. The reactions also produce carbon dioxide and water as waste. The sites at which these chemical reactions occur in the cell are the mitochondria.

Under powerful electron microscopes these appear as sausage-shaped structures with highly folded inner surfaces. The many folds increase the surface area for the energy-producing reactions to take place.

The energy produced by cells is used, for example, to make our muscles contract for movement or to build proteins for cell growth.

EATING AND DIGESTION

THE PROCESS OF living requires a constant supply of fuel in the form of food. Without it we could no longer replace dead cells, provide the energy our muscles need for movement, or carry out the thousands of other tasks necessary to maintain a healthy body. The digestive system is designed to turn food from the table into molecules small enough for the body to use.

The digestive system consists of two main parts. The digestive tract is a long, hollow tube from mouth to anus. For much of its length, it is folded. Its narrowest part is the esophagus, and the widest part is the stomach. The second part of the digestive system includes the organs, glands, and other structures that play a vital role in the digestive process. These are the salivary glands of the mouth, the liver, the pancreas, and the gall bladder.

Digestion begins in the mouth. Food is broken down into smaller pieces by the teeth, thereby increasing the surface area that can be worked on by the digestive juices. The digestive fluid present in saliva begins the chemical breakdown of food, and the tongue rolls it into a ball ready for swallowing.

After Swallowing

From the esophagus food then enters the stomach. It remains here for about three hours while it is churned over by the stomach muscles and mixed with digestive secretions from the stomach walls. These include pepsin, which breaks down protein; lipase, which breaks down fat; and hydrochloric acid, which kills bacteria and assists pepsin. The food is released into the duodenum—the first part of the small intestine—in bursts.

In the duodenum the food is mixed with more enzymes (chemicals that help in the breakdown of food) from the intestinal walls as well as

Teeth

Food taken into the mouth is first cut and ground up by the teeth. Teeth are fixed into the jawbones at their roots with a hard cement. The enamel that covers the teeth is the hardest substance in the body. At birth human babies normally have no teeth, but during the first two years of life they grow 20 milk teeth. From about six onward these are replaced by the 32 permanent adult teeth.

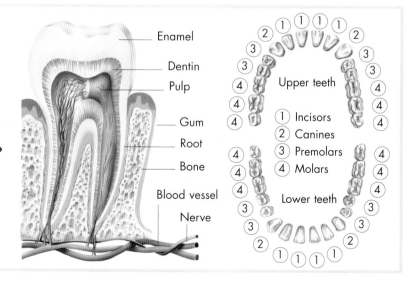

Enamel

Dentin

Pulp

Gum

Root

Bone

Blood vessel

Nerve

Upper teeth

1 Incisors
2 Canines
3 Premolars
4 Molars

Lower teeth

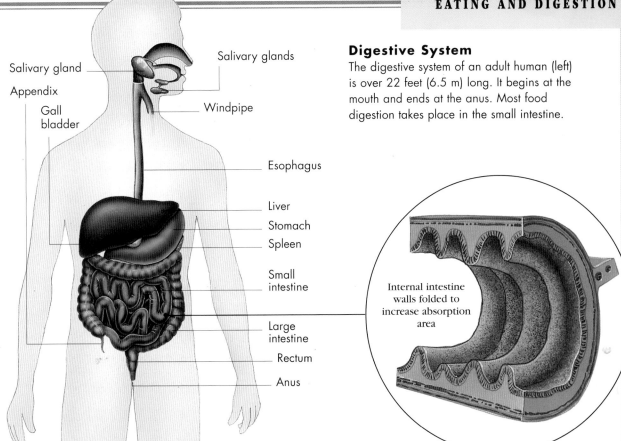

Salivary gland

Appendix

Gall bladder

Salivary glands

Windpipe

Esophagus

Liver

Stomach

Spleen

Small intestine

Large intestine

Rectum

Anus

Digestive System

The digestive system of an adult human (left) is over 22 feet (6.5 m) long. It begins at the mouth and ends at the anus. Most food digestion takes place in the small intestine.

Internal intestine walls folded to increase absorption area

enzymes from the pancreas. Amylose breaks starch into maltose, a sugar. Trypsin and chymotrypsin break proteins into smaller molecules. Some absorption of food takes place in the duodenum, but most occurs in the last part of the small intestine, known as the ileum. Here sugars are first converted into simpler forms, and proteins are broken down into individual amino acids. Absorption of food in the small intestine is aided by the highly folded walls, together with the fingerlike projections called villi (singular: villus), which increase the surface area. Every villus has its own rich supply

of tiny blood vessels. Digested proteins and carbohydrates pass through the intestinal walls and into the bloodstream.

After passing through the small intestine, the majority of the useful food products have been absorbed. The remains, which include mucus and various digestive fluids, pass into the large intestine. In the part of the large intestine known as the colon, water is absorbed back into the body. The remaining waste products, now known as feces, pass on to the rectum, the last part of the digestive tract. Here they may be stored briefly before they leave the body via the anus.

Peristalsis

Food is pushed down parts of the digestive system, such as the esophagus (below), by waves of contractions and relaxations of the surrounding smooth muscle.

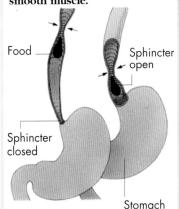

Food

Sphincter open

Sphincter closed

Stomach

THE LIVER

THE LIVER IS the largest internal organ. It is also one of the most important and complex. A living chemical laboratory and factory, the liver carries out over 100 different tasks for the body, including protein production, iron and vitamin storage, and toxic waste removal. The body cannot survive for more than a few hours if the liver fails completely. Closely associated with the liver are the gall bladder and the pancreas.

The liver is a large, soft, roughly pyramid-shaped organ lying in the upper part of the abdomen, on the right-hand side. It is loosely attached to the diaphragm by connective tissue. The liver is divided into four lobes by the structures that run through it. Right underneath the liver is the gall bladder, which stores a greenish substance called bile.

Bile is a product made by the liver's chemical processes, but it also helps to digest fats. Bile is emptied into the duodenum.

The liver has a very rich supply of blood. It receives about one-fifth of its blood supply from the hepatic artery, a branch of the aorta. The remainder enters the liver from the hepatic portal vein. This blood is rich in food substances that have been first broken down and then absorbed through the walls of the intestine. The liver processes these food substances, and the remaining blood passes to the heart via the hepatic vein.

fact file

The word "hepatic," which is used to describe anything related to the liver, comes from *hepar,* the ancient Greek word for liver.

During fetal life, red blood cells are manufactured in the liver.

The importance of the liver was known to Chinese doctors over 2,000 years ago.

Liver and Associated Organs

An adult human liver weighs about 3.3 pounds (1.5 kg). The pancreas lies close to the liver. The gall bladder is a small, saclike organ under the liver with many branching ducts leading from the liver lobules (left).

Liver
Stomach
Pancreas
Gall bladder
Duodenum
Small intestine

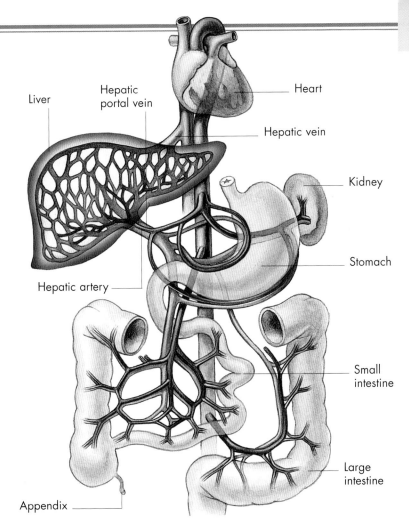

Liver

Hepatic portal vein

Heart

Hepatic vein

Kidney

Stomach

Hepatic artery

Small intestine

Large intestine

Appendix

Liver Blood Supply

The aorta, the main artery from the heart, brings oxygen-rich blood to the liver along the hepatic artery. The liver also receives blood rich in food materials from the intestines along the hepatic portal vein. Blood leaves the liver by the hepatic vein (left).

liver uses these amino acids to make new proteins for blood plasma (see page 18). Urea is formed as a waste product of this process. Unlike glucose or fats, proteins cannot be stored in the body and must be used right away.

The liver also plays a vital part in breaking down harmful chemicals in the blood. Many poisons, including drugs and alcohol, are changed into harmless substances by a process known as detoxification before being passed out of the body in the urine.

When viewed under the microscope, the liver can be seen to be made up of a great many hexagon-shaped units called lobules, each of which is about 0.04 inches (1 mm) in diameter. Each lobule is made up of millions of individual liver cells. Running in between the lobules are branches of the hepatic artery, the portal vein, bile ducts, and lymph vessels.

Blood from the hepatic artery and the portal vein passes into the lobules through channels known as sinusoids and then drains into a central vein in the liver lobule.

Food Processing

The liver stores fats, proteins, and carbohydrates. It is also the place where each of these food substances is processed for use by the body. Some vitamins, for example, vitamins A, D, and B_{12}, are also stored in the liver. The sugar glucose is stored in the form of glycogen—a starchlike carbohydrate. It is released into the blood, when needed, to provide cells with the fuel for respiration (see page 23). Fat is broken down by the liver and is also stored in the liver cells. Proteins are brought to the liver in the form of amino acids. The

The Pancreas

The pancreas is a slightly elongated organ about 6 inches (15 cm) long. It produces a digestive juice containing enzymes that break down carbohydrates, fats, and proteins. The digestive juice is poured into the first part of the small intestine, the duodenum. It also produces salts that neutralize the digestive acid secretions of the walls of the stomach (see page 24).

The pancreas also secretes insulin into the bloodstream. This is used to regulate the amount of glucose released by the liver into the blood.

THE URINARY SYSTEM

THE URINARY SYSTEM is the part of the body that controls the water volume and chemical content of the body's fluids. This ensures that the chemical processes that take place in the cells and tissues always work at the correct concentration and therefore at maximum efficiency. It also removes waste protein from the body by the process known as excretion. The organs responsible for these tasks are the kidneys.

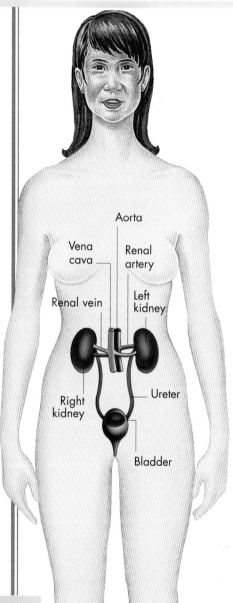

Aorta

Vena cava

Renal artery

Renal vein

Left kidney

Right kidney

Ureter

Bladder

The kidneys are located high up at the back of the abdomen. There is one on each side of the spinal column, partly encased by the lower ribs for protection. Each kidney weighs about 5 ounces (140 g) and is a dark-red organ shaped like a kidney bean. The kidneys receive their blood supply from the renal arteries, which are branches of the aorta. Filtered blood leaves the kidneys along the renal veins to rejoin the vena cava going to the heart.

Internal Structure
Each kidney has an outer layer called the cortex. The cortex consists of many tightly knotted blood capillaries known as glomeruli (singular: glomerulus). Each glomerulus is surrounded by a small cup

Urinary System
The urinary system (left) consists of the kidneys, the ureters (which carry urine from the kidneys to the bladder), and the bladder. The kidneys receive blood from the renal arteries.

of tissue called a Bowman's capsule. The Bowman's capsule leads into a long, looped, collecting tubule. Each glomerulus, together with its Bowman's capsule and collecting tubule, is called a nephron. There are approximately a million nephrons in each kidney.

The collecting tubules pass through the next layer of the kidney, the medulla, and eventually go into the pelvis. The pelvis is a funnel-shaped tube that acts as a collecting system for the urine made by the kidney.

How the Kidneys Work
The kidneys are basically filtering mechanisms. Their main task is to remove soluble waste products from the body by producing urine. At the same time, the kidneys help control the levels of various chemicals and water in the body so that the body fluids are maintained at the correct concentration.

Blood enters a kidney through the renal artery and travels to the mass of tiny blood vessels that make up each glomerulus. As the blood

Kidney

Each of the paired kidneys in the human body is approximately 4 inches (10 cm) long and 2 inches (5 cm) wide (right). Within the kidney there are three major regions. The outer layer is known as the cortex. Inside this is the medulla. The center of the kidney is called the pelvis. The renal arteries carry blood to the kidneys; blood is taken from the kidneys by the renal veins.

Glomeruli in cortex

Cortex

Renal pyramid

Medulla

Collecting tubule

Glomerulus

Capsule

Renal artery

Renal vein

Pelvis

Ureter

passes through the glomerulus, it is filtered, under pressure, into the collecting tubule. Blood cells and large protein molecules remain in the blood, but water, glucose, potassium, sodium, and amino acids are filtered out, along with urea (the waste product of protein breakdown and digestion) and uric acid. The filtered fluid passes down the collecting tubule to the ureter. As it does this, water, glucose, and amino acids are absorbed from it back into the bloodstream.

Formation of Urine

When the remaining liquid reaches the ureter, it is called urine. Urine is about 95 percent water, 2 percent urea, 1 percent sodium chloride, and 2 percent uric acid and other salts such as those of calcium, potassium, and ammonia.

Approximately 1 quart (1 liter) of urine is produced each day. Urine passes from the ureters and collects in the bladder, which stretches as it fills. When the urine can be passed from the body, it leaves via the urethra, a tube from the bladder. The amount of urine we produce also varies according to how much water we lose through sweating.

Water Loss by the Body

More than three times as much water is lost from the body in the form of urine and with the feces than is lost through the respiratory surfaces while breathing. About 8 percent of the body's total water content is lost through the skin by sweating.

Water lost in urine and feces

Water lost in breathing

Water lost in sweating

GLANDS AND HORMONES

GLANDS ARE STRUCTURES that release certain chemicals to help control the body. Some types of glands empty their chemicals directly onto a body surface through a duct, but others release their products, known as hormones, directly into the bloodstream.

There are two different kinds of glands in the human body. They are classified, or grouped, according to the way in which their substances are released:

Exocrine glands release their substances through tiny ducts. They include sweat glands (which produce sweat to cool the skin), salivary glands (which produce saliva in the mouth), and tear glands (which wash the eye). The internal walls of the stomach and intestine also contain glands. These pour enzymes into the digestive tract to aid digestion.

The second type of glands are called **endocrine glands.** They do not have a duct, but instead, the cells of these glands release their products—called hormones—directly into the bloodstream. Hormones (sometimes called chemical messengers) are then carried in the bloodstream to other glands and organs in the body.

The Role of Hormones

The task of hormones is to control the body processes; each hormone is designed to regulate a specific process or activity. The pineal gland controls activities such as waking and sleeping.

Endocrine Glands

Glands that empty their contents directly into the bloodstream are called endocrine glands. The chemicals they produce are called hormones. The main endocrine glands of the body are shown left.

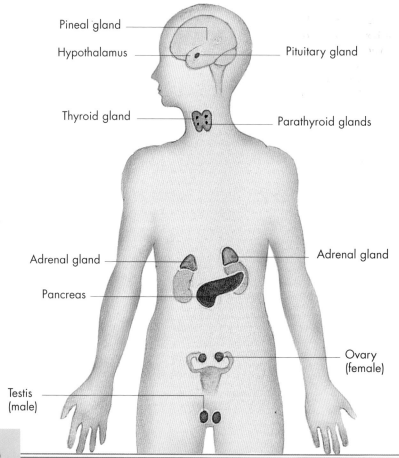

Pineal gland

Hypothalamus

Pituitary gland

Thyroid gland

Parathyroid glands

Adrenal gland

Adrenal gland

Pancreas

Ovary (female)

Testis (male)

The pituitary gland is often called "the master gland," since it controls the activities of many other glands. It is controlled by the hypothalamus in the brain. Pituitary gland hormones control the function of the kidneys, the body's growth rate, and the activity of the sex glands—the ovaries in females and the testes in males. In puberty they produce sex hormones in preparation for reproduction. The pituitary gland also controls the color of the skin by stimulating cells called melanocytes to produce the pigment melanin in response to sunlight. The thyroid gland, also under pituitary control, produces the hormone thyroxine, which controls how energy is used by cells. Calcium use is controlled by the parathyroid glands; they ensure that the bones maintain their strength.

The pituitary gland also influences the adrenal glands.

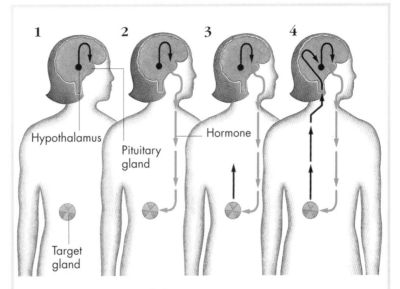

Hypothalamus

Pituitary gland

Hormone

Target gland

Hormone Control System

Once a hormone has triggered the required cellular action, it must be "turned off" until needed again. This occurs as follows: a hormone in the hypothalamus of the brain (1) stimulates the pituitary gland to release one of its hormones (2). The pituitary hormone travels to the target gland in the bloodstream, causing the release of another hormone (3), which is taken by the bloodstream to where it is needed. Some of this hormone also reaches the hypothalamus, switching off the original pituitary-stimulating hormone (4).

They produce two hormones: epinephrine and norepinephrine. These control the body's reaction to stress and prepare it for emergency action. The adrenal glands also regulate growth and metabolism.

Fight or Flight

Some situations, such as fright or anger (left), make the brain send a message to the pituitary gland. This stimulates the adrenal glands to release epinephrine. As a result, other changes occur in the body, preparing the muscles to help you fight or flee.

SEX ORGANS AND FERTILIZATION

THE STARTING POINT of all human life is the fertilized egg, or ovum. This is produced when the nucleus of a single male sperm fuses with the nucleus of the female egg. The egg is released from the ovary during the process known as ovulation.

Sperm and male sex hormones are produced in the testes, a pair of rounded glands situated in a pouch called the scrotum. Each day a man produces 300 million sperm cells. These pass down a coiled duct, the epididymis, during which time they mature and are stored until they leave the body or are broken down.

Each sperm is approximately 0.002 inches (0.05 mm) long. It consists of a head region containing genetic material, covered by an outer layer called the acrosome. This contains material that prevents other sperm penetrating the egg. A tail, or flagellum, moves the sperm along.

A female egg is released from the ovaries once a month during the process known as ovulation. The egg passes down a narrow duct, the fallopian tube (or oviduct), to the uterus. The tiny egg is helped on its way by thousands of cumulus cells that surround the egg and beat their cilia (tiny hairlike structures) to waft it along.

Chromosome Numbers

The genetic material in the chromosomes of the sperm and egg carries hereditary information that shapes the characteristics of the offspring (see pages 36–37). All body cells, except for sperm and eggs, have 46 chromosomes arranged in 23 pairs. Sperm and egg cells have only 23 chromosomes each— half of a complete pair. When the egg is fertilized by the sperm, the two "half sets" of chromosomes join together to form a complete set of 23 pairs.

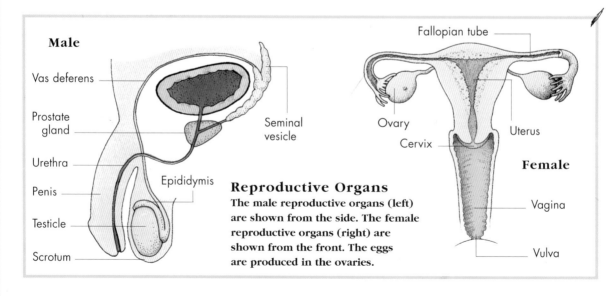

Male — Vas deferens, Prostate gland, Urethra, Penis, Testicle, Scrotum, Epididymis, Seminal vesicle

Female — Fallopian tube, Ovary, Cervix, Uterus, Vagina, Vulva

Reproductive Organs
The male reproductive organs (left) are shown from the side. The female reproductive organs (right) are shown from the front. The eggs are produced in the ovaries.

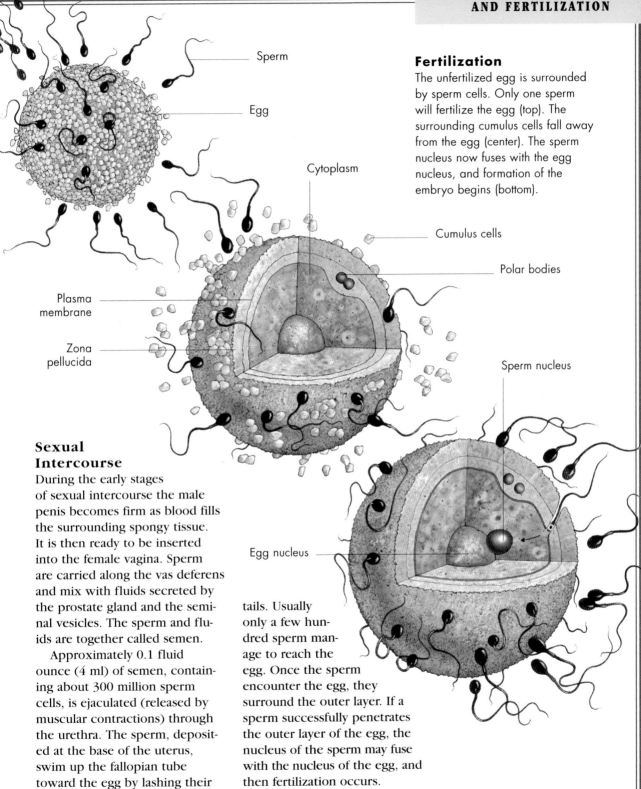

Sperm

Egg

Cytoplasm

Cumulus cells

Polar bodies

Plasma membrane

Zona pellucida

Sperm nucleus

Egg nucleus

Fertilization

The unfertilized egg is surrounded by sperm cells. Only one sperm will fertilize the egg (top). The surrounding cumulus cells fall away from the egg (center). The sperm nucleus now fuses with the egg nucleus, and formation of the embryo begins (bottom).

Sexual Intercourse

During the early stages of sexual intercourse the male penis becomes firm as blood fills the surrounding spongy tissue. It is then ready to be inserted into the female vagina. Sperm are carried along the vas deferens and mix with fluids secreted by the prostate gland and the seminal vesicles. The sperm and fluids are together called semen.

Approximately 0.1 fluid ounce (4 ml) of semen, containing about 300 million sperm cells, is ejaculated (released by muscular contractions) through the urethra. The sperm, deposited at the base of the uterus, swim up the fallopian tube toward the egg by lashing their tails. Usually only a few hundred sperm manage to reach the egg. Once the sperm encounter the egg, they surround the outer layer. If a sperm successfully penetrates the outer layer of the egg, the nucleus of the sperm may fuse with the nucleus of the egg, and then fertilization occurs.

33

PREGNANCY AND BIRTH

A PREGNANCY IS the name given to the period of time during which
a fertilized egg, embedded in the female uterus, undergoes a series of repeated
cell divisions and growth to become a fully formed baby. This period is usually
about 38 weeks. For the first eight weeks of pregnancy the developing baby
is called an embryo. After that time it is known as a fetus.

After fertilization, which occurs in the fallopian tube, the fertilized egg (or zygote) begins cell division as it travels down the fallopian tube. In about a week the embryo reaches the uterus. Here it secretes enzymes that break down the uterine lining, forming a hollow into which it embeds itself. This stage is known as implantation. Once implantation has occurred, the placenta begins to form. The placenta is an organ that provides the developing fetus with a supply of oxygen and nutrients, and disposes of the waste products of the fetus. It also acts as a barrier to harmful substances. As pregnancy goes on, the umbilical cord develops. It connects the placenta with the baby, and through it the baby receives nourishment from its mother.

At about the end of the third week of pregnancy the spinal cord has formed. The heart normally starts to beat by about the fourth week, and the lungs and liver are visible. By the eighth week the embryo is called a fetus. It has fingers and toes, and may begin moving now.

Fetal Development

From this stage until birth the baby develops inside a protective, saclike structure within the uterus called the amnion. The amnion is filled with amniotic fluid, which cushions the baby against injury.

During the first few months of pregnancy, as the limbs and organs develop, the baby is susceptible to infectious diseases such as German measles, which can cause deafness and heart defects, as well as to poisons like alcohol and tobacco, which are absorbed by the fetus and can be harmful.

By 12 weeks the fetus's internal organs have developed, and nails are visible on its fingers and toes. By 16 weeks the external genitals are visible. Development and growth of the fetus continue steadily, and by about 32 weeks it has turned to a head-down position.

Birth

When the baby is ready to be born, hormones in the mother's body begin to prepare her for the event. First, the muscles of the uterus begin to contract. This is the start of the stage known as labor. The cervix widens to enable the baby to pass through, and the amniotic membranes rupture. Stronger contractions of the uterus now begin to push the baby out head first. Once it has left the mother's body, the umbilical cord is cut, and the baby will be fed on milk from the mother's breasts or on artificial milk. The mother's milk provides substances that help protect the baby against disease.

fact file

The menstrual cycle, which occurs approximately every 28 days in mature females, prepares the body for conception and pregnancy by transferring an egg from the ovary to the uterus. If fertilization does not occur, the uterine lining is shed, causing the monthly blood flow known as a period.

The muscle of the uterus is the strongest in the human body.

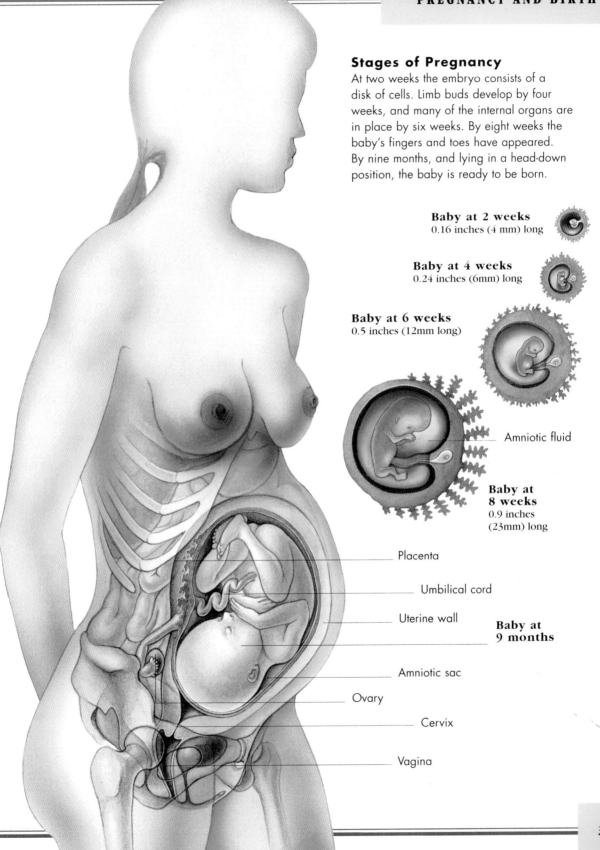

Stages of Pregnancy

At two weeks the embryo consists of a disk of cells. Limb buds develop by four weeks, and many of the internal organs are in place by six weeks. By eight weeks the baby's fingers and toes have appeared. By nine months, and lying in a head-down position, the baby is ready to be born.

Baby at 2 weeks
0.16 inches (4 mm) long

Baby at 4 weeks
0.24 inches (6mm) long

Baby at 6 weeks
0.5 inches (12mm long)

Amniotic fluid

Baby at 8 weeks
0.9 inches (23mm) long

Placenta

Umbilical cord

Uterine wall

Baby at 9 months

Amniotic sac

Ovary

Cervix

Vagina

HEREDITY AND GROWTH

THE GENES IN our body cells are inherited, or passed on, from each of our parents.
As we grow, the genes help shape what sort of basic characteristics and personality
we will develop, but our environment plays a part in our development, too.

The newly formed cell that results from the fertilization of an egg by a sperm contains all the genetic codes not only to form a new individual but also to shape many of that individual's physical and mental characteristics. These characteristics include height, hair color, ability in sports, resistance to certain diseases, and temperament.

Each time the cells in the developing embryo divide to form two new daughter cells, each new cell will also carry on its chromosomes a complete copy of the genes from the original fertilized egg. This ensures that the blueprint for that particular person is known to every cell that will be formed in his or her body throughout life.

Since there are millions of genes, there is an even greater number of combinations of them possible when they combine during reproduction. Therefore, with the exception of identical twins—who each have identical genes—everyone in the world is different from everyone else because they do not have identical genes.

Eye Color

Eye color is one of the characteristics inherited from our parents and is determined by genes. For example, there are genes that control blue eyes and genes that control brown eyes. "Brown eyes" genes are dominant over "blue eyes" genes, which means that if a person inherits a "brown eyes" gene, they will have brown eyes. For a person to have blue eyes, they must inherit two "blue eyes" genes, one from each parent.

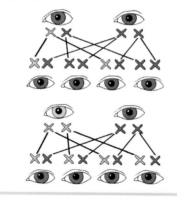
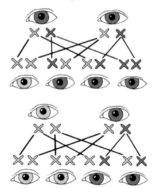

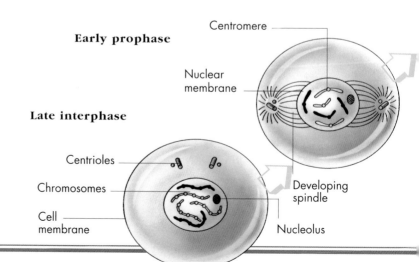

Early prophase

Centromere

Nuclear membrane

Late interphase

Centrioles

Chromosomes

Cell membrane

Developing spindle

Nucleolus

Development

Babies are born with certain abilities. These include rooting (searching for a nipple) and grasping reflexes, as well as sight and hearing. During the early years of life they develop motor skills (such as walking), speech, and social skills such as toilet training. As children progress into early teens and beyond, many of these early skills are refined and further developed. The environment in which we grow plays an important part in determining how this happens.

From the early years of life through to old age our bodies change, too. Hormones control the way our bodies grow, when we become sexually mature and how—much later in life—we age and finally die.

Daughter cells

Telophase

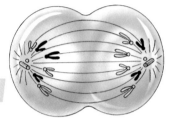

Anaphase

Early Development

Although babies are born with certain inherited abilities, they develop and learn many of the skills for later life in the first few years. These basic skill-learning stages are shown below.

Metaphase

Late prophase

How Cells Divide

Growth occurs when a cell divides to form two new cells. The process is called mitosis, and there are several stages (left and above). During inter-phase the chromosomes of the nucleus replicate themselves. During later stages they shorten and move to the center of the cell before drawing apart. Finally, the cell separates.

Early Child Development

Age	Movements and Abilities	Behavioral Traits
1 MONTH	When not feeding, sleeps most of the time with head turned to one side. Will grasp finger placed into palm.	Studies mother's face. Begins to smile at about 6 weeks.
6 MONTHS	Can sit upright when supported. Holds objects and passes them from hand to hand.	Tests objects by placing in mouth. Reacts to familiar voices.
1 YEAR	Walks if one or both hands are held. Likes dropping and throwing toys.	Understands certain words. Begins to indicate his or her wishes.
18 MONTHS	Climbs stairs if help is provided by hand or rail. Can scribble on paper.	Uses some words. Indicates toilet needs.
2 YEARS	Can run around unaided, kick a ball, and open doors. Builds brick towers.	Uses simple sentences.
3 YEARS	Rides tricycle or pedal car. Able to copy simple shapes like circles.	Plays with others. Begins to understand the concept of sharing.
5 YEARS	Can skip, dance, and climb ladders. Can form many letters and copy more complicated shapes.	Ready to begin formal primary schooling.

INTRODUCTION

OUR BRAIN CONTROLS our movements and keeps our body systems functioning properly. Using information relayed by our senses, the brain also interprets the environment and enables us to respond appropriately to it. But uniquely, our brain allows us to have reasoned thought, and it is this feature, above all others, that sets us apart from all the other animals on the planet.

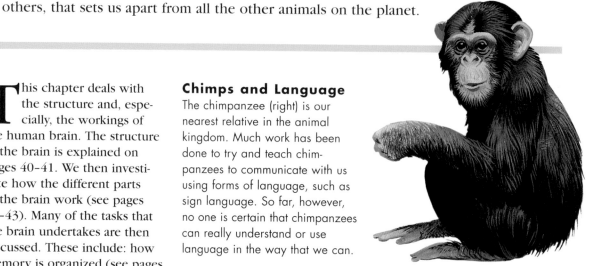

This chapter deals with the structure and, especially, the workings of the human brain. The structure of the brain is explained on pages 40-41. We then investigate how the different parts of the brain work (see pages 42-43). Many of the tasks that the brain undertakes are then discussed. These include: how memory is organized (see pages 44-45); how we learn (see pages 46-47) and how learning can be improved (see pages 52-53; and how we think and how we measure intelligence (see pages 48-49). For our

fact file

The human brain contains 25 billion neurons (nerve cells).

20 percent of the body's blood supply goes to the brain.

Over 100 million nerve fibers link the cerebral hemispheres.

The brain weighs about 3 pounds (1.3 kg).

Chimps and Language

The chimpanzee (right) is our nearest relative in the animal kingdom. Much work has been done to try and teach chimpanzees to communicate with us using forms of language, such as sign language. So far, however, no one is certain that chimpanzees can really understand or use language in the way that we can.

brains to work efficiently we need sleep, and the importance of sleep and how it is studied are described on pages 56-57.

This chapter also looks at the organs most closely associated with the brain—the eyes (see pages 58-65) and ears (see pages 66-67), and the organs of smell, taste, and touch (see pages 68-69). They are the body's means of sensing the world around us and relaying information to the brain so that we can react accordingly.

The Human Brain

The brain is the largest and most complex organ in the human body. Although some other animals (for example,

elephants and dolphins) have larger brains, humans are the most intelligent animals on Earth. This is because the cerebrum, the part of the brain responsible for our thoughts and actions, is at its most highly developed in humans (see pages 39-43).

The brain consists of billions of nerve cells linked by millions of nerve fibers, forming a highly complex organ that can mastermind an extraordinary range of tasks from conscious thought to highly coordinated physical activities. At the same time, the brain unconsciously regulates the body processes.

The complexity of our brains is what makes us different from other animals. We have achieved our position as the dominant creatures on Earth through our greater intelligence. Other species may be physically stronger or have more finely developed senses, but our unique capacity for thought and reason has enabled us to overcome our physical shortcomings and, intellectually, to tower over all other animal species.

Although many other animals can also learn, remember, and communicate, humans have developed these activities in far more complex ways.

It is our use of the human brain, rather than our physical strength, that has enabled us to modify our planet so that we can exploit its resources and live in otherwise inhospitable environments.

Studying the Brain
Our knowledge of the anatomy, or structure, of the brain and the senses is fairly strong. We also know much about how these organs function. We know, for example, how messages in the form of electrical impulses are passed from one brain cell to another. Yet there is still much to discover about how the brain organizes its activities and how certain brain diseases occur. The human brain is such a complex subject that separate branches of science and medicine have developed in order to study it and try to understand it fully. Two of these major areas of study are psychology and psychiatry.

Psychology is the branch of science that deals with the study of why human beings behave as they do. We look at many aspects of human behavior in other chapters in this series. (See *Communication* and *The Mind and Psychology*.)

Psychiatry, closely linked to psychology, is the branch of medicine that is concerned with the diagnosis and treatment of mental illness. It is still a fairly recent form of medicine. Various methods are used by psychiatrists to try and cure different mental illnesses.

Comparing Vertebrate Brains
The cerebrum (the part of the brain in vertebrates that is responsible for our thoughts and actions) becomes relatively larger the further up the evolutionary scale the animal is to be found. Notice in the human brain that the cerebrum is so enlarged that it overlays many of the other parts of the brain. The outer cortex also becomes highly folded to increase its area.

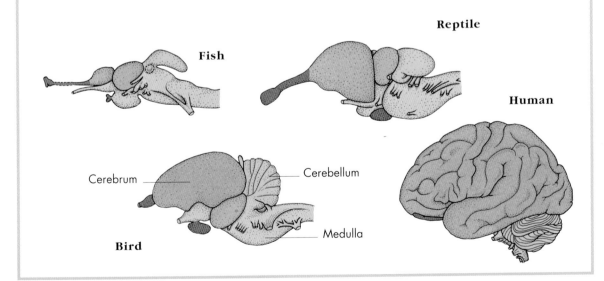

Fish

Reptile

Human

Cerebrum

Cerebellum

Medulla

Bird

BRAIN STRUCTURE

SHIELDED BY THE thick bones of the skull, the brain lies within three membranes called meninges and floats in a special nourishing fluid that also helps cushion and protect it against damage should the skull receive a blow. The brain is the largest part of the nervous system and the most complex organ in the human body. It uses 20 percent of the body's total energy resources, yet weighs only about 3 pounds (1.3 kg).

The human brain contains billions of interconnecting neurons (nerve cells) as well as other cells known as neuroglia. Neuroglia help support and protect the neurons. There are three main parts to the brain. The **cerebrum** is the largest part and accounts for 90 percent of the whole brain. The outer surface of the cerebrum is called the cortex. It is highly folded, and each fold is called a gyrus. The grooves formed by the folds are called fissures

fact file

The two separate halves, or hemispheres, of the cerebrum can be seen clearly. They are connected by millions of nerve fibers.

The brain makes up only 2 percent of the body's total weight.

The brain is the fastest-developing organ in the embryo.

(if large) and sulci (if small). The pattern of folding varies in every person. The cortex consists of neurons known as gray matter. Beneath the cortex is the white matter. This consists mostly of long nerve filaments or axons (see *Body Systems,* page 15). The cerebrum is divided into two halves, called hemispheres, linked by nerve fibers. Each hemisphere is further divided by fissures into four lobes—occipital, temporal, parietal, and frontal.

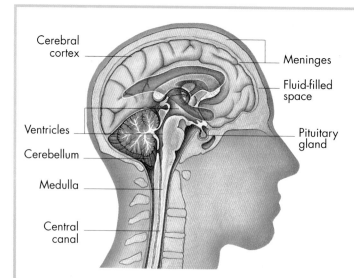

Cerebral cortex

Meninges

Fluid-filled space

Ventricles

Pituitary gland

Cerebellum

Medulla

Central canal

Protecting the Brain

The delicate brain is protected within an outer casing of cranial bones (the skull) and by three membranes (the meninges). Between the middle and innermost layers of the meninges is the cerebrospinal fluid. In addition to providing a cushion against physical injury, the fluid is rich in glucose and proteins that provide energy for the brain cells. The fluid also contains lymphocytes that help to protect the brain against infections. The cerebrospinal fluid circulates around the brain and spinal cord and also through the brain via four cavities known as ventricles.

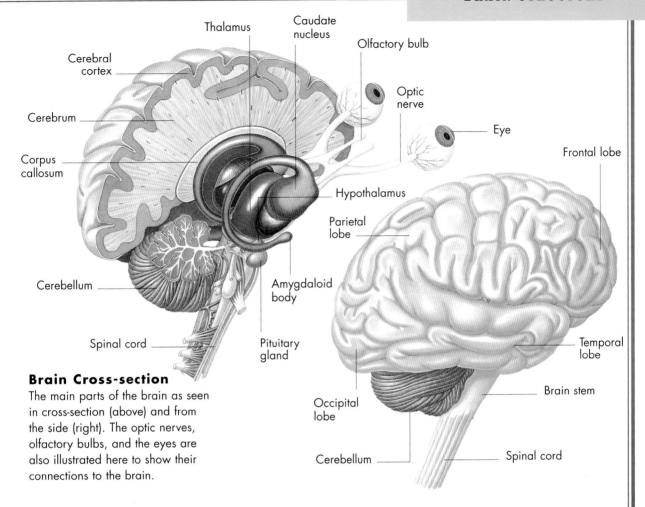

Thalamus
Caudate nucleus
Olfactory bulb
Cerebral cortex
Optic nerve
Cerebrum
Eye
Frontal lobe
Corpus callosum
Hypothalamus
Parietal lobe
Cerebellum
Amygdaloid body
Temporal lobe
Spinal cord
Pituitary gland
Brain stem
Occipital lobe
Cerebellum
Spinal cord

Brain Cross-section
The main parts of the brain as seen in cross-section (above) and from the side (right). The optic nerves, olfactory bulbs, and the eyes are also illustrated here to show their connections to the brain.

The second largest part of the brain is the **cerebellum**. It is situated toward the rear of the cerebrum. The cerebellum resembles a butterfly with wings folded; it has a central region and two cerebellar hemispheres, one to each side. The surface of the cerebellum consists of gray matter, folded into ridges known as folia. Beneath the gray matter are areas of white matter that give the appearance of branches of a tree. Within the white matter there is more gray matter, whose purpose is to transmit information to the spinal cord and other parts of the brain.

The third part of the brain is the **brain stem**. It consists of the medulla oblongata, the pons, and the midbrain, and extends downward to merge with the spinal cord. The nerve fibers of the brain stem connect the spinal cord to various regions of the brain.

A cross-section through the brain also reveals other structures. Above the brain stem is the bulbous thalamus. The thalamus acts as a relay center for messages received by the cortex from the spinal cord, brain stem, cerebellum, and other parts of the cerebrum. The hypothalamus is a small structure located near the base of the brain. It plays a vital role in controlling the release of hormones. Another structure, the amygdaloid body, is concerned with controlling some of the body's basic functions, while the caudate nucleus assists with movements. The mass of nerve fibers connecting the two cerebral hemispheres can be seen near the base of the cerebrum; it is called the corpus callosum.

BRAIN FUNCTIONS

EVERY SECOND WE are awake the brain receives a huge amount of information, sent to it by our eyes, ears, and the senses of touch, taste, and smell. It quickly classifies and sorts all this sensory data and then uses it to control our thoughts and actions. In addition to this conscious activity the brain's autonomic, or unconscious, processes keep us alive by ensuring that body systems function properly.

The brain is sometimes likened to a complex computer—issuing commands, processing and storing data, and providing us with the information we need to think. Almost simultaneously, the brain can consider an action, send a signal instructing muscles to contract and move our limbs to carry out the action (see *Body Systems*, pages 14–15), while at the same time, we engage in another complex activity such as talking. Then it stores the memory of the events and enables us to recall them at a later date (see page 45). And at the same time as this, it is also carrying out many other subconscious tasks, such as keeping the heart beating and monitoring all the other body processes.

Each of the different parts of the brain plays a different role in its overall functioning, although the contributions of the parts are often linked and coordinated.

The cerebrum (see page 40) is the part where higher thoughts—such as learning, memory, and reasoning—take place. The four lobes of the cerebrum are each associated with a particular mental activity. The frontal lobes, near the forehead, control judgment,

Fighter Pilot
Millions of neural pathways within the brain produce thought processes enabling this pilot (left) to fly the airplane, scan his instruments, talk to other pilots, and think about what he will do next.

thinking, and reasoning. Just behind the frontal lobes is an area that controls speech. At each side of the brain, the parietal lobes process incoming messages concerned with touch, temperature, and pain. The temporal lobes are responsible for hearing (see pages 66–67). They are also involved in the storage of memory. Close by are groups of cells associated with taste and smell (see pages 68–69). At the back of the brain, the occipital lobes control vision (see pages 58–65).

Each of these lobes interacts with areas known as associative areas. These process information relayed to other parts of the brain and are vital in developing intelligence.

The cerebellum (see page 41) is responsible for enabling us to maintain our balance and coordinating muscular movements such as walking. The third region of the brain, the brain stem (see page 41), has within it several centers that

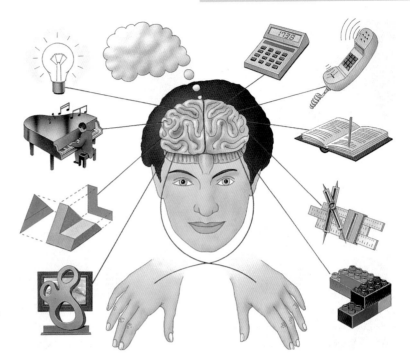

are important for our basic survival. These centers control breathing, heart rate, blood pressure, and digestion. They also control some of the body's reflex actions, such as vomiting. The brain stem is also responsible for the control of sleeping and waking.

Different Thoughts

Logical and creative activities are each controlled by a different hemisphere of the brain (above). The left hemisphere controls our understanding of numbers, language, and technology. The right hemisphere allows us an appreciation of shape, movement, and art.

Reflexes

Some stimuli require such quick responses to protect the body from danger that there is no time for the message to go to the brain first. In these situations a reflex reaction occurs. Stepping on a nail, for example, sends a sensory nerve impulse to the spinal cord, where it connects with a motor neuron. A message is sent straight back to the leg muscle, which contracts. The brain receives information about the event after it has occurred.

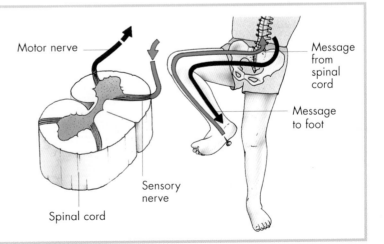

Motor nerve

Message from spinal cord

Message to foot

Sensory nerve

Spinal cord

MEMORY

OFTEN AN EVENT that occurred fleetingly in childhood—perhaps many years ago—can be recalled vividly. So, too, can an event such as a dream that we may never have experienced at all while conscious. Yet a telephone number dialed only a few hours ago, or someone's name, may no longer be remembered. These are just a few examples of the fascinating features of the human memory and the way that it works.

Memory is the ability of the brain to store the experience of past events and then recall them or to use the stored information in ways that enable us to carry out specific tasks. Memory is a very complicated system of storage and often relies on various interconnected activities working together.

There are three main types of memory. The first, **sensory memory**, is used as part of our equipment for perceiving the world. Sensory memory includes the recognition of sounds—for example, those used in words so that we can understand speech. Some sensory memory impressions may be transferred to the other memory systems, the short-term memory or the long-term memory.

Short-term memory is used, for example, when we want to perform a simple task such as multiplying two numbers together. We need to remember the number long enough to carry out the mathematical task. Studies have shown that short-term memory has three parts to it: the articulatory loop (which is used for storing verbal information and may be used in calculations); the visuo-spatial scratchpad (which helps us deal with visual images); and the central executive (which controls the other functions).

Long-term memory is used for retaining information over

The Brain's Memory Systems

Information received by the brain is processed and then either quickly lost or stored in the short-term or the long-term memory (below). Various factors determine into which memory system the experience is stored.

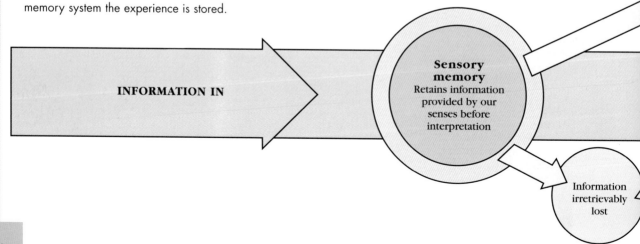

INFORMATION IN

Sensory memory
Retains information provided by our senses before interpretation

Information irretrievably lost

much longer periods of time, even permanently. It has two parts. Semantic memory remembers general facts, such as what the word "dog" means. Episodic memory is used for remembering things such as what you did earlier in the day.

How Memory Is Stored

Different regions of the brain are used to interpret different sensory experiences. For example, one part of the brain seems to recognize faces, and another objects. It seems likely that the part of the brain where an image is processed is also where it is stored as memory. In other words, no part of the brain specializes in memory storage.

When the brain stores the memory of something, changes take place in the neurons responsible for processing the information. If the event is stored in the short-term memory, a temporary biochemical change occurs. If the event becomes part of the long-term memory, however, a more permanent change seems to occur in the protein structure of the neurons involved. The process of committing events to the long-term memory is called consolidation. For an event to become part of the long-term memory, it needs to be reinforced in some way—perhaps by repetition or by association with another important event.

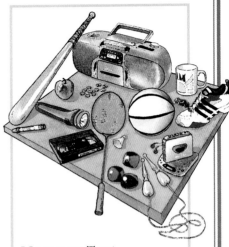

Memory Test

Look at the objects in the illustration above for about a minute, and try to memorize them. Now look away, and write down as many of the objects as you can remember. This will test your short-term memory. To find out how many of these objects have been stored in your long-term memory, see how many you can remember one hour, 24 hours, or one week later.

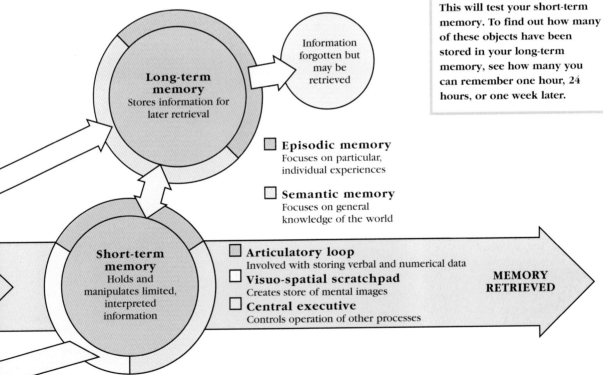

Long-term memory
Stores information for later retrieval

Information forgotten but may be retrieved

☐ Episodic memory
Focuses on particular, individual experiences

☐ Semantic memory
Focuses on general knowledge of the world

Short-term memory
Holds and manipulates limited, interpreted information

☐ Articulatory loop
Involved with storing verbal and numerical data
☐ Visuo-spatial scratchpad
Creates store of mental images
☐ Central executive
Controls operation of other processes

MEMORY RETRIEVED

LEARNING

LEARNING IS THE process by which past experiences are used to acquire knowledge and determine our future behavior. Learning begins as soon as we are born and continues throughout our life. Nearly everything we do as humans is learned, although we are born with certain basic behavior patterns. Much of our learning is shaped by the society in which we live; we can even learn to override many of our instincts.

When we say we have learned something, what we mean is that we have set up a new pattern of behavior. There are several different ways by which we acquire learning, each of which has been extensively studied by psychologists.

Operant or instrumental learning usually involves the use of rewards to reinforce the activity; the person learns to behave in a certain way because of what follows if they do. An example of this kind of learning is a child asking for some candy. Each time the child receives some, it reinforces the activity. The child has learned that asking for candy produces the result that it wants.

Learning by Example
Children like to imitate the actions of adults, especially those of their parents. By copying the car-cleaning actions of her father, this young child (right) is learning, through repetitive behavior, how to hold and manipulate the sponge. She is also learning what effect her actions have on the dirty car.

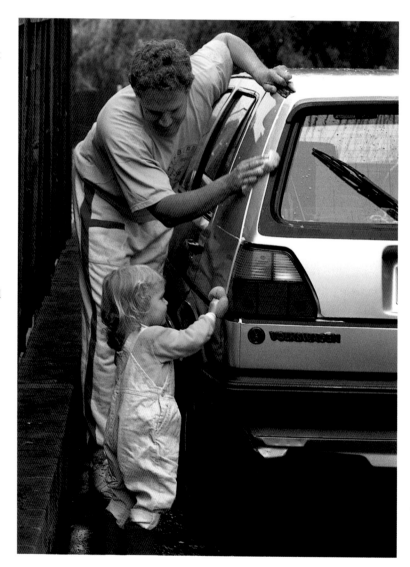

In classical learning or conditioning the new behavior comes about without the use of any reinforcement. A young child who is repeatedly chased by geese in a farmyard may cry whenever she sees the geese, even if she is not being chased at the time. Classical conditioning is involved when we learn emotional responses such as fear, anxiety, or happiness in particular situations.

Using What You Know

Your existing knowledge can influence how much you learn about something new. Someone interested in, and with some

Positive Reinforcement

When a pupil receives attention, praise, and encouragement (right), the learning process is often improved. This is known as positive reinforcement. The pupil feels more motivated and encouraged, and tries to maintain his or her standards so that the teacher will continue to praise the efforts.

knowledge of, say, automobiles, can learn more quickly about some new type of engine than someone with no previous knowledge of automobiles. The main reason for this is that adding to a familiar area of knowledge makes it possible to form improved links between existing knowledge and new information. The basic concepts are already known and can act as a platform on which to build. This same technique applies to many other skills, such as learning to play a musical instrument or even to speak a language.

The things we learn help us use our intelligence. For example, a child may want to turn a door handle but is too small to reach it. But he has learned that standing on a chair makes him taller. So he stands on the chair and thus reaches the handle. The child's actions are a form of intelligence application called problem solving (see page 55).

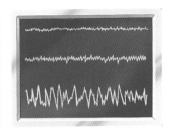

Brain Waves

Learning usually involves thinking, too; and when the brain is active, the electrical activity of the nerve cells in the brain also increases. This can be recorded as brain waves, like the ones shown above. When the brain is working hard—for example, when we are learning a complicated task—the brain waves are fast and irregular (top row). As the mental activity decreases, they become slower and more regular (middle row). During some of the stages of sleep they become even slower and deeper (bottom row).

THINKING AND IQ

THINKING MEANS USING the extraordinary mental powers of our brains. It enables us to imagine things we cannot even see; plan a course of action before undertaking it; solve problems; perform complicated calculations: understand others and communicate back to them; reason; and create everything from pictures to spaceships. One of the measures of how we think is the intelligence quotient, or IQ.

Our ability to think, as well as our ability to learn and remember, is limited partly by the mental apparatus with which we were born. But many people who may appear less intelligent than others have simply not reached the limit of their brain potential. This may be because they have never been given the chance to discover what they can achieve or perhaps lacked encouragement in the critical preschool years.

There are many different kinds of thinking and many different situations in which we do it. We may think alone or as part of a group. We may think using numbers or reason with thoughts, words, or symbols. (Reasoning means making judgments beyond the information given.) We may create something visual for others to think about, too. The speed at which one thinks also varies. It depends on who you are, what you are thinking about, the time of day, and even your mood. We sometimes need to understand other people's thinking before we can organize our own thoughts properly.

Intelligence

Intelligence is a combination of many aspects of human ability. It includes thinking ability, the power of reasoning, understanding, and memory, together with the speed at which all these tasks can be carried out.

One of the ways in which intelligence can be measured is by an intelligence test. This is often called an IQ test. IQ tests are usually divided into two parts: a set of verbal tests and a set of performance tests. The verbal tests look at general knowledge, comprehension,

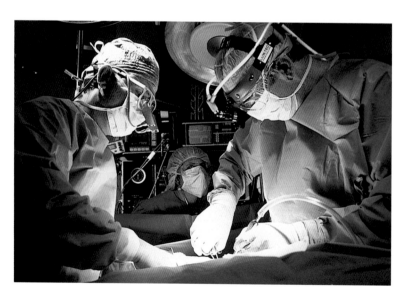

Levels of Intelligence

Intelligence is a term which covers a wide range of abilities. These surgeons (left) require a high level of specialist knowledge and the ability to make decisions under pressure. They also need good coordination. Many other types of jobs require different, but no less demanding, skills.

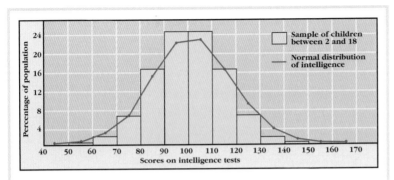

Intelligence Distribution

The graph above shows what percentage of the population belongs in each IQ range. The blue bars show the IQ range of a group of nearly 3,000 children between the ages of two and 18 who were tested. The red line is the normal average distribution of intelligence. The estimated and tested IQs are very similar.

Dodging Dinosaurs

Two students are looking at the skeleton of a giant, meat-eating *Tyrannosaurus rex* (below) in a museum. "Those creatures could swallow a prehistoric man in one gulp," says the first student. "They could, but they never did," says the second. Is he right, and if so, why?

Which Set?

The five numbers (above) give the answer 18 when one of the sets of +, −, and x are inserted into the four blank spaces. Is it set A, B, C, D, E, or F?

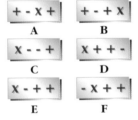

Make the Box

Which box (1, 2, 3, or 4) can be made from the opened-out design shown on the right?

arithmetic, reasoning, memory, and vocabulary. The performance tests cover assembling puzzles, analyzing abstract forms, completing pictures, and decoding tasks. The problem with IQ tests is that they usually only measure certain skills and not others, and do not take account of the cultural and language differences that exist between people. Some IQ-style tests are shown here. (The answers are on page 71.)

Crack the Code

One of the disks below is the correct one to put in the sequence on the right and should replace the disk in the center with the question mark. Is it disk A, B, C, D, E, or F?

GENDER DIFFERENCES

ARE THE BRAINS of males different from the brains of females? In other words, do males and females really think and behave differently, and if they do, what are the factors that determine those differences? Are they inherited through our genes, or is our upbringing an important factor? Or if there are no real differences, is it the way society expects us all to behave at work and at home that causes variations?

Throughout history men and women have carried out roles according to their sex. From earliest times stronger men provided the meat—hunting wild animals and defending their territory. Females had the gentler tasks of homemaking, rearing the family, and gathering plant foods.

Today the assumption that males and females will perform different roles persists. It is called gender stereotyping. A male is likely to be regarded as tough, ambitious, and scientific in his approach to problems. A typical woman is regarded as more sensitive and ready to compromise. Her interests may more often be in the arts than in science. These perceived differences affect the way males and females are treated by their employers. Men may be seen as more competitive and likely to put their career before family. Women, it is often thought, are seen as less competitive and therefore perhaps less effective, and likely to put their family before their career. But what real evidence is there for these differences in thinking?

Biological and Environmental Evidence

Scientists think that some abilities may be passed only to either the sons or the daughters through their parents' genes (see *Body Systems*, page 36). For example, the gene controlling the ability to catch a ball well may always be inherited by male offspring. There is also the possibility that the male and female sex hormones are in some way able to influence the way the brain works and therefore how we think. It has also been suggested that male and female brains are somehow organized differently. But the evidence for all this is inconclusive so far.

So perhaps gender stereotyping during upbringing encourages different thinking between the sexes? As soon as a child is born, it is likely to be dressed in colors and to be given toys

Whose Job?

This young woman (above) works on high-performance cars. She shows clearly that one's job need not be determined by one's sex.

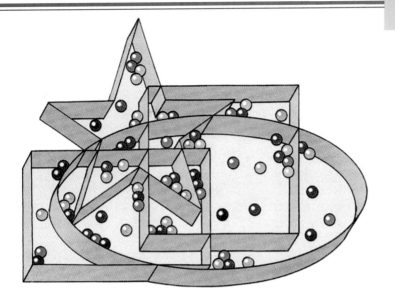

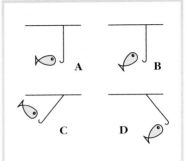

Fish on a Hook

Look at the four figures A, B, C, and D. Which is the odd one out? This is a logical test.

How Many Balls?

This will test your eye for detail. How many balls are there in the star, the square, the oval, and the rectangle (above). How many balls are there altogether?

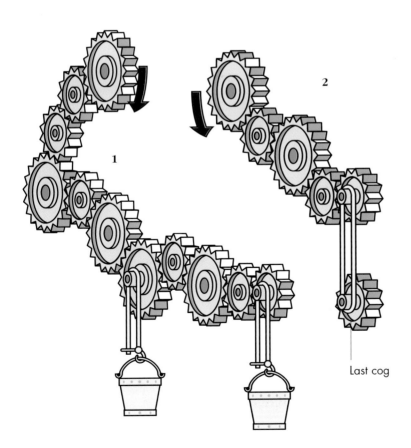

1

2

Last cog

"appropriate" to its sex. As it grows, it will be expected to behave in the ways society expects. It would be unusual if all of these pressures did not in some way influence the manner in which a person behaves and thinks. It is these factors, probably more than any biological ones, that determine how each of us thinks and behaves, and that play a large part in shaping the roles we adopt in later life.

Try the puzzles on this page and see if each can be solved more quickly by females or males. Compare your times with those of your friends. (The answers are on page 71.)

Turning Cogs

Here are two groups of cogs (left). If you turn the first cog of each group in the direction of the arrow, will the two buckets of group 1 go down or up, and will the last cog of group 2 turn clockwise or counterclockwise? This puzzle tests spatial ability.

IMPROVING LEARNING, MEMORY, AND IQ

SOMETIMES, THE PEOPLE who seem the most clever are simply those who have developed effective ways of learning and remembering and are prepared to study hard to achieve good results. Many of these techniques are straightforward and available to us all.

Why is it that some people seem to be rather "brainier" than others and always do best on exams and tests? Partly it is because the brains that they were born with have the kind of neural connections that enable them to learn quickly and recall facts easily. It probably also provides them with the power to reason and calculate effectively. But what is probably also true is that they learn and study effectively and—very importantly—that they actually want to learn. There are strategies that we can all use to assist our mental powers, and by doing so, we will increase our own ability to learn, memorize and recall facts, and even master skills that we might have thought were beyond us.

Can we also improve our intelligence, then? To an extent we can, by undertaking training and education in the skills that make up intelligence. For example, verbal intelligence requires an extensive vocabulary. Vocabulary building (learning and using new words in spoken and written sentences) and

reading more to also increase your vocabulary, will improve your powers of self-expression.

Hints for Studying and Remembering

• Repeat to remember. The more times that you repeat something, the better your long-term memory will become.
• Learn in short bursts. Many short sessions are better than one long session. Only study for

Study Time

The right environment is important for effective studying. A college library (above) provides a quiet setting with plentiful access to reference materials.

as long as you feel that you can concentrate.
• Learn by association. Try to think of something already familiar to you that you can link

with what you are trying to remember.

• Learn logically. Learn in a structured, systematic way. This will help establish logical memory patterns in the brain.

• Write it down. Writing out facts, or carrying out calculations on paper, helps you focus on the material more clearly and helps to reinforce it in your memory.

• Break it down. Once you have studied something, reduce the material into smaller units by a series of key words and short notes. In time, the key words should be all you need to remember in order to recall the rest of the material.

• Transform the information. Write notes, using your own words and phrases, rather than simply copying the exact words in a book or from a computer screen.

• Analyze the material. First, scan the contents, text headings, etc., to gain an overview of the subject matter. Next, skim through the text looking for key phrases and pieces of information. Then, study selected areas carefully, making notes. Last, make your own shortened version of the information.

• Don't study when you feel ill or are becoming very tired. Try to regard studying as an enjoyable, challenging part of your daily routine—not something that must be endured.

• Look elsewhere. If a subject seems too difficult to grasp, read about it in a different resource. One author may have a better way of getting the

information across than another.

• Study at a regular time. Make yourself a timetable and try to keep to it. The timetable should have reasonable, achievable targets. If you find you are falling behind your schedule make a revised timetable. It is often a good idea to delete items as you achieve them; this lets you see how you are progressing.

• Believe in yourself. Any studying you do in a conscientious way will help you learn. Don't worry if others seem to

Learning to Play
Learning to play a musical instrument like the violin (above) will take time. As well as the one-to-one instruction she receives at her regular lessons, this student must spend many hours practicing by herself.

have learned more than you. You will be amazed at how much you can achieve if you are prepared to enter into the activity in a motivated and fully committed manner.

Exam-writing Techniques
Here are some tips that may help you pass those exams!
• Read *all* the questions on the exam paper.
• Plan your answer before you start writing.
• Keep your answer confined to the question.
• Where relevant, have an introduction, main text, and conclusion.
• Don't write more than is necessary to fully answer the question.
• Write as legibly as you can.
• From time to time, refer back to the question as you write.
• Use large, labeled diagrams where appropriate.
• Include plenty of facts, figures, and other data.
• Time yourself; ensure you allow time to answer all the questions.

PROBLEM SOLVING

THE ABILITY OF human beings to find solutions to problems has been, arguably, the principal reason for the huge advancement of civilization in such a relatively short period of time. It has enabled us to conquer life-threatening diseases, to survive in hostile environments, to unravel many of the mysteries of time and space, and to explore worlds beyond our own.

Everybody faces problems. A toddler may have a problem working out how to turn that door handle he can't quite reach yet. A student may have a problem organizing her revision so that she can pass an exam. Someone in business may have a problem concerning how to fund the expansion of a factory. All problems have one thing in common: they are unsatisfactory situations we want to change. Fortunately, we find solutions to most of our everyday problems because problem solving is just another form of thinking (see pages 48–49). However, there are various methods and strategies that almost all of us can learn and use to make problem solving an easier and more effective task. Indeed, for some people the prospect of a problem is something they regard as an exciting challenge. In fact, many organizations exist simply to offer solutions to people's problems.

Stages In Problem Solving

Problem solving can be broken down into a number of stages. First, there is the problem itself: it must be identified and the situation assessed. Second,

fact file

Problems can be solved successfully only if they are properly identified at the outset.

Plan a series of achievable steps toward solving the problem, and work steadily.

If no progress is made, try a different approach.

Treat each problem as a new one—solutions to earlier problems may not work.

Choosing a Route

These soldiers (left) are faced with the problem of how to get from one place to another in difficult, snowy conditions. The map is part of the solution; it helps them choose the best route to reach their goal.

there needs to be a goal: how would we like the situation to be? Third, there needs to be a route or pattern that can be followed to get from the problem to the goal. It is important to be clear and precise about defining the problem so that time and effort are not wasted pursuing the wrong goal.

Now we must think of some routes to the goal. These can be rehearsed and imagined in our heads, perhaps even acted out, or we can write down a series of staging points—small tasks to be achieved on the route toward our goal. Very difficult problems may require several attempts before the goal is achieved. It may even be necessary to approach the problem from an unusual angle. In other words, to redefine the problem in a new way and to ignore the

12-Straw Problem
Make six equal-sided squares using 12 straws (below). Hint: you will need some Scotch tape.

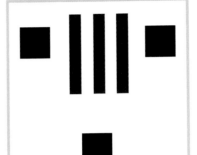

Off the Ground
The planks of wood (shown red) are too short to reach from one pillar (shown purple) to the next. Arrange the planks so it is possible to cross from one pillar to the next without touching the ground.

usual assumptions about the problem. This may help you reach a more imaginative solution. This form of creative thinking is often called lateral thinking. Here is an example of lateral thinking. Imagine you owned a gravel pit, and all the gravel had been used. How could you continue to make a living from your land? One solution might be to fill the hole with water, and stock it for use as a fish farm.

Another way of solving difficult problems sometimes is to work backward. The goal now becomes the starting point, and a series of reverse steps can be identified. Imagine you need to assemble something: you could start by carefully taking apart another similar item to see how it is put together. Can you solve the problem puzzles on this page? (Answers on page 71.)

Link Up
The five pieces of chain below must be linked together to make a continuous length. By opening link C (first move) and attaching it to link D (second move), then opening link F, and so on, it will take eight moves. How can it be done in less?

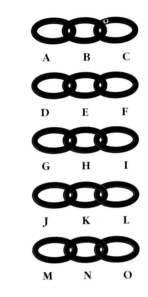

Reach Out
Tie a piece of string to a tree or post. Now tie another piece to a second tree or post positioned so that by holding onto one piece of string, you cannot reach the other (above). Using only a piece of modeling clay, how would it be possible for you to hold both pieces of string at the same time?

SLEEP

WE SPEND ABOUT one-third of our lives sleeping, and our regular sleep periods are an integral part of the human 24-hour activity cycle. Sleep rests the body and restores the mind. During sleep more of the body's defenses can be diverted to repairing cells and tissues and fighting illnesses. As we sleep, we drift from one level of unconsciousness to another and back again, with corresponding changes in our brain activity.

Humans, in keeping with other mammals, have two types of sleep. In rapid-eye-movement (REM) sleep the eyes move backward and forward rapidly behind the closed eyelids, and this is the period of sleep when we dream and when brain activity is greatest. Non-REM sleep, which usually accounts for most of our nightly sleep, is interspersed with shorter bursts of REM sleep, occurring in a cyclic pattern throughout the night. The stages of sleep are marked by different brain wave patterns

and by changes in body processes and muscular activity.

Why We Sleep

There is still much that we do not understand about why we sleep, but it is generally thought that during this period of relative inactivity, the body has an opportunity to rest and restore itself. We sleep longer during infancy and adolescence—the times of maximum growth. People suffering from diseases and other illnesses sleep more deeply at this time, too, as the

Sleep Time

The amount of sleep we require varies with age. We need more when very young but less as we grow older. Children around the age of one (above) sleep for about 13 hours each night.

body's repair systems work hard to help combat the disease or illness and return the body to full health.

It is also believed that REM sleep is in some way involved in the brain's learning process

fact file

People whose sleep patterns are disrupted—for example, shift workers—suffer more illnesses on average.

Insomnia is the name given to the chronic inability to sleep.

Each year over 10 million people in the U.S. consult their doctor about sleep problems.

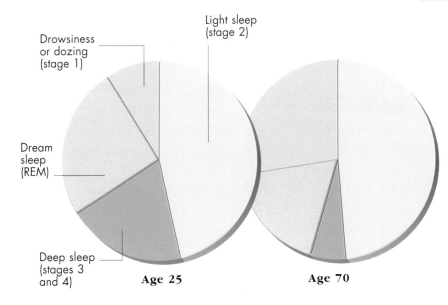

Drowsiness or dozing (stage 1)

Light sleep (stage 2)

Dream sleep (REM)

Deep sleep (stages 3 and 4)

Age 25 **Age 70**

Effect of Age on Sleep

The chart far left shows the proportions of a nightly sleep pattern for a 25-year-old, while the chart near left shows the pattern for a 70-year-old. The 70-year-old spends only a quarter as much time in deep sleep (stages 3 and 4) but spends nearly four times longer in the period of dozing, drowsiness, or awake (stage 1). The older person also dreams for a shorter time. Light sleep (stage 2) remains approximately the same in both cases.

and in the formation of memory patterns (see pages 44–45).

On average we sleep for eight hours each night, although this varies considerably with age and also slightly less widely between different people of the same age. Newborn infants typically sleep for 16 hours or more each day. One-year-olds sleep for 13 or 14 hours, and between the age of five and fifteen this drops to nine or ten hours per night. Elderly people often need only about six hours sleep. Being deprived of sleep on a prolonged basis can seriously reduce our alertness and performance in tasks, and it can also affect our moods and behavior.

People who cannot sleep properly are said to be suffering from insomnia. This may occur due to stress, illness, or broken sleep patterns. The other major sleep problem is hypersomnia, or excessive sleepiness.

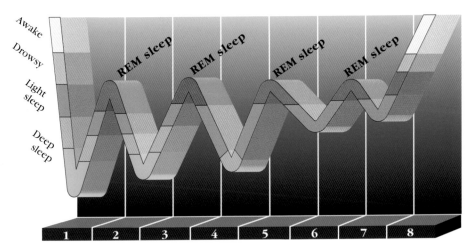

Awake
Drowsy
Light sleep
Deep sleep

REM sleep REM sleep REM sleep REM sleep

1 2 3 4 5 6 7 8

Hours of sleep

Sleep Patterns

A normal sleep pattern follows a cycle of peaks and troughs as shown (left). We fall from light sleep to deep sleep and back again several times, the stages gradually becoming less deep as sleep progresses. During REM our eyes move rapidly, and breathing and heart rates increase. During deep sleep, muscle activity is at its lowest, and heart rate and blood pressure also reach their lowest points.

EYE STRUCTURE

THE EYE IS similar in many ways to a camera. The iris at the front of the eye acts like a camera shutter to control the amount of light entering the eye. There is also an adjustable lens to focus the images. The retina is like a camera's film; it captures images, but unlike camera film, it can be used time and time again. Also like a camera, the images formed must be processed in some way so that we can see them.

The eyes are paired, light-sensitive organs, each about 1 inch (2.5 cm) in diameter. Each eye lies within a bony socket of the skull called the orbit. The eyes are richly supplied with blood vessels and nerves. Different muscle groups move the eyeball within its socket. Other muscles alter the size of the iris and the shape of the lens.

The outer wall of the eyeball consists of three layers. The outermost, the sclera, is composed of fibrous tissue. At the front of the eye the outer layer becomes the transparent

cornea. The middle layer includes the iris, the ciliary muscle, and the choroid. The iris is colored by pigments and is the part used to describe a person's eye color. The iris surrounds the pupil, the aperture through which light enters the eyeball. Muscles in the iris control the size of the pupil and therefore the amount of light that enters. The ciliary muscle pulls on the lens to alter its shape. Changing the shape of the lens allows images to focus on the retina. The choroid is richly supplied with blood vessels, that also nourish the other layers of the eyeball.

The innermost layer of the eye is called the retina. The retina contains the light-sensitive nerve cells of the eye that are connected to the brain by the optic nerve.

There are two types of nerve cells in the retina. Rods are long, thin cells that are sensitive to low light conditions. They are particularly important for night vision. Cones are narrow at one end and wider at the other. Unlike rods, which are found all over the retina, cones

fact file

Each eye contains about 125 million light-receptive rod cells and 7 million cone cells.

The human eye is capable of distinguishing more than ten million different colors.

Tears contain an antibacterial agent to help protect the eyes against infection.

pupil size

The size of the pupil changes automatically according to how much light is entering it. Cover one eye for several seconds while looking in a mirror. Now uncover the eye. Notice how the pupil quickly becomes smaller as it reacts to the extra light coming into the eye.

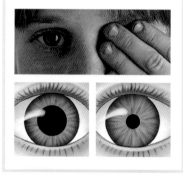

are concentrated in a part of the retina called the macula. Cones are sensitive to bright light. They allow us color vision and form the sharpest images. The rods are extremely sensitive to light. Once the eye has adapted to the dark, it can see a candle flame from 5 miles (8 km) away.

The Human Eye

A human eye in cross-section (right). The lens divides the eyeball into two parts. In front of the lens is a chamber filled with fluid, known as the aqueous humor. Behind it is a chamber filled with a jelly-like substance, known as the vitreous humor. Light entering the eye passes through the cornea, aqueous humor, lens, and vitreous humor and is focused onto the retina. The optic nerve goes to the brain.

Protection for the Eyes

In addition to the orbital bones of the skull that surround the eyes, they are also protected by the eyebrows, the eyelashes, and the eyelids. They help prevent mechanical injury and also keep dust and other harmful bodies out of the eye. The lacrimal (tear) glands produce a fluid that washes the cornea and conjunctiva (the inside part of the eyelid) and helps fight bacteria.

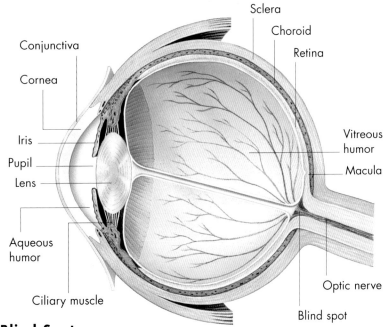

Conjunctiva
Cornea
Iris
Pupil
Lens
Aqueous humor
Ciliary muscle
Sclera
Choroid
Retina
Vitreous humor
Macula
Optic nerve
Blind spot

Blind Spot

Stare at the cross with your left eye closed. Hold the page at arm's length, and move it toward you until the spot disappears. It has focused on the "blind spot" (a part of the retina with no light-sensitive cells).

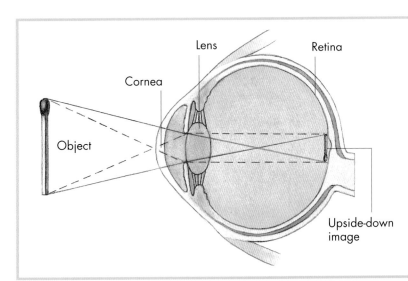

Object
Cornea
Lens
Retina
Upside-down image

Images on the Retina

As rays of light from an object pass through the cornea and lens, they become inverted—in other words, the image that is focused on the retina is turned upside down. (Exactly the same process occurs when an image falls on the light-sensitive film in a camera.) The visual cortex of the brain turns the image around again, however, so we see it the correct way up.

PERCEPTION

WHEN WE LOOK at something, light reflected by the object passes through the eye and strikes the millions of light-sensitive cells on the retina at the back of the eye, forming an image. The cells act like electrical switches, turning on as light hits them. Instantly, they relay messages to the brain containing information about the object—such as its shape and color. The brain then interprets this information, enabling us to see.

The first part of the process we call seeing occurs when light from an object strikes our eyes. The light then passes through the pupil, which regulates the amount coming into the eye. When the light rays pass through the lens, they are refracted (bent) so that they will focus the image we are looking at onto the retina. The lens is slightly elastic and is able to change its shape through the action of the ciliary muscle pulling on it to allow it to focus on near and distant objects. This is known as accommodation. The lens is able to focus on only one object at a time and changes its shape slightly whenever we look at objects at different distances from the eye in order to bring them into focus. This effect is noticeable if one views various objects placed at different distances on a table, for example. When one object is held sharply in focus by the eyes, other objects will still be visible but will only come into sharp focus when viewed directly.

At the Retina

After passing through the lens, the light waves hit the light-receptive rods and cones in the retina, which are stimulated by the energy contained by the light. The rods respond to light, dark, and movement, whereas cones are sensitive to color. Not all areas of the retina are equally sensitive to light, however. The greatest concentration of cones is to be found in a small

Binocular Vision

Each of our eyes has a slightly different field of view, but the fields overlap in the center. This is the area of binocular vision. It enables this mother and baby to gauge the distance from each other (above).

area called the fovea, in the center of the macula (see pages 58–59). This is where the sharpest focus of images occurs.

The area of the retina surrounding this provides us with our peripheral vision.

Once stimulated, the rods and cones produce electrical signals that are then transmitted by neurons. The nerve cells of the retina converge at the blind spot and leave the eye as a bundle of fibers, called the optic nerve, to travel to the brain. Before reaching the brain, the two optic nerves split at the optic chiasma (see below).

In the Visual Cortex

When the nerve impulses reach the brain, they pass to the visual cortex. In the visual cortex, the nerve impulses are then converted into mental images, enabling us to see. Different parts of the visual cortex are designed to interpret the information received by the brain. For example, certain areas specialize in interpreting shape and brightness. Other parts are concerned with pattern recognition.

Seeing Colors

At normal reading distance the red, blue, and black dots (right) are easy to distinguish. Now move the page further away. The red dots still stand out clearly, but it is harder to distinguish the black dots from the blue dots. This is because the cones, that are sensitive to blue light, are scattered thinly in the retina, making it hard to pick out the color from a distance.

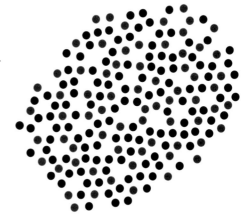

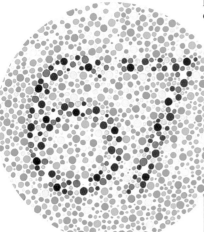

Color Blindness

Are you able to see the number 67 in the pattern of dots above? Don't be too alarmed if you can't, because some people are red-green color blind. This means that they are unable to tell some colors apart because they have only two types of cones instead of three. This affects about 4 percent of people.

Optic Chiasma

The optic nerves from each eye meet at a "crossroads" called the optic chiasma. Each nerve then divides, with fibers from the inner half going to the hemisphere on the opposite side of the brain. Thus messages from the left visual fields of both eyes go to the left hemisphere, and those of the right visual fields of both eyes go to the right hemisphere. This arrangement improves three-dimensional vision.

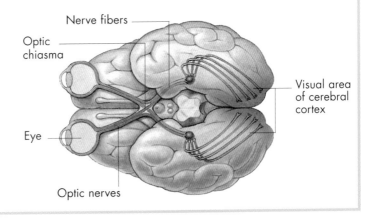

Nerve fibers

Optic chiasma

Eye

Optic nerves

Visual area of cerebral cortex

INTERPRETING THE VISUAL WORLD

THE BRAIN MUST make sense of all the visual information that is relayed constantly to it by our eyes. It must recognize objects for what they are and must separate objects from their backgrounds. The process by which it does this is called visual perception.

On previous pages we have looked at the structure of the eye and the way in which the images on the retina are relayed to the brain. Here we examine how the brain is able to make sense of the world we see. From all the pieces of sensory information the brain receives, it must ignore some, enhance others, or even fill in missing details.

Survival Pack

Do we, as babies, have to learn how to interpret visually what we see, or are we born with an instinctive understand-ing of how our visual world works? From experiments in which babies showed distress if presented with an object that appeared to be coming toward them on a collision course, it appears that we are born with a kind of distance perception. This is probably a basic survival mechanism. Babies have also been shown to track (follow with their eyes) facelike patterns for much longer periods of time than nonfacelike patterns, which suggests that they pay attention to objects that they recognize as important to them (in this case a potential provider of food).

Recognizing Objects

Recognition may be based on the overall size of the object, on being able to identify important parts, or on an understanding of the relationship between the parts and the overall shape. Recognition also involves matching the object that we see, or the parts of it, with our knowledge of what it should look like. There must also be

Catching a Ball

To catch the ball, this fielder (left) must first use his eyes to pick the object out from its background. He must then constantly alter his focus on the ball as it heads toward him, "looking" it into his glove.

What Is It?

What do you see when you look at the picture on the right? Perhaps you see a skull, with eye and nasal sockets and some teeth. You may also see some confusing detail to either side of the jaws. Or maybe you see two people—a man and a woman—wearing berets and leaning toward each other over a table with some glasses on it. You may be able to make out both images if you concentrate on one or the other, but not at the same time. This is because the brain is alternately jumping between deciding that the various parts of the picture are really the elements making up the skull or that they are part of the scene with the two drinkers. There are many other examples of these so-called ambiguous pictures.

some way in which the brain matches up our memory of an object with whatever view of it we see. It may be that the brain has a range of memories of the object seen from very different viewpoints. If this matching process did not take place, we would think that every time we saw an object from an unfamiliar view, we were looking at the object for the first time.

How do we recognize faces? The difference between all the millions of people's faces on the planet are often tiny, yet we can pick out a familiar face among thousands of remarkably similar ones. Partly this is a result of our society—we need to be able to recognize faces, and so it is a skill that we all practice daily without even realizing it. Also, it is likely that everyone's face reflects slightly different emotions—the eye can pick up the tiny unique social signals in facial gestures that identify a particular individual. Research has shown that recognizing these so-called secondary features has to be learned. We are all better at distinguishing members of our own society because we are more used to doing it. The brain must also make many other judgments about what the eye sees. It must notice detail, separate objects from backgrounds, and account for movement and perspective. Furthermore, it must recognize that an object seen dimly lit or at a distance is still the same colored and sized object even when seen in bright light and close up.

Visual Cliff

Babies who are old enough to crawl will refuse to cross a transparent bridge if they can see a drop (below). This raises interesting questions. Is our ability to perceive depth instinctive, and at what age do we begin to associate depth with danger?

VISUAL PUZZLES

SOMETIMES OUR BRAIN is fooled by the information being sent to it from our eyes. What we think we see isn't always there. In some cases there may be confusing pieces of information that fool the brain. In other cases there may just not be enough information for the brain to make the right judgment about an object or picture. These puzzling pictures are often called optical illusions.

Visual puzzles can be fun and even challenging to do, but there is a scientific principle underlying the way they work connected with how the brain processes the information it receives from the eyes. Visual puzzles that fool the brain are often called optical illusions. There are various kinds, and the five puzzles shown here each demonstrates

Spiral Trick
Look at this spiral (right). Now try to follow the spiral to the center. You can't! The spiral is really just a series of circles, but your brain, confused by the background, mistakenly joins them together.

Color Strength
In the squares (left) are four colors against either a black or a white background. Look at each pair of colors. Are they the same, or does one of the pair look brighter? Your brain is influenced by the light from the surrounding colors as well as the light reflected by the colored squares themselves, making the colors on the black background appear brighter.

Magic Spots

Look at the blue squares below. You will see small, gray, flashing squares at the corners, especially at the edge of your field of vision. The gray squares are caused by the brain combining the light and dark images falling on the retina.

a different way in which images can play tricks on the brain. It is interesting to note, however, that not everyone is affected by illusions to the same degree.

How Illusions Work

Our brains, through past experience, often take it for granted that things are really as they seem. We can interpret a few brush strokes as a picture of, say, a person, because the brain has enough clues about what the picture should be and fills in the gaps. But occasionally the brain interprets the visual information wrongly. Most optical illusions work because the brain has insufficient data or is confused or fooled by the other information it receives.

Some illusions are based on the fact that the brain cannot separate an image from its background. Others rely on the brain combining images together, making it see something that isn't really there. Sometimes, one part of a picture influences the brain so much that it misjudges or misinterprets another part.

Which Is Taller?

Is the corner of the building, from the ground to the top, higher or lower than the corner of the room, from the floor to the ceiling, in the illustrations above? Measure them and see. (Answer on page 71.)

Illusions of Nature

In this underwater scene there are 18 sea creatures concealed by camouflage. Can you find them all? In nature some animals use these tricks to look like something else to fool their enemies. (Answer on page 71.)

HEARING

OUR EARS ARE the organs that enable us to hear. Vibrations in the air produce energy sound waves that stimulate special receptors inside the ear. These receptors then transmit nerve impulses to the brain, turning them into sounds. Other parts of the ear are responsible for helping us maintain our balance, or equilibrium. Surprisingly, our hearing reaches its peak at about ten years of age and then starts to slowly decline.

O ur ears are one of the body's major sense organs. Like the other sense organs, they supply information about the world around us to the brain. The small time difference taken for a sound to reach each ear enables us to locate the source very accurately. For humans, particularly, the ears also play a major part in communication, for it is with our ears that we hear speech.

How the Ears Work

The fleshy, outer part of the ear is called the auricle, or pinna. Its job is to collect sound waves so that they can be channeled along the auditory canal to the middle ear. At the inner end of the auditory canal is the eardrum, or tympanum. This is a sheet of tissue. When sound waves reach the eardrum, they make it vibrate, and these vibrations are then passed to the middle ear. The middle ear consists of three tiny bones that magnify the vibrations by 20 times. The first bone, the malleus, or hammer, is attached to the eardrum at one end and to a bone called the incus, or

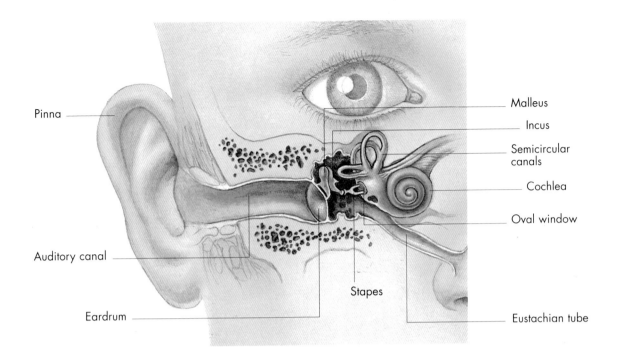

Pinna

Malleus

Incus

Semicircular canals

Cochlea

Oval window

Auditory canal

Stapes

Eardrum

Eustachian tube

anvil, at the other. The incus in turn is attached at its other end to a bone called the stapes, or stirrup. The other end of the stapes is attached to a membrane called the oval window.

Vibrations from the eardrum set the middle ear bones in motion, and the sound waves are then transmitted into the inner ear. Inside the inner ear is the cochlea. This is a fluid-filled structure containing the organ of Corti. The organ of Corti is lined with special hair cells that are sensitive to sound waves. When the hair cells are stimulated, they turn the sound waves into nerve impulses that are carried to the brain along the auditory nerve. The brain then interprets these impulses as sound.

The human ear is able to hear sounds within a broad range— between 20 and 20,000 cycles per second. By comparison, a dog's range is 15–50,000 cycles per second. Our ears are also extremely sensitive to sounds. They can detect movements of the eardrum of one-billionth of a centimeter—less than the diameter of an atom.

Maintaining Balance

Inside the inner ear there are also structures known as semi-circular canals. The canals are

Ear Structure

Each ear has three parts: the outer ear, the middle ear, and the inner ear (above). For the eardrum to vibrate freely, air pressure must be equalized on both sides of it. Air reaches the inner part of the eardrum through the eustachian tube, which connects with the throat. If this becomes congested—when we have a cold, for example— hearing may be impaired.

set at right angles to each other. When a person tilts or turns their head, the fluid in these canals moves. The movements cause nerve impulses to be relayed to the brain. The brain responds to these impulses by moving the body's limbs so that it maintains its balance.

Piano Tuning

This piano tuner is using his ears to listen carefully for the small difference in sound called pitch that is made by each piano key. By using a special tool, he makes adjustments to retune the instrument (left).

SMELL, TASTE, AND TOUCH

JUST LIKE THE eyes and ears, the organs of smell, taste, and touch are merely detectors, collecting information from the environment for the brain to interpret and use. The sense of touch can also tell us about what is happening inside the body.

Touch, like the senses of sight and hearing, is a sense that works by responses to physical stimuli. Smell and taste, however, are senses that are stimulated by chemicals. Smell and taste have been less well studied than the other senses, and as a result, our understanding of exactly how they work is not complete.

Smell

Our sense of smell is more sensitive than our sense of taste, and we can detect about 10,000 different odors. A sense of smell is important to us for detecting dangerous odors. It also plays a part in attracting the opposite sex and in simply enjoying the rich experience of pleasant smells in our everyday

Sense of Smell

The senses of smell and taste (right) are quite separate, but both are stimulated by chemicals. Receptors in the nasal cavity detect molecules of scent present in the air. The receptors are attached to nerve endings that relay messages to the brain.

lives. We also use our sense of smell as part of the process of tasting, although smell and taste are entirely separate sensory systems. When we smell something, the odor particles reach specialized, sensitive tissue at the top of the nasal cavity. This contains millions of tiny olfactory nerve endings that are stimulated by the particles. The nerves are connected to the olfactory nerve, that runs to the base of the brain. Once it has been

received, the message can be interpreted by the brain as a specific smell.

Taste

What we commonly call taste is really a combination of taste and smell resulting in flavor. We are able to distinguish only four basic taste qualities: sweetness, saltiness, bitterness, and sourness. These combine together to form specific tastes. Special taste cells known as taste buds

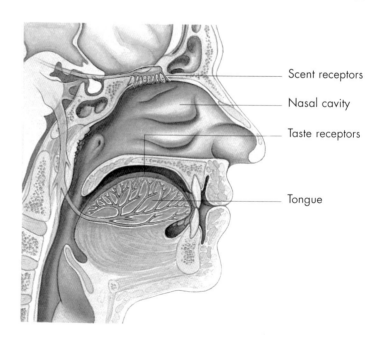

Scent receptors

Nasal cavity

Taste receptors

Tongue

taste buds

Different parts of the tongue are sensitive to each of the taste sensations of bitter, sweet, sour, and salt, as shown below. You can test this yourself by placing small amounts of coffee powder, sugar, lemon juice, and salt on different areas of your tongue and discovering where you can taste them.

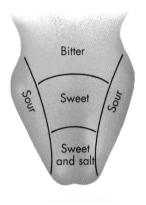

are stimulated when they are in contact with the substance being tasted. They are connected to nerves that send a signal to the brain for it to interpret as taste. The tongue, the organ most concerned with taste, has different areas that are receptive to each taste quality. There are about 10,000 taste buds on our tongue, palate, pharynx, and larynx. To enable a taste to be experienced, the substance must first be dissolved in saliva.

A sense of taste is important to our survival. We can detect decaying (sour) and poisonous (bitter) flavors in much lower concentrations than sweet and salty flavors.

Touch

The brain also receives information about our surroundings through the sense of touch. As well as the pleasant sensations associated with touch, the ability to feel pain or extremes of heat and cold is also vital for survival. Touch is brought about by the touch receptors that pack the skin and the deeper tissues. If they are stimulated by something coming into contact with the skin, they send messages to the spinal cord. From here, the message passes to the brain. The touch receptors differ from one another in the way in which they are surrounded by protective "packaging" and in the depth they are found beneath the skin. These two factors determine whether the nerve ending is stimulated or not by various types of contact —light touch, pressure, pain, vibration, heat, or cold. The sensation of touch fades quickly, which is why we can wear clothes without being aware constantly of them. The brain

also receives information about the internal environment—for example, a stomach pain is the body's way of telling us that something is wrong with the digestive system.

Touch Receptors

Nerve endings in the dermis, just beneath the skin's surface (below), provide sensory information about temperature, pressure, and texture, and can also detect pain. The most sensitive areas of the body are the fingertips and the face.

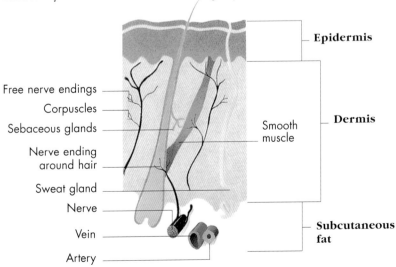

Free nerve endings
Corpuscles
Sebaceous glands
Nerve ending around hair
Sweat gland
Nerve
Vein
Artery

Epidermis
Smooth muscle
Dermis
Subcutaneous fat

CHANGES CAUSED BY ENVIRONMENT AND AGE

WHAT EFFECTS, IF any, do our upbringing and the environment in which we live have on brain development? Also, what effect does the aging process have on the way our senses function and on our mental abilities?

Although humans all share many characteristics, our individual personalities are very different. Each of us has our own likes and dislikes, and our own way of thinking about things. But where does this unique personality come from? Do we learn to be outgoing, shy, mild-mannered, or aggressive?

Some researchers point to evidence suggesting that our environment is the key to the development of personality. How we are brought up as children determines how we develop in later life. Others believe that our inherited genes provide each of us with a basic personality framework, and that our upbringing enhances and develops certain characteristics already present in each of our personality profiles.

This may also be true for many tasks involving thinking

and reasoning. It is possible that we are born with particular aptitudes—which might include skills in mental arithmetic, for example—and the right teaching environment will help us develop such abilities and will offer opportunities to learn more successfully. There are, however, many examples

throughout history of people being born into impoverished conditions with little obvious opportunity for extensive formal education, who have risen to positions of prominence through their inherent mental abilities and sheer determination and wish to succeed. Indeed, we can all improve our knowledge by our own efforts through study and also by practicing learning and remembering techniques (see pages 52-53).

Signs of Aging

Not everyone ages at the same rate, but for many people old age is characterized by a reduction in physical abilities (left) that may include impaired hearing and eyesight and diminished senses of taste and smell.

The Aging Process

If we live and work in a healthy environment, with adequate medical care available to treat any illnesses that may occur, our brain and senses should remain healthy. However, like all the other biological systems, the brain and senses can become prone to disease. They will also eventually become victims of the aging process.

Exactly when "old age" begins varies from person to person. Often the signs of aging can start to show themselves from about the age of 55. The signs are often gradual, and lifestyle can often play an important part in reducing or delaying the effects of old age. A sensible diet and exercise can improve blood flow and therefore help organs remain healthy. Having a range of activities and interests and keeping a positive mental attitude can also be effective.

Inevitably, though, the senses can deteriorate with

Learning Environment

Even though the conditions in which these Sudanese students (above) are learning is poor by Western standards, it is still possible to use this basic education as a springboard for further learning. However, social and political pressures may prevent further learning.

age. Long- or shortsightedness—the inability of the lens to focus properly—can often occur between the ages of 40 and 50. More serious eye diseases, such as cataracts (clouding of the lens) and glaucoma, may also occur in later life. A loss of hearing—particularly the loss of higher-pitch sounds—is fairly common in elderly people. There is often also a reduction in the ability to taste and smell.

Brain diseases associated with old age include dementia (loss of memory) and Parkinson's disease, which affects the muscles (see *Health and Illness*, pages 172–173).

fact file

Page 49:
Which Set? E.
Crack the Code A.
Dodging Dinosaurs Dinosaurs became extinct before prehistoric man appeared on Earth.
Make the Box 2.

Page 51:
How Many Balls? Star—20; square—30; oval—49; rectangle—30; 68 balls altogether.
Turning Cogs 1—both buckets go down; 2—counterclockwise.
Fish on a Hook B—end of tail not parallel to fishing line.

Page 55:
12-Straw Problem Make a cube—it has four square sides, a square top, and a square bottom.

Off the Ground

Link Up Undo links A, B, and C. Link remaining four lengths together with them (six moves).
Reach Out Squeeze the modeling clay onto the end of one piece of string. Set it swinging toward you. Now, holding the end of the other piece of string, catch the end of the first piece as it comes toward you.

Page 65:
Which Is Taller? Both the same.

Illusions of Nature

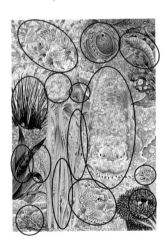

INTRODUCTION

EVERYONE HAS A personality that makes them unique in the way they think, feel, and behave. But where does someone's personality come from? For hundreds of years philosophers and scientists have tried to answer this question. Most psychologists now believe that we inherit part of our personality from each of our parents, but that the world in which we live (our environment) affects our behavior, too.

In this chapter we look at what is meant when we talk about someone's personality. We also study the way we think and behave in different situations and the reasons for this.

Each of us inherits, via our parents' genes, many different characteristics, or features. They include a set of instincts that make us do certain things in a preprogramed way, an individual temperament that determines our moods and feelings, and a personality. The word "personality" describes the set of individual characteristics that makes each person unique, or different. On pages 76 and 77 we look at some of the methods psychologists have used to study personality and to look

for similarities and differences between people.

Everyone studies human personality and behavior, often without being aware of it. Every day we take in huge amounts of information about where we are, ourselves, and other people. This chapter describes how we organize and then use those experiences so that we can interact appropriately with all

the different people that we encounter. For example, on pages 78–83 we look at how we see others and also how others view us. We also examine the ways of thinking we develop that lead us to group similar people together using what are known as stereotypes.

Everyone is an individual, and the way we behave as individuals is discussed on pages

Judging by Appearance

Even when we do not know someone, we start to form ideas about their personality just by looking at their faces and actions. We can do this even when the people are from different racial and cultural groups, like the boys shown right. How would you describe them—sporty, sociable, mischievous, showoffs?

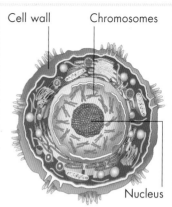

Family Likeness
The children in this family (above) have inherited physical features from each of their parents. Most scientists think that our personalities are inherited, too.

90-91. The factors that change our behavior when we are part of a group are looked at on pages 94-95.

Thoughts and Feelings
Although the characteristics we inherit make it likely that we will react to situations in certain ways, the environment we live in and our individual experiences have the biggest influence on our behavior. Between pages 108 and 111 we will investigate feelings and emotions.

We all experience some of the same emotions, like grief, but we each react differently. We will look at the ways our temperament and early relationships influence how we learn to interpret and deal with our feelings (see pages 108-109). Learning that our thoughts affect our feelings enables us to take control in situations when we experience unpleasant emotions like anxiety (see pages

Nature or Nurture?
The nucleus of each cell in the human body contains chromosomes made up of hundreds of genes. We inherit our genes from our parents, and they determine the characteristics we develop. In addition to physical features, like eye color, we also inherit our personality and some of our behavior. But psychologists are interested in studying how much of our behavior we also learn through our interactions with other people and the world around us—in other words, through our environment. This is called the nature versus nurture debate.

116-117). Understanding more about human personality and behavior gives us the chance to make the best of ourselves and others. In this chapter you will find ways to help you reach your goals (see pages 118-119).

Finally, you will see that there is still much to discover about human personality and behavior—like why we dream and what dreams mean (see pages 120-121).

INSTINCT AND HUMAN NATURE

PEOPLE OFTEN SAY that they reacted instinctively to something. By this they mean they seemed to know what to do without any previous experience. But experts continue to disagree about how much of human behavior is instinctive and how much is learned.

An instinct is a pattern of behavior that makes us do certain things in a particular way. We are born with instincts. Instincts have also been described as unconscious forces over which we have no control. When an instinct is triggered, we act in a preprogramed way. It is thought that instincts are passed on genetically (see *Body Systems*, page 36), and that their purpose is to increase our chances of survival.

Basic instincts include hunger, thirst, and the drive, or need, to reproduce. It is easy to see that without these instincts the human race would not survive.

But there is disagreement about how much of our behavior is the result of instincts and how much of it is learned. For example, some psychologists (see *The Brain and Senses*, page 39) believe that aggression is a basic instinct that we are constantly producing. You can think of it as a tank of water that is continuously filling up. If the water is not released from time to time, the tank

will overflow. In the case of aggression the "overflow" results in aggressive behavior.

Others believe that it is how we live that makes us aggressive. From this point of view it is thought, for example, that inner city violence results from overcrowding and limited

Caring for Others
When we see people cry, we often comfort them (above). This urge to care for others when they cry evolved so that family members would be looked after if they cried and therefore survive. This caring activity also extends to strangers— people outside the carer's family.

human responses, too, it is difficult to see what purpose they serve. One explanation is that our instincts are not as strong as we once thought they were, and that experience (in other words, what we learn) and our environment (where we live) may be as important in determining what we do.

Most experts agree that we have inherited the likelihood to behave in particular ways, but that we can take some control of these patterns and change our behavior (see *The Brain and Senses*, page 70). It is likely that our environment influences our behavior as much as our instincts do.

Survival Instinct

These families fleeing from danger (above) are increasing their chances of survival. It is instinctive for parents to protect their offspring because children carry their parents' genes. Ensuring their children's survival increases the chances that their own genes will pass to future generations.

opportunities to achieve goals, and not from a natural instinct to be aggressive.

Make your own list of what you do during the day, and then think about how much of your behavior may be the result of your instincts and how much of it is a result of things that you have learned to do.

Genetic Influences

Some of the instinctive things we do seem to have more use for survival than others. We are probably instinctively concerned with our own survival and the survival of people closely related

to us. Those who share at least some of our genes—especially sons and daughters—matter most of all. This explains why a mother may go hungry in order to feed her child. She is making sure that her genes are passed on to future generations.

But some mothers abandon their babies or mistreat them, and we often hear of people who show unselfish behavior, risking their own lives for strangers. If these are instinctive

Channeling Aggression

Many psychologists think that aggression is an instinct, more often seen in males than females. If aggression is not released regularly, it may build up and come out as even more aggressive behavior. Competitive sports (below) are a safe way to release aggression.

TYPES OF PERSONALITY

WE GENERALLY USE the word "personality" to describe what we know about a person's character. We often make guesses about people's behavior, and we talk about people "acting out of character" if they do not behave as we expect. We also tend to group certain characteristics together—for example, we are not surprised if someone who is quiet is also shy. But do predictable personality types really exist?

We commonly use the word "personality" when we talk about the characteristics of people. For instance, we may say that someone has a kind personality or an aggressive personality. It was once thought that people's general appearance—their facial features and body build, for example—told us what their characters were like. And even though this has been found not to be true, some of us still make assumptions about people based on their appearance (see page 78).

Over the years scientists have developed different theories, or ideas, of personality in an attempt to explain the similarities and differences between people. Two things are generally agreed: we each have a unique personality made up of many different characteristics, and our personalities remain more or less the same over long periods of time.

One well-known theory is called the trait theory (see page 77). Trait theories look for particular characteristics,

or traits, that tend to be found together in people. According to these theories it is possible to identify different personality types and group people according to type. Studying groups of people with similar types of personality provides information about how different characteristics affect behavior. This is useful because it lets us imagine how people we do not know very well are likely to behave in different situations.

Self-actualization needs

Self-esteem needs

Need for belonging and love

Safety and security needs

Physiological needs

Freud's Theory

Another well-known personality theory was developed at the beginning of this century by the Austrian physician Sigmund Freud. His theory states that there are three parts to the human personality. Freud called these the **id**, the **ego**, and the **superego**.

The id develops first and is the self-centered part of our character. It is driven by unconscious instincts like hunger. The id wants immediate satisfaction. For example, babies cry when they are hungry, demanding to be fed.

During childhood the ego develops. This part of the personality tries to satisfy

Maslow's Pyramid

The American psychologist Abraham Maslow thought that our behavior is driven by our basic needs. We have to satisfy the needs at each level of the pyramid (left) before moving to the next. People who reach the top of the pyramid are said to be fulfilled. (This is called self-actualization.)

Eysenck's Theory

The psychologist Hans Eysenck developed a well-known trait theory of personality. He thought that all the different types of people there are could be fitted into two major aspects of personality. He called these extroversion/introversion and stable/unstable. Eysenck argued that much of our personality is inherited from our parents, so our individual characteristics are more or less decided before we are born. This chart shows how he thought different characteristics were grouped together. For example, an unstable extrovert would be excitable and possibly aggressive, whereas a stable introvert would be calm and reliable. Can you locate yourself and members of your family on the diagram on the right?

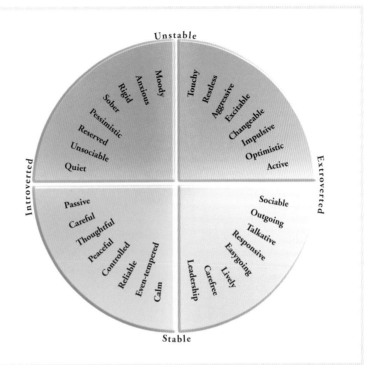

Unstable

Moody
Anxious
Rigid
Sober
Pessimistic
Reserved
Unsociable
Quiet

Touchy
Restless
Aggressive
Excitable
Changeable
Impulsive
Optimistic
Active

Introverted

Extroverted

Passive
Careful
Thoughtful
Peaceful
Controlled
Reliable
Even-tempered
Calm

Sociable
Outgoing
Talkative
Responsive
Easygoing
Lively
Carefree
Leadership

Stable

What Sort of Person?

How would you describe this boy's character (left)? We often make assumptions about how people are likely to behave based on what type of personality we think they have, which is often based—in turn—on their appearance.

the needs of the id but in a way that is socially acceptable. For example, we learn that we sometimes have to wait to eat when we are hungry.

Finally, the superego develops. It acts as our conscience and is made up of ideas we have learned from our parents and others about what is right and wrong. The superego demands perfection from us.

In fact, both the id and the superego make demands on us that it would be impossible to meet. The ego, the realistic part, helps balance out the other two unrealistic sets of demands. This theory is still popular with some people, although it is not very scientific, and there is no way of testing if it is true.

HOW WE SEE OTHERS

THROUGHOUT OUR LIVES we meet many people, and it is important to be able to judge what they are like. After only a brief meeting we may decide that we do not want to see someone again. Many factors affect how we see other people, and first impressions can often be wrong. We have probably all lost the chance of making good friends because we "got the wrong impression" of someone.

When we first meet someone, we look for obvious features in their personality to help us begin to figure out what they are like. We first look for the main characteristics, sometimes called central traits, that will describe them broadly. For example, we may call someone a friendly person and someone else an unfriendly person.

Once we have established these central traits, we then add to them other features that we know from experience often go together. These groupings of information in the brain are called **schemata** (singular: schema). For instance, if you are going to meet someone who has been described as shy,

you immediately think of your shy schema. This is probably made up of a number of traits that you group together such as "quiet," "unsociable," and "loner." When we get to know a person better, we replace the general schema with the right one for that person.

Schemata are not always an accurate way of assessing someone's general personality,

however. We tend to include the positive features of someone with other positive features we think they might also have, and negative features with other negative ones. This explains the so-called Halo Effect, which occurs when we generalize a person's central traits. For instance, if someone is considered good and likeable, we tend to think that all their

First Impressions

We make judgments about what people are like within the first few seconds of meeting (right). Clothes, appearance, voice, and mannerisms all help make up this process. Once we have formed an impression, it affects how we think the person will behave in the future.

fact file

The first information we see or hear about someone has the biggest effect on our overall impressions. This is called the Primacy Effect.

We tend to like people who also like us.

The longer we are with someone, the more we like them.

behavior is like this. They can do no wrong. Similarly, if someone is perceived as bad, we tend to dislike whatever they do. But once we know people well, any important new piece of information about them is likely to change how we see them in the future and will replace our first impressions.

Forming Impressions

There are some features that seem particularly likely to affect our thinking about people. This is partly due to the effect of stereotypes (see pages 84–85 and *The Brain and Senses*, pages 50–51). Stereotypes are preset views we have about the way certain groups of people will behave. For example, there is a stereotype that assumes that boys are better at games than girls.

We can also attach too much importance to an unusual or distinctive feature. If a man has a black eye, we might decide that he has been in a fight or has been attacked. This thought, true or untrue, will then affect our overall impression of him.

Our impression of people is also sometimes affected by what is going on around them. If a group of people are generally thought to be boring, we might

Making Sense of What We See

To make sense of unusual scenes (like the one above), we often go beyond the facts. For instance, we may think this man is just attention-seeking, whereas the reality could be that he lost his car keys.

overestimate how much we like the least boring person in the group.

There are a number of things about you—the observer—that can affect how you see others. For example, we tend to think that people who are like us in one way will also be like us in others, and that they will think and generally behave as we do. Our own behavior can have an effect, too. If we like someone, we are more likely to behave in a friendly way, and they are more likely to be friendly toward us, which strengthens our view of them as friendly.

HOW OTHERS SEE YOU

WHETHER WE ARE aware of it or not, most of us have different "faces" that we put on to suit the occasion. But even when we consciously try hard to create a particular impression, we never really know how others see us. No one can actually read our minds, although some people are very good at seeing things about us that we do not realize we are revealing.

People observing us take in not only our general appearance but also our mannerisms, speech, and constantly changing facial expressions (see *The Brain and Senses*, page 63). They may notice things we do of which we ourselves are not aware— like playing with our hair when we are anxious or worried.

In general we care about what others think of us and usually try to present ourselves in a favorable light. The art of self-presentation is like acting in a play. We put on a face for the world, and we often change what we wear, how we talk, and the words we use to create a particular impression. We sometimes do this on purpose, but at other times we are not aware that our presentation is being adapted to suit a particular situation.

Our awareness of ourselves also changes depending on our surroundings. For instance, in unfamiliar situations, when we are ill at ease, we become more aware of our behavior and monitor the way others react to us more closely than we do

The Real You

The face you see when you look in the mirror is not the same as the face that others see. First, it is reversed from left to right. Most faces are not symmetrical (not exactly the same on both sides), and reversing features can make a difference in the overall impression. Second, a mirror only lets you examine your face from one angle. Faces are very expressive. Humans have more muscles for moving their faces than does any other animal, and our facial expressions can change very rapidly. Some expressions may last for only one-fifth of a second, yet they still convey meaning to another person.

when we are relaxing with friends or family.

People who observe themselves a lot are called "high self-monitors." They tend to be better at judging how they appear to others. They change their presentation if they feel things are not going well.

The term given to the ability

to present the image we want is **impression management**. Successful impression management depends on being aware of what kind of behavior is expected in the social situation you are in, as well as being able to observe yourself.

However good we are at impression management,

we often communicate things about ourselves of which we are unaware. People cannot know exactly what you are thinking, but they can subconsciously pick up signals, or cues, from your voice and body language (see *Communication*, pages 140–141), which add to the overall impression of you.

Subconscious Signals

These verbal and nonverbal signals can give us away when the image we are trying to present is not what we actually feel. Nonverbal signals are very powerful. It has been found that the look on our faces when we are talking has a much bigger impact on the listener that the actual words we speak.

There are a number of ways in which the observer picks up information about our mood. As we have already seen, fidgeting with objects in our hands suggests that we are anxious. We are also very good at subconsciously assessing someone's feelings by the emotion in their voice, even if we do not know the person.

Much of our self-image (in other words, what we think of ourselves) is also based on what we believe others think of us— although we rarely check out the truth of our assumptions by finding out what people really *do* think of us.

Try writing down a list of features that you think a friend would use when trying to describe you, and see if your version matches what they actually say.

Clues in Clothes

The way we dress gives out information about us and the lives we lead before we have even spoken. Judgments about status and profession are often made on the basis of clothes.

We also use clothes to create an impression. For example, we may dress in formal clothes when attending an interview. We may also sometimes wear particular styles of clothing to help ourselves feel and act the part, as for a wedding.

People who wear clothing associated with high status tend to have more influence than those wearing low-status clothing. A person wearing smart

Putting on a Face

A clown's makeup (above) is designed to hide true expressions and create a face that always looks happy or sad. We create a public face in much the same way. We may also choose to enhance certain features by using makeup, but sometimes we simply hide our true feelings behind a false smile.

clothing—for example, a suit— will usually be more likely to be given help from strangers. Color also plays a part; we expect ambitious people to wear clothing with hues of gray, dark blue, or brown rather than red, yellow, or green.

HOW YOU REACT TO SITUATIONS

THE WAY YOU react in different situations is governed by several factors—
for example, your mood, your past experiences in a similar situation,
and also what kind of behavior society expects of you.

When we encounter a new situation or meet someone for the first time, we use a set of values, or beliefs, formed by previous experiences, to help us react in the right way. These values may include our views on what we consider to be good and bad, for example. Values like these are called **personal constructs**.

For example, if we meet people who speak in a very forthright manner, we may either think that they are rude and upsetting or that they are talking in a straightforward and trustworthy way. The construct

fact file

Refusing a direct request is difficult. In one study people on the subway were asked to give up their seats without any explanation. Half of them agreed to do so.

Breaking social rules often makes us feel anxious.

We tend to obey people wearing "official" uniforms.

Sports Fans
At a sporting event like an exciting tennis match (above) it is quite usual for spectators to dress casually and to react openly to the action with gasps, groans, and cheers. Sometimes the umpire even has to remind them to keep quiet.

Formal Events
At a formal social occasion (right) we are expected to behave in a more dignified and controlled manner. In this situation people clearly react very differently from the sports fans above.

we use to interpret their behavior will direct our actions and affect how we interact with them. With the first interpretation we might avoid them, but with the second we might ask their opinion if we had a problem. In both cases the same people are acting in the same way, but the way in which we interpret their behavior can be very different depending on our personal constructs.

Social Roles

From an early age, through the process of socializing, or mixing with others, we learn rules that direct our behavior in different situations. Some rules are personal to your family—such as not wearing outdoor shoes in the house, perhaps. Others are social rules—often called social or cultural norms. These include obeying laws. We learn to expect people to behave in predictable ways in different situations, and they expect the same of us.

When we first do something new, like starting to attend school, we feel as if we are acting out a role. Gradually the acting becomes easier, and in the end we adopt the role more or less automatically. When this happens, it is said that the role

Keeping a Distance

In public places we keep a distance between ourselves and people we do not know (right). We find it strange and unsettling if someone breaks this unwritten rule and sits too close.

The situation you are in

Social rules/norms

How you are feeling

Your reaction

Past experiences

Your personality

has been internalized. Taking on roles allows us to respond automatically most of the time. Think of a typical day and how many roles you have. They may include being a son or daughter, car passenger, friend, and student. Each of these roles carries its own set of behaviors, which are appropriate and relevant for

How You React

Individual and social factors work together to influence how we interpret and react to different situations (above).

a particular situation. If we do not stay "in role" and break the rules, our behavior is often met with social disapproval.

STEREOTYPING

IMAGINE SOMEONE IS asked, "What are college students like, and how do they behave?" It is very unlikely that the reply will be, "It is not possible to say in general, because all students are different." This is because we often apply beliefs we hold about a group to everyone within the group. This is called stereotyping. Often we are not aware that we are stereotyping people, but we do it frequently.

A stereotype is a belief that all the people who belong to a particular group behave in the same way. Although stereotypes are rather rigid, they serve a purpose. They help us "file" in our brains the vast amount of information we receive about different people on a daily basis. This lets us begin the process of interacting with other people.

We all use stereotypes until we get further information that

1

At first glance we begin the process of deciding what a person is like. We look for key characteristics to help us form an overall impression.

2

If the person belongs to a group for which we hold a stereotype, this will influence our impression. We automatically apply the stereotype and ignore other information.

3

The stereotype we apply immediately prompts us to assume the existence of other characteristics, often mistakenly. Someone who is a vegetarian is assumed to care for animals, for example.

Appearance

We often apply stereotypes based on a person's appearance. For example, we usually think that fat people will be more jolly than thin people (left).

Stereotyping in Action

We stereotype people all the time, usually without realizing we are doing so. This automatic process (left) can lead us to gain the wrong impression of someone.

changes or disproves what we first think. There are a number of common stereotypes, or prejudgments, of groups in our society. They include stereotypes about males and females, racial groups, ages, and reli-gions. Can you think of any other groups that we have stereotypes for?

There are a number of reasons why stereotypes can cause us to judge people wrongly. On page 78 we looked at the importance of first impressions. Once we have applied a stereo-type to someone, we are more likely to notice what we expect to see and to be unaware of evidence that contradicts this. For example, if someone gets most of the answers right at the beginning of a quiz, we see them as more intelligent than another person who did badly at the start of the quiz—even if the person who started badly ends with a higher score.

Stereotypes can also be self-fulfilling. When we expect people to behave in a certain way, we behave differently toward them. For example, it has been shown that we tend to expect "feminine" behavior from girls and "masculine" behavior from boys (see *The Brain and Senses*, page 50).

Changing Stereotypes

As roles in society change, so do our stereotypes. There are now many more women in what were in the past considered to be "men's jobs." Once a female surgeon was unusual; and if we had continued to meet only male surgeons, the stereotype of a surgeon as male would have been reinforced. But as female surgeons have become more common, the stereotype has weakened.

Stereotypes based on a person's racial group are common. When the stereotype is a negative one, there can be disastrous effects, particularly when the stereotypes are held by a group rather than by an individual (see page 89).

There are a number of ways in which we can challenge

Glasses and Stereotypes

It has been found that people who wear glasses—particularly women—are judged to be more intelligent than people who do not. Look at these two pictures of the same woman (above and below) and see if you agree.

stereotypes. One way is to get to know people better from a group that you stereotype. Another way is to make changes in society. This can be done, for example, by introducing laws that make employers give all job applicants an equal chance whatever their sex or ethnic group. Being aware of our stereotypes is the first step toward challenging them and changing them.

fact file

We treat boys and girls differently from birth, which reinforces stereotyped behavior between the sexes.

Our clothes have a strong influence on how people judge our personalities.

Getting to know people better is a good way of breaking down stereotypes.

SELF-AWARENESS AND SELF-ESTEEM

WE ALL HAVE ideas about ourselves and how we would like to be. In order to develop confidence in our ability to succeed and to believe that what we do is worthwhile, we need to feel that we are valued by others.

Self-awareness in humans probably developed in our very early ancestors as a means of survival. First, the most self-aware individuals would be best at hiding from, or avoiding, wild animals and other enemies. Second, because our society favors individuals who are thought of as attractive or useful, it would be a distinct advantage for anyone who could project such an image of themselves.

Self-awareness begins with the realization by a baby that some objects, like hands and feet, belong to it and are always there, whereas other objects are not part of it and are present only some of the time.

Self-awareness

The beginnings of self-awareness usually appear after about age six months. At about 18 months of age children recognize their faces (right) and point to pictures of themselves when their names are spoken. Shortly afterward they begin to use the pronouns "I," "me," and "you," suggesting an awareness of themselves and others.

As they get older, children begin to understand who they are and what they can do, developing as they do so their self-image (see page 87).

Self-esteem

Self-esteem is a person's sense of what he or she is worth. It comes from recognizing our own achievements and feeling

Your Self-image

We each develop a self-image, or view, of ourselves. It is made up of our own observations of our appearance, feelings, and behavior, as well as what we think of the reactions of others toward us. Feeling valued by others increases our feelings of worth. We try different ways of presenting ourselves and observe other people's reactions. The most successful self-presentations then become part of our self-image. But our self-image may not be a true reflection of what we are really like or want to be.

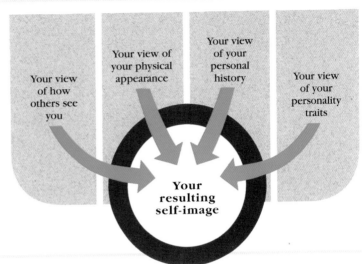

Your view of how others see you

Your view of your physical appearance

Your view of your personal history

Your view of your personality traits

Your resulting self-image

valued by other people. For self-esteem to develop, we need to be made to feel special when we are young. For example, feeling accepted and valued by our parents for who we are encourages feelings of self-worth and gives us confidence to explore our abilities.

It is important that our parents encourage us to try new things and praise our achievements. But sometimes parents expect too much. If a child feels valued only when it is achieving, it will often feel that it has failed. The child may then view itself as worthless

and never develop confidence.

In addition to our self-image we each have an idea of who we would like to be—an "ideal-self." When our self-image is very different from our ideal-self, self-esteem is likely to be low. Some people set themselves unrealistically high goals that are impossible to achieve, and others have an inaccurate self-image. For example, a person may be thought of

as successful and popular by his or her friends. But the person may have unrealistic expectations and may believe that the only way to be successful is to always be top of the class, and that the only way to be popular is to be liked by everyone.

The closer your ideal-self and self-image, the more fulfilled and happy you will feel. This subject is considered again on page 90.

Public Recognition

Recognition by others of our achievements increases our own sense of worth and encourages us to persevere (right). We value skills and other achievements that get rewarded. It is important to value different skills. We cannot all be good at everything, but we are each good at something.

HUMANS AS INDIVIDUALS

ALTHOUGH WE LIKE to live together in groups and share many common interests,
it is the fact that humans are all so different from each other and are able to express
the differences that set them apart from the other animals on the planet.

Humans have always been concerned with their personal hopes, fears, and feelings. They have expressed their individual feelings in literature and art, as well as in the fury of battle. But in ancient societies, as well as in many modern ones, personal interests have often been submerged by those of society (see pages 80–81) as a whole. In times of war or famine day-to-day survival is the priority.

In the early medieval world individuals were expected to fit within a strict social framework. If you broke the law, you faced severe penalties. If you were a peasant, you worked on the land. In Europe during the 1300s a series of plagues killed many people and created a labor shortage. The peasant was now in a position to bargain for

Faces in a Crowd

Soccer supporters gather for a match at the Arsenal team's stadium in London, England (below). When individuals are in a crowd, they behave differently than they would on their own. They like to show they belong to the group by wearing the same clothes and singing the same songs.

Renaissance Man

Leonardo da Vinci (right) was born in 1452 at Vinci, in Italy, as the European Middle Ages were drawing to an end. He lived in an exciting new age of scholarship, art, and invention that was inspired as much by humanity as by religion. This period has been called the Renaissance, or "rebirth." Leonardo's life shows how much an individual human is capable of doing. He was one of the greatest artists of all time. He produced plays at the royal court. He was a brilliant architect, engineer, sculptor, botanist, mathematician, and inventor.

better wages as an individual.

As the old feudal system collapsed, a new age of individualism began. There was a burst of creative activity. Artists now celebrated humankind for its own sake, rather than as just a part of a social or religious system. By the 1790s the rights of the individual within society were being championed for the first time. The 1880s saw the foundation of a new science,

psychology (see *The Brain and Senses*, page 39). Psychologists such as Sigmund Freud and Carl Jung delved into the mind of the individual, studying how humans behaved within society.

To Rebel or Conform?

During the 1930s political systems such as fascism tried to crush individualism. However, by the 1960s individualism was a potent force

within society. Popular music, art, film, and new ways of thinking about society in general all encouraged people who wanted to be different to express themselves.

But another side of individualism was selfishness and greed. In the 1980s many politicians encouraged individuals to make money for themselves and to let the less fortunate look after themselves. Some people even declared that there was no such thing as society.

Individualism was very much a feature of North America, the Western nations of Europe, and Australia. This concept was at odds with the religions and traditional cultures of countries such as India, China, and Japan. In Japan, particularly, people had always been expected to conform to social traditions.

But now many western and eastern traditions are being challenged and changed as the spread of global communications, international economics, and greater opportunities for travel mean that different peoples and cultures are brought increasingly close together.

fingerprinting

Each of us is different, physically as well as mentally. For example, no two fingerprints are the same. By making fingerprints as shown here, you can compare those from different people.
1. Scribble on some paper with a soft, black pencil. Rub your finger over it.
2. Press some Scotch tape (sticky side down) onto your finger to make a print.
3. Stick the Scotch tape onto some white paper.

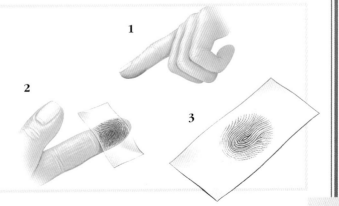

INDIVIDUALITY

WHEN SOMEONE IS said to show individuality, it means that they use their own unique beliefs and values to guide their thoughts and actions. We notice differences between ourselves and others, and usually value people whose individuality sets them apart. But it is not always easy to stand up for your beliefs and assert your individuality, particularly when your views are different from those of the majority.

Our personality is mainly the result of character-istics, or features, that we inherit through our parents' genes (see page 72). However, individuality, which is an important aspect of a person's personality, is something that we develop as we grow. We form our own opinions, some-times with help from others, and learn to express ourselves in words and deeds.

On page 76 we looked at a diagram of Maslow's pyra-mid. The psychologist Maslow believes that what we are all aiming for in life is the chance to achieve our true potential. Part of being an individual is about setting your own goals. By achieving these goals, we are able to reach our full potential and stand out as individuals.

An important aspect of individuality is the ability to recognize that other people's individuality—in other words, their views and beliefs—are as important as your own. This means not forcing your values and beliefs on others just as you would not wish to have others impose their beliefs on you.

Achieving Individuality

Individuality is not about being different for its own sake. Rather, it means having your own set of values for what is right or wrong—and sometimes defending them if necessary.

It is not always easy to say what you believe about things without being easily persuaded to change your mind. This is particularly true when your beliefs differ from those of the majority. Social pressures can prevent us from developing our own individuality. You can probably think of times when

Leadership

Many leaders, like former South African president Nelson Mandela (above), show exceptional individu-ality. A good leader needs a clear vision of the goals he or she wishes to achieve and a strong will to pur-sue them in the face of opposition.

your actions have been influ-enced more by social pressures than your own beliefs. For example, it is common during school years to join in teasing someone, even when we know it is unkind.

Individual Style

Someone who dresses creatively to please himself or herself has individual style (right). Most often what people choose to wear is not a reflection of individuality. Instead, we tend to use clothes to give a message to people around us—for example, when we dress to fit in with a group, to stand out in a crowd, or to create a particular impression.

The pages on group behavior (see page 94) describes how we all seek social approval. To please other members of a group, we often take on the beliefs of the group rather than develop our own. Experiments have shown that fewer than 30 percent of us are willing to support an idea that is different from the majority view. Asch's experiment (described on this page) demonstrates this.

Similarly, some children face pressure from their families, for example, to follow a particular profession. If we try simply to achieve the expectations of others, we are less likely to discover our personal strengths. One of the tasks of adolescence is to develop our own beliefs, values, and goals, which may be different from those of our parents and peers.

Believing in yourself, being creative in thinking about solutions to problems, and standing up against social pressures will help you find out what you believe in and where your strengths lie.

Asch's Lines

Stimulus line

This experiment shows how hard it is not to agree with the majority view. A psychologist asked groups of people to look at three lines (called test lines) like the ones bottom right. He then showed them another line (called the stimulus line) like the one top right and asked each person in turn which of the three test lines (A, B, or C) was the same length as the stimulus line. All the people in the groups except for one person (called the subject) had been told beforehand deliberately to give the wrong answer. When it was their turn, the subjects felt uncomfortable disagreeing with the majority view, and many of them eventually "gave in" and agreed with the rest of the group, even when it was clear that they were wrong.

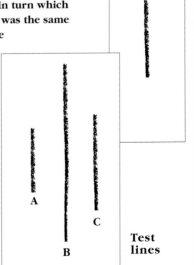

A

C

B

Test lines

SOCIALIZATION

SOCIALIZATION IS THE process whereby a person learns the social skills, roles, and values that enable him or her to become integrated into society. Socialization starts at birth and continues throughout a person's life. It is especially important from birth through early adulthood, since during this time children and young people are developing rapidly and learning many new things about themselves and the society in which they live.

Socialization is a gradual process that is influenced by many factors. For the newborn infant the strongest influences come from parents and other caregivers. As the infant grows older, other family members and friends become increasingly important. Nursery school, later school life, and wider social and cultural circles also play important parts and help shape attitudes. For example, children growing up in a city are likely to have very different experiences from those growing up in rural communities. As a result, their values (the things they consider important) may differ widely.

Early Social Behavior and Interactions

Many of the actions of very young infants are designed to help them form social bonds with adult caregivers. For example, infants prefer to turn their heads toward the sound of familiar voices. Some studies have shown that newborn infants can tell the difference between the sound of the voice of their own mother and that of an unfamiliar female voice.

Infants are especially interested in images that resemble the human face (see *The Brain and Senses*, page 62).

Influences on Socialization

Our immediate family usually has the strongest influence on our socialization because it is through our relationships with those who love and care for us that we learn about what is expected from us in society. As we get older, school and work life also add to the process of developing our social skills (left).

Development Through Life

The process of socialization also shapes our development. (Development is the process by which an individual grows and changes throughout his or her life span.) This is because as we grow up, we have many different experiences and learn more complex skills, roles, and values. For example, the influence of

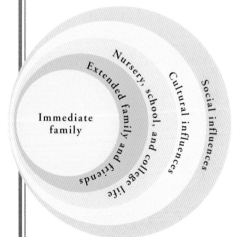

Immediate family

Extended family and friends

Nursery, school, and college life

Cultural influences

Social influences

Phases of Development

As time passes, we move through different phases of development. With each phase come new challenges and changes. As we become older, our social network widens, and we become increasingly involved in activities outside the family home. This finally turns into the phase when many young people choose to leave home for college, a new job, to live with friends, or to marry.

Early childhood	Middle childhood	Late childhood	Adolescence

| 0 | 3 | 5 | 7 | 9 | 11 | 13 | 15 | 18 |

Approximate age (in years)

our family affects how we understand and show our feelings and emotions.

The development of an individual can be divided into three different types. They are: emotional development, social development, and cognitive development.

Emotional development refers to the child's understanding of his or her own emotions, as well as those of other people around them.

Social development refers to children's ability to interact (in other words, to form relationships) with those around them.

Cognitive development is concerned with how we develop our intellectual knowledge and reasoning skills (see *The Brain and Senses*). Much of what we know about how the young child gains his or her knowledge of the world comes from the work of a well-known psychologist called Jean Piaget.

Playing Together

Play (left) provides many opportunities for children to learn about themselves and each other. Playing encourages children to discover and practice new skills as well as experiment with different kinds of behavior and social roles. Between the preschool ages of three and five there is a rapid increase in play and use of language. As children get older, play can help them learn about sharing, cooperation, and games with rules.

Feeling Sad or Angry

The little boy above is not very happy. Learning how to deal with upsetting feelings is an important part of growing up and socialization. From a very young age children discover that they cannot always have what they want. We usually learn how to respond to such situations with the help of parents and other family members.

GROUP BEHAVIOR

THROUGHOUT OUR LIVES we will be part of many groups. They might include family, friends, sports teams, clubs, religions, and political organizations. Humans seem to have a strong need to belong to social groups. And groups can have a powerful effect on what we think and how we behave. They often bring out some of the best, and the worst, examples of human behavior.

We learn from an early age to cooperate in groups, working together with others toward common goals. In groups we often achieve things we could never achieve on our own. In childhood we play team games with rules that are shared by all the members of the team. We also show a distinct preference for, and loyalty toward, members of our own team.

In many ways other groups we belong to in later life work in a similar way. We tend to agree with what most of the other members of the group think, and we run the risk of social disapproval and isolation if we do not.

But while membership in a group often helps us achieve a feeling of worth and belonging, some of the effects of being in a group can be negative. Being a member of a group can make us feel less of an individual, for example. It can also affect how we react to members of other

fact file

If we see someone in trouble, we are less likely to go to their help if there are other people standing nearby.

We tend to accept majority decisions made by a group we belong to, even if we do not personally agree with them.

We often behave "out of character" when part of a group.

Cooperation

Learning to cooperate is a vital part of becoming a member of society. Working with others to achieve a common goal has many benefits. It is usually quicker and more fun, and problems can be solved together along the way (left).

groups. Intergroup rivalry often occurs, for example, between supporters of rival football teams.

Even when the values and beliefs of a group are not actually true, if a large enough number of people accept them, all the members of the group may act as if they are true. This may lead, for example, to excessive nationalism of the type shown by the Nazis in Germany in the 1930s and 1940s.

Expressing Yourself

In a crowd excitement is catching. We become aroused and feel less shy. We feel anonymous and less concerned what others think of us. This can be liberating and provides an outlet to behave in ways we would not normally do, such as feeling free to scream and wave our arms around (left).

Crowd Behavior

The mere presence of lots of other people around us can have an effect on our behavior, even if we do not know them. Being in a crowd can lead to behavior you might not normally expect of yourself. In a crowd the high levels of excitement generated by the people around us may reduce our normal ability to monitor and control our behavior. We become part of what is going on around us.

The effect of a crowd on the people in it can be dramatic. It can cause a rapid change in mood from mere excitement to one of mass hysteria, panic, or violence.

Bystander Apathy

We would all like to think that we would go to the aid of someone in trouble. If there were other people around, do

you think you would be less likely to do this? Perhaps surprisingly, it has been found that this is the case. The effect has been called bystander apathy, and there are two factors which are thought to explain why it happens.

First, we may be uncertain that there is a real emergency, so we wait to see what others will do. The second factor has been called diffusion of responsibility. This refers to the knowledge that others are there, and as a result responsibility does not fall on any one individual. We each think that someone else will do something, with the result that often nobody does anything.

On the positive side, once people are aware of bystander apathy, they are much less likely to be affected by it and will instead take the necessary action to help a situation.

Risky-shift Effect

Decisions made by groups, rather than an individual, tend to be riskier. This is known as the risky-shift effect. It may happen because the responsibility for making a risky decision can be shared by the group as a whole.

SOCIAL UNITS

THE FAMILY IS the most important social unit, or grouping of people. Families tie us together and link generations. They usually provide love, care, and responsibility. The structure of the family has varied greatly over the ages and is continuing to change all the time. Families are building blocks for society—but not the only ones. Age groups, friendship groups, partnerships, and communities also play their part.

In many countries the typical family unit is made up of a mother, father, and two or three children—or many more in some cases. In more traditional societies the family group also keeps close contact with many other relatives, too, such as grandparents, cousins, aunts, and uncles. However, modern transportation and working practices mean that family members are less likely to remain living within the same communities than they were 100 years ago. The traditional family ties are weakening.

Variations of the family group include societies where the man takes several wives (polygamy) or the woman takes several husbands (polyandry).

In many modern societies divorce rates have risen sharply in the last 30 years. Couples may remarry, and the children of the first marriage may live with a stepparent. Many couples live together without marrying. In an increasing number of societies same-sex relationships are also tolerated. Many children are raised by one parent only or by foster parents (people who take the place of a child's real parents).

Many people claim that the traditional family is the only secure and balanced environment in which to raise children. Others point out that rigid family values in some traditional families have led to unhappiness, tension, and violence in the home. They

fact file

In many societies people's surnames indicate their parentage. In some the surname reflects the appearance, trade, or position in society of their ancestors.

The U.S.A. has the world's highest divorce rate.

Vanuatu has the world's highest marriage rate.

Single Mothers

Fifty years ago Western society believed that it was shameful for unmarried people to have and raise children. Today, attitudes have changed, but single-parent families (left) still face an economic struggle.

argue that love and affection are more important than the structure or legal status of the family.

Social Connections
The Masai people are cattle herders who live in Kenya and Tanzania, in East Africa. Traditionally, Masai men take several wives. But they are also part of another social structure —age-sets. When they come of age at about 16, they join the first age-set as junior warriors. They move away from the family and live with other members of their age-set for a period. This arrangement is a formalized version of what tends to happen to children everywhere as they grow toward adulthood. They begin to look less toward their family for support and more toward friends of their own age.

Similar groups of equals (called peer groups) exist at all age levels and in all societies. They may be senior citizens meeting to play cards or young people at a pop concert.

Strengthening the Ties
The importance of all these units in human society is emphasized by special rituals. People wear their best clothes and eat cake and drink champagne at weddings. They hold christenings or other naming ceremonies for their babies. They sometimes celebrate a

In the Longhouse
In parts of Borneo, in southeast Asia, an extended family can become a whole community. Dozens of families live under the same roof in a traditional "longhouse" (above), and small children have the run of the place, playing with the other children.

child's coming of age, as at the Jewish bar mitzvah ceremony. Peer groups may also have their own, less formal initiation ceremonies, which are necessary if you want to join certain clubs or go to a new school. All these links may strengthen society, providing a sense of continuity in a changing world.

SOCIAL SKILLS AND BEHAVIOR

INTERACTING WITH OTHER people is a central part of everyday life. As we grow up we learn, mostly from our parents and other caregivers, how to behave in relation to other people and according to the different social situations in which we find ourselves.

We saw earlier in this book how infants begin to learn to interact socially very early in their lives. Simple games such as peekaboo teach children how to use eye contact in social interactions and also let them practice taking turns to do something. Dressing up and pretending to be a doctor, nurse, or cowboy, for example, allows children to practice different kinds of behavior, speech, and gestures.

Most important of all in learning social behavior are our parents, caregivers, and friends. By observing other people's behavior, we learn what to do in similar situations. From a very young age we are also told to say "please" and "thank you" as a way of beginning to learn about manners.

How Others React to Us

Social skills are important because they affect how other people react to us and help us meet new people and make friends. The reaction of other people to us is very important because it also affects the way

we feel about ourselves. Eye contact (looking the person you are addressing in the eye), smiling, listening properly during conversations, and being sensitive to other people's feelings are among the social skills we should try to practice.

Our friends and family usually help by telling us if we are behaving in ways that other people do not like. We learn quickly that certain behavior— for example, interrupting when people speak—is not acceptable.

We act in different ways toward professionals such as teachers, nurses, and anyone in a position of authority. The

Mealtimes

When we are very young, we learn the basics of eating—how to use a knife and fork and how to eat food properly (below). As we get older, we learn other social skills related to food—such as that on occasions people often get dressed up for dinner, and that it is polite to thank the cook or host for a meal.

Formal Relationships

This boy is being cared for in a hospital (right). The relationship between a nurse and a patient means both of them use different social skills than the ones they would use when talking to friends.

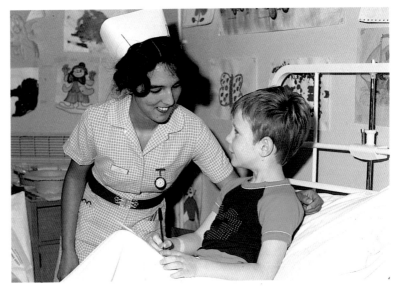

relationships we have with these people are sometimes called formal relationships.

Shyness

It is not unusual for any of us to feel shy in situations where we are unsure how to behave, what to wear, or what to do. Shyness can often be overcome by watching what others do and copying them or by asking someone the correct way to behave in a particular situation.

Knowing how to begin a conversation is an important part of overcoming shyness (see *Communication*, pages 128–129). As we grow older, we learn the many different ways to behave in different situations, and our confidence increases.

Sometimes shyness can keep us from meeting others and doing new things. When this happens, it can make us feel less confident about our social skills. This can lead to us feeling even more shy. Being aware of this cycle (below) can help break it. Talking with friends and family about shyness can help us understand that we are not alone in feeling shy and can often help us find ways of overcoming the problem.

The Shyness Cycle

A's self-image is of an unattractive or socially unskilled person

A assumes people like **B** are favorably impressed only by very attractive or socially skilled people. **A** is pessimistic about making a good impression on people like **B**

A's pessimism is reinforced

Shyness is reinforced by repeated social failures that are due partly to shyness itself. One step toward breaking out of this cycle is to become aware of it.

A believes that **B** has a poor impression

A behaves shyly or anxiously

A knows **B** is forming an impression and feels anxious

A wants to make a good impression on **B**

EMOTIONAL DEVELOPMENT

FROM THE MOMENT a newborn baby enters the world, emotions start to develop through interactions with others. Healthy emotional development depends on feeling loved and cared for early in life. With it children feel safe to explore the world of emotions.

Babies are born ready to respond in ways that encourage interaction with other people (see page 104). In the first few months of life, infants respond to people with smiles, cooing noises, and eye contact. But at this stage they do not show clear preferences for any particular person.

During the second six months of life they begin to show attachments to particular people. A special relationship develops with the person—usually the mother—who provides the baby with food and comfort. A secure attachment to someone early in life lays the foundations for healthy social and emotional development.

Behavioral scientists have observed a series of interactions between mother and baby in which each takes its turn imitating the other's facial expression. In this way babies get their mother's attention, which helps the attachment between them develop. For a secure attachment to develop, the mother must be sensitive to the baby's needs. It seems to be

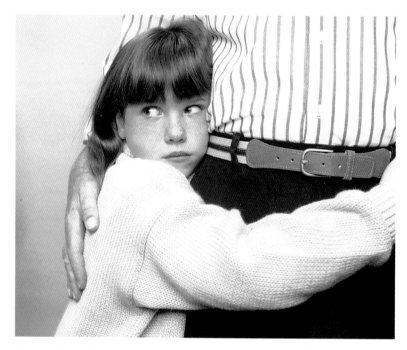

the quality of interactions that is important rather than the amount of time spent together. Babies are more easily comforted by their mothers than anyone else and rely on them to interpret and respond to their feelings. In this way the baby begins to learn about emotions.

There are individual differences between babies—for example, in how much they cry, how easily they are

Comfort Seeking

Young children become distressed when separated from people they have a strong attachment toward, especially when they are in unfamiliar places. As they get older, they are physically and psychologically more able to cope with this, and their fears of the unfamiliar lessen. But when reassurance is needed, they will still seek comfort from people with whom they feel safe (above).

To primary caregiver

To friends

To intimate partner

The Kinds of Attachment

Our first attachment is to our primary caregiver, usually our mother. It develops over the first seven months and lays the foundations for healthy emotional development. As we get older, we are encouraged to make friends outside the home. During play we explore our emotions and learn to express them. During adolescence we explore more complex emotions and our sexual feelings. We get to know ourselves and others on a deeper level. Close relationships prepare us for establishing lasting intimate relationships in adult life (above).

comforted, and how they react to new situations. These differences are partly a result of the sort of temperament with which they are born, and partly a result of the type of interactions that they have with those around them.

Naming Emotions

Babies cannot describe how they feel, but they show different sorts of behavior that suggest they experience increasingly complex emotions as they grow older. They begin with reactions to cold, hunger, and pain. They then go on to show fear of the unfamiliar and anger or frustration when an activity that they are enjoying is stopped or interrupted.

As children mature, they begin to interpret and give names to how they feel, often using descriptions taught by other people. Adults "label" feelings for children—saying, for example, when they think a child is tired, angry, or happy. The child learns to associate feelings and particular situations with these labels.

When self-awareness (see pages 86–87) emerges during the second year, children become capable of identifying with the emotional state of another person. This suggests that they are aware of their own emotional experiences.

Feeling Safe

In infancy our mothers encourage us to play with others. But we still need them nearby to give us confidence to explore and develop our social skills. You can often see children seeking reassurance by checking that Mom is there or by asking to be watched (below).

CHILDHOOD FRIENDSHIPS AND PLAY

MAKING FRIENDS AND playing together provide important ways to learn about ourselves and others, and how to get along with others in later life. The way we make friends and the things we do when we play change and develop as we grow up.

Making friends and playing start in the first year of life and then continue for the rest of our lives. The development of a trusting relationship between the infant and its parent or caregiver in the first two years of life is an important step toward forming friendships later.

Children under two often look at each other, perhaps smile, show each other a toy, or make noises. They often imitate each other. For example, if one child picks up a toy, the other child will also pick up a toy. Imitation helps maintain communication between children at this young age.

Between the ages of two and four many children go to nursery school. It is during these years that toddlers develop many of the skills that help them play more with their peers—for example, rough-and-tumble games. As children grow older, they become less and less focused on themselves and

their own needs, and gradually become more able to understand the needs of others. Beginning to have an understanding of what others may be thinking or feeling makes it easier to make friends and play.

School Friends

Through the middle school years (six to 11) children mostly choose same-sex friends. Some studies show that boys more often play in larger, mixed-age groups, while girls play in smaller, same-age groups. Girls often attach importance to the uniqueness of their friendships, while boys are more likely to place importance on playing competitive team games. However, girls can also be very competitive with each other and also like to play team games.

Between the ages of 12 and 14 most young people spend more time with friends and less time in the family home. This is often a transitional period when, for example, young people have moved from elementary school to junior high school. It is also the beginning of adolescence (the period of development that starts at about the ages of 12 and 14 and goes on into the early 20s).

Young Friends

Play between young boys and girls often involves the sort of behavior shown left. The boy is teasing the girl with his water pistol, and she is doing her best to keep dry by shielding herself with the umbrella.

A Common Pattern of Friendship

Most of us have a pattern of friends like the one shown below. Many friendships are formed throughout our childhood years. Very close friends are usually few in number, up to about five. We tend to have slightly more good friends. We know an even greater number of people who are "friends of friends" or people from school or work.

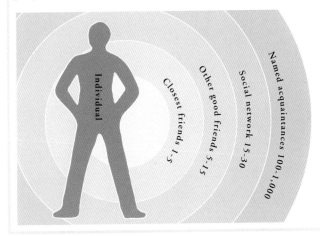

Individual

Closest friends 1-5

Other good friends 5-15

Social network 15-30

Named acquaintances 100-1,000

Adolescent Friends

The nature of friendship groups changes again at adolescence. Same-sex groups or gangs are common in early adolescence. They usually change to mixed-sex groups later, as relationships with the opposite-sex become more important.

Throughout early adolescence children tend to choose friends not only of the same sex but also the same ethnic background and academic achievement as themselves. This type of behavior can mean that some children are left out of friendship groups.

Factors affecting popularity during the adolescent years vary. For boys there is often social pressure to be an active athlete. In some schools owning a car is a factor reported as affecting popularity.

Young people can feel enormous pressure to be part of the group or crowd. This is one of the reasons why groups tend to dress in similar clothes and behave in similar ways (see *Communication*, page 122).

Girls tend to develop special friends particularly in adolescence. This is also a time to try out new activities, such as arranging a night out to go dancing with their friends.

However our friendships might change over time, they are important for all of us. Friends give us companionship and support, help us think about things in new ways, help us work problems out, and let us have more fun. Most friends fight or argue sometimes. Learning how to make up and resolve arguments is also an important part of friendship.

GROWING UP

OUR RELATIONSHIPS CHANGE as we become older and meet different people. Our first relationship is with our biological mother as we grow in her womb. Once we are born, we develop strong relationships, known as attachments, to those who care for us. We also form very close relationships with other family members. Later, we develop a broad network of friends and other acquaintances independent of our kinship ties.

Many psychologists and others have tried to trace the course of emotional and social development by identifying key stages and phases, but they can only be generalizations because we are all unique and develop in our own time. For example, some people achieve certain skills before others, some people develop physically faster than others, and some children are slow to start walking and talking, while others are much faster.

An important study of emotional and social development comes from the work done by the psychoanalyst Erik Erickson in 1968. He identifies several distinct developmental stages from birth to old age.

From birth to around one year old Erickson sees the development of trust between the baby and caregiver as the main relationship to be established (see page 101).

The ability to trust people who we consider to be important to us is a vital part of making and keeping friends and developing relationships.

Preschool Years

These are marked by the rapid growth of play and language. Children like to start activities and create things (above). There is often a sense of purpose and great satisfaction at accomplishment.

Between the ages of one and two the young child interacts mostly with his or her caregivers and begins to discover what he or she is able to do—developing a self-image in the process (see page 86). Between the preschool ages of three and five the toddler begins to develop a sense of conscience that guides its actions toward others and helps it distinguish right from wrong (see page 77).

From about age six until the start of adolescence, most children's interactions shift increasingly away from the home to school, and it is there that many new relationships occur.

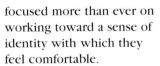

Between the ages of six and 12 there is more understanding about cooperation and a realization that friends do things for one another. From about the age of eight, friendships start to have a more enduring quality; we begin to feel sadness at the loss of a special friend if a relationship is broken—perhaps by a family move to another neighborhood. From about the age of 12 friends start to become liked because of attractive personal qualities we see in them.

Middle Childhood

Around the age of nine, children begin to share secrets and show loyalty and self-sacrifice. They start to see things from the other person's point of view and begin to undertake joint ventures for the good of both. At this age they can become very possessive about their "best" friends.

Adolescence

Our self-identity is important throughout life, but the start of puberty (sexual maturity) and entry into adolescence are often the times when young people are focused more than ever on working toward a sense of identity with which they feel comfortable.

Group membership helps young adolescents learn the roles they will take as adults and to establish identities separate from the ones provided by their families. The ability to think about abstract issues and hypothetical situations also develops in adolescence, and therefore it is not surprising that young people reflect more on how others see them.

Many young people worry if their body is not changing as fast as their friends'. However, everyone has a different body clock, and so it is quite natural for changes to occur at different times. The start of puberty for girls generally comes between 10 and 14 years of age and for boys between 12 and 16 years.

Early adulthood is a time when adult role commitments and responsibilities are taken on. The young adult has a clearer sense of self-identity, is often involved in an intimate relationship, and has identified certain goals that he or she would like to achieve in life. Preparing for new roles (see pages 106–107) becomes a central focus.

Young Adulthood

The transition, or change, from adolescence to young adulthood (left) is a time of intense interest in relationships. Attraction between the sexes is strong, as we practice intimacy and consider a choice of life partners.

GENDER ROLES

MOST SCIENTISTS AGREE that females and males behave differently in certain situations. There is evidence that this is due to a mixture of the biological differences that exist between females and males, and—perhaps more importantly—that it is also caused by the way we are brought up and the expectations placed on us. These differences mean that women and men may vary in the way they approach some relationships.

There are two major influences on behavior. First, there are the biological differences between males and females that we inherit through our genes. Second, there are the expectations of family, friends, and society about how girls and boys should behave (see *The Brain and Senses*, pages 50–51). Different outlooks, values, and ways of thinking about things sometimes affect the ways in which we interact with others.

By three years of age most children know whether they are a boy or a girl and can tell if their friends are boys or girls. In other words, they have learned that there are differences in the way each sex behaves and have begun to develop stereotyped ideas (see *Personality and Behavior*, pages 84–85) about females and males. Research has shown that children of this age believe that girls cook, clean the house, and talk a lot, while boys like to help father and say things like "I can hit you."

It is not surprising that sex-role stereotypes start early. One of the important ways children learn is by watching and imitating their parents and people close to them. While many mothers work, and fathers are increasingly involved in child care, male and female stereotype sex roles are still common

In the Workplace
Once, few women held senior management positions in companies. Now it is much more common for a woman to be in a position of authority (right). The way women deal with their staff may be different from the way men might deal with them.

on television, in films, and in books and magazines.

The role of parents is very important in encouraging particular types of behavior, and studies show that parents tend to behave differently in their own relationships toward boys and girls. Girls are often encouraged to dance, dress up, and play with dolls, while boys are engaged more in play fighting and sports, and are encouraged to build and play with things like trucks.

These learned stereotypes can show themselves in many ways in our later relationships. For example, men's friendships tend often to be "activity-oriented"—built around doing things together, such as sports. By contrast, friendships between women usually involve more affectionate behavior and discussions about personal issues—in other words, they are more "person-oriented."

So far we have talked about sex differences in Western societies. However, in many non-Western societies girls tend to be encouraged more to be caregivers and boys to be self-reliant high-achievers. These sex differences seem to be particularly strong in societies where male strength is important for herding and hunting.

At Work
The ways in which females and males deal with their relationships toward other staff members at work can also differ markedly. Although the stereotype of the tough, competitive

Child Care
Traditionally it was women who had the main role of looking after children. This has changed, and today fathers often become very involved in child care (above).

Learning to Care
This little girl (left) is feeding her baby doll. She has watched her mother, and perhaps father, too, and knows what to do. Boys are not often given dolls to play with and are much less likely to be encouraged than girls in play that involves caring for babies.

male boss is often just as likely to be mirrored by female bosses, there is nevertheless a strong likelihood that female supervisors and managers will be instinctively more caring and considerate, and more willing to take an interest in their sub-ordinates' (the people they manage) personal well-being.

As all managers, regardless of sex, improve their management skills and recognize the importance of a contented workforce, however, even these differences tend to disappear.

UNDERSTANDING YOUR FEELINGS

WE HAVE MANY feelings in common with each other, but we each experience them differently. Feelings can be confusing and difficult to understand. Sometimes we can describe our feelings easily, but at other times we cannot do so.

Everyone is capable of experiencing a range of feelings. Some of them may come and go quickly, and others may remain longer. Sometimes we have a number of different feelings at the same time.

Language allows us to name our different feelings and to distinguish between them. Humans do not always simply respond to their feelings by actions. They will often discuss their feelings with others and try to interpret them. Talking to other people can help us work out where our feelings come

fact file

There are seven major groups of facial expressions: anger, happiness, surprise, interest, fear, sadness, and disgust. They are recognized by almost all human societies.

The left side of your face shows the most emotion.

No two people experience feelings in the same way.

from and can make it easier to understand and describe them.

All feelings are accompanied by physical changes in our bodies. Sometimes these intrude on our thoughts, like the anxiety reaction described on page 117. At other times, when we feel relaxed or peaceful, we may not be aware of any particular physical sensations.

Different feelings can also be accompanied by the same physical sensations. For example, you might think that fear and excitement are completely different sensations. Yet in fact

Describing Feelings

Three things help us understand our feelings: what is going on around us, our thoughts at the time, and our physical response. This girl (above) could be feeling a number of different things. She may be crying because she feels sad, frightened, lonesome, or angry.

both are characterized by an increase in pulse rate. It is how we interpret our reactions that determines if we feel fear or excitement. On a roller coaster we may at first interpret our physical reaction as excitement. But if we begin to think about falling off, our interpretation may alter to fear. The physical sensations and situation remain the same, but our thoughts have changed dramatically.

We use three pieces of information to name a particular feeling. First, the situation in which we experience it; second, the thoughts we have at the time; and last, our physical reactions. For example, if you see a ferocious dog, your thoughts might be about being bitten, and the physical changes might include an increase in your pulse rate. (This particular combination of thoughts and feelings is usually called fear.)

How Feelings Develop

We saw on page 101 how we learn to name our feelings or emotions. All societies develop a language that is used to identify and describe feelings. The process of experiencing a feeling and describing it to ourselves and others goes on throughout our lives. We usually agree on the names of feelings, but the physical sensations we each experience are different.

People often react differently to the same thing—for example, what one person finds annoying another may not. Both our individual temperament and previous experiences affect our emotional reactions. Our temperament influences how easily we become aroused, and we therefore differ in how emotional, unemotional, or moody we are.

We each have different past experiences that affect our feelings in future, similar situations. Sometimes we are aware of our past feelings and anticipate how we think we will feel in a situation similar to one we have experienced before. Have you ever looked forward to something and then found it disappointing? It may be that your expectations were too high, or that the mood you were in that day affected your feelings.

Sometimes we are aware of the process of past feelings affecting how we feel in the

Sorting Out Feelings
Teenagers must often balance seeking new experiences with their parents' natural feelings of protectiveness. Arguments may leave the teenager and the parents both feeling misunderstood (above).

present. For example, we may take a dislike to someone because they remind us of someone else that we do not like. At other times our feelings toward a person or place may be influenced by past experiences without us realizing it.

DEALING WITH EMOTIONS

EMOTIONS ARE THE strongest feelings we experience, and they are often accompanied by intense physical sensations. It can be hard to deal with these feelings. Learning how to channel emotional energy can turn negative feelings into positive ones.

Intense feelings are usually referred to as emotions. They can be pleasant—like joy—or unpleasant—like fear. The way we interpret and respond to our emotions is influenced by our upbringing and by social rules. We learn that some emotions, such as jealousy, are negative. Others, such as joy, are positive.

In a similar way we learn acceptable and unacceptable ways of expressing our emotions. For example, if something disappoints us greatly when we are young, our parents may teach us that crying is not going to solve anything, whereas smiling may make us feel better. Over time we learn to hide or control many of our emotions, especially when in the company of other people.

Defense Mechanisms

The physician Sigmund Freud, whose theory of personality was discussed on page 76, said that we sometimes hide our real feelings even from ourselves. He thought that we use "defense mechanisms," or alternative ways of thinking about things, to protect ourselves from unpleasant emotions.

Defense mechanisms are sometimes useful. For instance, someone who has been in a bad car accident may repress, or forget, what happened. The memories usually return when the person has recovered enough emotional strength to deal with them.

At other times we may use a defense mechanism to protect our self-esteem by fooling ourselves about the reasons for our behavior. For example, you may say that you ate the last cookie so that your sister would not spoil her supper, rather than admit to yourself that you were acting selfishly. Such ways of dealing with emotions are not good for our general well-being.

Road Rage

Sitting in a traffic jam can be frustrating for the driver (left). We usually have no control over this situation, and emotional energy can build up. If we do not find the right way to release it, it can spill out as uncontrollable anger.

Emotional Energy

Expressions of emotion, such as shouting, singing, and laughing, release emotional energy. But if we have to deliberately suppress, or hold back, emotional energy because it is not appropriate to release it in a particular situation, we tend to find other ways of releasing it.

One common way is to "displace" the emotional energy—in other words, to release it somewhere else. For example, if we are angry with a friend but do not say so, we might slam a door or snap at the next person we meet. As result, people may think of us as moody and unpredictable.

Displacing emotional energy in this way is usually unhelpful because it does not deal with the real cause of the unpleasant feelings.

During a school day we are required to behave in particular ways and may have to suppress some of our emotions. Having the opportunity to "let go" and have fun with friends gives us a chance to release emotional energy in positive ways. Taking part in sports, music, and drama groups, for example, can be useful ways of doing this.

Helping Yourself

Just because you feel an emotion, it does not necessarily mean that the best thing to do is act on it. To deal with emotions effectively, we first need to understand why we have a particular emotional reaction to a situation in the first place.

For example, if a friend is

annoyed with you for being late, your own immediate response may also be annoyance. If you acted on this emotion, you might remind your friend that he or she was also late the week before.

Such a response is a defense against feeling bad about yourself—both for being late and for upsetting a friend. If you realize this, you can apologize and then talk about why you were late. If you have a good reason for being late, you now have an opportunity to explain. If you did not have a good reason for being late, you have the chance

Comfort Eating

Children are often given cookies or other treats to comfort them when they are upset. In later life feeling upset can trigger eating for comfort (above). This response is not helpful for our emotional well-being because we do not learn to deal with the cause of our unhappiness.

of admitting this to yourself and taking control (in other words, working out a way to avoid being late again).

Either way you will feel better about yourself and not be left with unpleasant feelings.

DEALING WITH RELATIONSHIPS

HUMAN BEINGS ARE social animals who prefer to live in groups and form relationships with those around them. Learning how to cope with the many different sorts of relationships that we encounter, and how they change, is an important part of living with others.

As we grow up, we encounter more and more people in our lives, and we become involved in an increasing number of relationships. Many of our relationships develop and change over time.

Some of our earliest experiences of relationships changing in our own families are likely to be when baby brothers and sisters are born. For the older child in the family a new baby means no longer being the center of attention. Jealous and confused feelings are common. Jealousy often comes about if we do not feel confident and secure in our relationships with others. It is therefore important at this time that parents and caregivers make special efforts to remind the older child that it is also loved and wanted.

Envy is another difficult feeling that can affect our relationships. We feel envious when we want things that others have and we do not. They do not necessarily have to be objects; for example, we may be envious of a friend's looks. Like jealousy, envy can prevent us from developing close relationships if we do not recognize, understand, and try to address these feelings.

Family Problems

Divorce has become more common in many Western societies over recent years. It is something that all children find very distressing and upsetting. The way these feelings are expressed to others varies greatly depending on the age of the children and the circumstances of the divorce.

The younger children are when they experience upsetting things, the more difficult they will find it to put their feelings into words. This is one of the reasons why adults we can trust are very important, for they can help us put our feelings into words. This is one of the ways we learn about difficult and complicated feelings.

Talking Things Over

Our relationships with others are a vitally important part of our lives. When relationships change, run into difficulties, or end, we can feel upset, angry, confused, and let down. Talking about the problem with the person involved can often be the best way to resolve matters (left). Talking to other people we trust can also help.

If parents divorce and begin to develop new relationships, this can result in many new and confusing feelings. Jealousy is common, since the new relationship may seem to threaten the existing one you have with your parent—particularly if you are used to being the center of attention from that parent.

Adolescence is often a difficult time for children. It is a time when young people are pulling away from their parents and trying to be independent, but still needing their help and support. It is when we are experiencing these opposing reactions that we can have negative feelings about our parents.

Lonesomeness

Difficulties in knowing how to deal with relationships can cause us to become isolated and alone. The first and most important step in overcoming lonesomeness is to recognize the things that you can do yourself to help. Negative and critical thoughts about ourselves such as "No one really likes me" are unhelpful and result in us avoiding social situations and becoming even more lonesome (see *The Mind and Psychology*, page 117). Instead, identify the negative thoughts you have about yourself, and think of alternative, positive thoughts. Remind yourself that you do not have to be clever or attractive to be liked. Accept invitations when they are offered. Call on someone, or invite them to visit. Try to be relaxed and friendly. Be responsive in conversation; show you are interested in what

Parental Conflict

It is not unusual for parents to have difficult times in their relationship with each other. Talking to professionals who are experienced in helping people resolve their problems can be helpful (above).

people say by smiling and nodding. Ask questions to keep conversations going. Be open to the interests of others. Draw attention to interests you have in common. Try to overcome your shyness (see page 99).

Adolescent Uncertainty

This chart shows the percentage of boys and girls aged between 11 and 17 who indicate negative feelings about their relationship with their parents. It is very common for young people to hold mixed feelings toward their parents. Adolescence is a period of change, when young people are developing their own identity—and perhaps beliefs—separate from those of their parents and family. But at the same time, they remain dependent on their parents for many things.

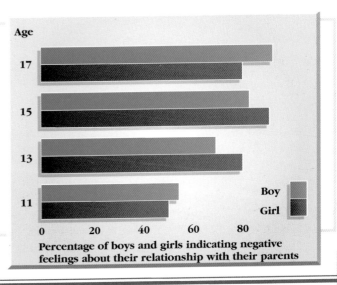

Percentage of boys and girls indicating negative feelings about their relationship with their parents

HAPPINESS AND SADNESS

HAPPINESS AND SADNESS are important human emotions that are expressed in similar ways by all cultures. Each has a place in our lives. Happiness helps build confidence and self-esteem. Sadness teaches us about the things we value most in life.

Feelings of happiness and sadness can range from a passing sensation, perhaps triggered by a memory, to a lasting mood. When we feel happy with ourselves and life in general, we can cope better with negative feelings such as boredom or frustration. We all have the ability to feel happiness, but the things that make us happy are different for each of us.

Both the temperament with which we are born and the way we react to situations affect how we feel. We cannot change our temperament, but we can sometimes choose a lifestyle that fits in with it. For example, having a job as a long-distance truck driver is not going to suit someone who likes to spend plenty of time at home.

We each develop an individual style of thinking that controls how we interpret events. Some people learn to approach situations thinking that the worst will happen. People like this tend to believe that they have no control over their lives. This is sometimes called learned helplessness and can lead to feelings of anxiety or even a

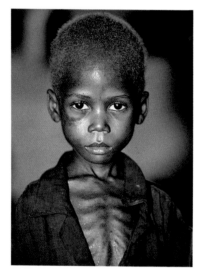

Empathy
Seeing other people in distress, like this young famine victim above, often triggers similar emotions in ourselves. This helps us understand what other people are feeling. This understanding is known as empathy.

lasting mood of deep sadness, called depression. On pages 118 and 119 we look at ways of recognizing and changing such negative ways of thinking.

Achieving happiness or fulfillment is not necessarily

about doing things that bring immediate satisfaction. For instance, you may prefer to go and see some friends rather than review for an examination. But if you do not review, you may not do your best, and your self-esteem could suffer. Everyone needs to balance immediate rewards with working toward goals that bring them happiness in the future. Making goals and working

toward them helps us feel in control of our lives. Success gives us the confidence to try new things, creating opportunities to achieve happiness in different ways.

Finding a Balance

Finding ways to lift our mood, relax, and take our minds off problems can stop us from being overwhelmed by worries. This needs to be balanced with allowing ourselves time to feel sad. Sadness provides a way of expressing and exploring our deepest feelings.

The most intense feeling of sadness is grief. We grieve after any sort of a loss but most strongly after the death of someone we love. It can take several years to get over the loss, and during that time we need to work through a sequence of feelings. People who cannot cope with such feelings and hide them away may suffer long-term despair or depression. When you feel sad, it is common to think that no one feels the same way. People who do not have support are more likely to get depressed. Talking with friends and family helps us accept our feelings and work out why we are sad.

Relaxation

Finding a balance between working toward our goals and relaxation keeps us emotionally healthy. Doing something we enjoy (below) can take our minds off difficulties. After a break we often see problems differently and find solutions.

Grieving Process

Grieving is a natural process that cannot be hurried. We experience a sequence of feelings that take time to work through. Although we are individuals, we all tend to experience these feelings in the same order.

Shock and Disbelief

Feelings of numbness and disbelief that the person has died. Everyday life comes to a stop. Things feel unreal.

Anguish and Despair

Intense sadness and longing for the lost person. Difficulty with sleeping and inability to relax. May feel unwell.

Anger and Guilt

Anger with the dead person for leaving. Feelings of guilt and thoughts of what you should have done.

Gradual Recovery

Acceptance of the loss. Feelings of sadness remain, but there is also hope for the future.

ANXIETY, STRESS, AND FEAR

A CHURNING STOMACH, dry mouth, goose bumps, racing heart, and scary thoughts are all automatic and normal reactions in frightening situations. Anxiety, stress, and fear are important instincts that, in the right circumstances, increase our chances of survival.

Anxiety is a normal, automatic reaction that is set off when we find ourselves in difficult or dangerous situations. The amount of anxiety we feel depends on the size of the challenge we face. When feelings of anxiety are intense, we feel fear. The purpose of what is called "the anxiety reaction" is to prepare the body for physical exercise, either to escape or to fight the threat to our safety. For example, if you are crossing a highway and see a fast car coming straight at you, it is your anxiety reaction that helps you jump out of the way quickly (see *Body Systems*, page 31).

Each challenge we face puts us under stress. Some stress is useful in our everyday lives. Meeting deadlines, devel-

Phobias

Intense fear of an object or situation, which in reality does not present a threat to your safety, is called a phobia. Fear of spiders (above) is a common phobia.

oping new skills, and taking tests can all be stressful situations that trigger the anxiety reaction. When we feel able to meet these demands, the anxiety reaction acts to increase our arousal, which helps us put in the extra effort required to meet the challenge. In this way anxiety can have a positive effect on performance.

However, when anxiety gets out of control, our performance gets worse. Our minds become

Stress and Performance

The physical changes in our bodies in response to stress can be useful, for we become aroused, which makes us more alert and helps us concentrate. But if our level of arousal gets too high, performance suffers, as shown below. Long-term stress results in exhaustion. If too great a level of stress is reached (point x on the graph below), it can result in a nervous breakdown.

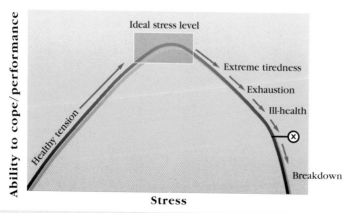

to supply more oxygen to our muscles, ready for action. Sweating increases to cool the body when it gets hot with exercise. Energy is diverted away from general activities in the body, such as producing saliva. These processes account for the feelings of anxiety: tense muscles, pounding heart, dry mouth, and churning stomach.

When we are alarmed by these normal physical reactions, we become more anxious, and the feelings get even worse. Our ability to cope and deal constructively with problems depends on how well we manage anxiety.

On the next page we will look at ways of preventing anxiety from getting out of control.

Enjoying Fear

During a fairground ride (above) we can enjoy the sensations of arousal that fear produces because we know it is for only a short time and that although we are frightened, there is no real danger. Screaming out loud releases nervous energy as it builds up.

preoccupied with problems, or we focus on the way our bodies feel. We may worry about making fools of ourselves or that we will lose control. A cycle of events is started in which our unpleasant thoughts increase our feelings of anxiety, which in turn increases our negative thoughts.

In these situations we have no hope of effectively coping with the original problem. All our energy is wasted on worrying. Unfortunately, these self-defeating patterns of behavior can be difficult to break. When we next have to face the same

situation, we remember the anxiety we felt and our inability to cope, and the cycle is set off again.

In a similar way, stress over long periods of time raises our general level of arousal so that it takes less to make us feel anxious. If we do not act to reduce our levels of stress, we end up unable to cope with even the slightest demand.

When we are generally very stressed, we can feel intense anxiety for no apparent reason. This is called a panic attack. Panic attacks always pass, but they can be very frightening at the time.

Physical Reactions to Anxiety

The physical reactions produced by intense anxiety can be uncomfortable. In response to a threat our bodies produce a great deal of energy very quickly. We breathe too fast, and our heart beats faster

What you think
about the situation

Knowing
what is going to
happen

Knowing what
to do

**The
stress you
feel**

How long the
situation lasts

People around to
support you

Stress Factors

Next time you feel stressed, think about the factors associated with stress (above), and how much each one affects your level of stress. Knowing why you are stressed, and then being able to take control by making positive changes, will improve your ability to cope and will help reduce stress.

POSITIVE THINKING

WHAT IS YOUR approach to life? Are you a pessimist (someone who expects the worst to happen) or an optimist (someone who always looks on the bright side)? Or maybe you try to keep an open mind. Whatever your way of thinking, your thoughts affect how you feel, what you do, and even what you see. Thinking positively can change how you view situations and help you achieve your goals.

We all develop ways of coping with situations that we find difficult. Some of these strategies are better than others in reducing the unpleasant thoughts and feelings we have when we are worried. On pages 116–117 we looked at the anxiety reaction. In the face of real danger this reaction is useful because it helps you escape quickly or face whatever is frightening you with increased strength.

But sometimes we feel anxious even when there is no danger, and our natural response may be to avoid these situations. Think about situations or things you avoid and why you do it. You will probably find that in many cases the things you avoid are not dangerous. For example,

What Do You See?

Is the glass below half full or half empty? How you see things reflects your style of thinking—positive, negative, or neutral. This, in turn, affects how you feel.

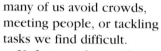

many of us avoid crowds, meeting people, or tackling tasks we find difficult.

Unfortunately, avoiding things often increases our feelings of fear. We may become so frightened that we do everything we can to avoid the thing we fear. This leads to a loss of confidence, which, in turn, leads to more anxiety and feelings of failure.

Negative or unrealistic thinking increases anxiety and stops people from doing their best. People who constantly blame

Looking on the Bright Side

Things do not always go according to plan. These women (right) are making the best of a wet day out. But they had prepared for the possibility of rain and went well equipped to have a good time whatever the weather.

or criticize themselves often feel helpless and think that they have no control over what happens to them. In a similar way people who expect always to be able to do things perfectly are also likely to feel disappointed in themselves much of the time.

Positive thinking can help not only when you are feeling anxious; it can also stop you from becoming anxious about things in the first place. But changing how you think takes practice. Negative ways of thinking can often become automatic.

Positive thinking can also help solve problems. Try not to think of a problem as something that has defeated you. Think of ways of tackling the problem and trying to defeat it instead (see *The Brain and Senses*, pages 54-55). Consider all the aspects of a situation and what options you have to change it. Talking positively to yourself leaves no room for negative thoughts. And tackling things you find difficult—even if you do not always succeed—will build your confidence.

Forward Planning

The next time you face a challenge, work out a plan of action toward your goal. Planning ahead can help you feel in control. It also helps ensure that your efforts are not wasted by doing things that were not thought through first. Be realistic about what it is possible to achieve, and try to be flexible so that you can change a plan if it is not working.

Positive and Negative Thinking

Are you a negative or a positive thinker? The way we think about things is often automatic, but there may be two ways of looking at problems—a negative way and a positive way. One failure does not mean you will always fail. If you are positive, you can turn failure into success.

How to Achieve Your Goals

Steps to Achieving Goals	Your Goals and Actions
Describe what you want to change and why you want to change it. Monitor where you are now.	I want to watch less TV so that I have time for other things. Last week I watched TV for 22 hours.
Decide on, and set, your final goal. Ask yourself if it is realistic and achievable.	I would like to watch 8 hours or less TV a week and spend more time with my friends.
Set small steps toward your goal. Make each step easy to achieve. Think how you can help yourself succeed.	Each week I will watch one hour's less TV. I will decide what I want to watch at the start of each week.
Think of a way of recording your progress. Give yourself "rewards" along the way.	I have made a chart to record my progress, with treats when I achieve each goal.

DREAMS AND
WHAT THEY MEAN

DREAMS ARE VIVID mental images that occur during sleep. Everyone dreams, even people who never remember doing so. Although there are many theories, scientists are still trying to discover exactly why we dream and what our dreams mean.

During the night we pass through four stages of sleep several times (see *The Brain and Senses*, pages 56–57). Dreaming occurs during the stage called REM sleep. This is also the stage when our brain is most active. During this period our closed eyes make fast, irregular movements called REMs (rapid-eye-movements).

Dreams can be influenced by events around us. In a series of tests dreamers were sprayed lightly with cold water. When they were roused later, they reported dreams about washing, floods, or being in the rain. You may have dreamed about a noise, only to wake and find the noise is real.

In our dreams we often seem to experience small glimpses of events from the previous day that are then pieced together in a new situation.

Dream Sequences

Many dreams consist of vivid, clear sequences that make up a complete event, such as this visual interpretation of an accident and emergency dream shown right.

Why Do We Dream?

Scientists do not really know why people dream, but dreams seem to be important. If we are waked from REM sleep during the night, we dream even more when we fall asleep again. It is as if we needed to make up for our lost dreaming time.

A common belief is that dreams come from our unconscious mind. The physician Sigmund Freud was the first to suggest this. He thought that dreams are a way of safely releasing desires and thoughts that we have hidden or suppressed in our unconscious mind. He said that in our dreams these thoughts appear in disguise in order to make them less frightening. In other

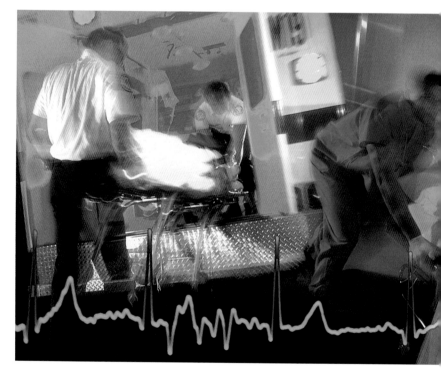

words, we use symbols to represent thoughts. In order to interpret our dreams, we must interpret the meaning of the symbols. So, for example, vultures might symbolize death.

More recent theories about why we dream say that dreams allow the brain to sort out the events that have happened during the day, to think about ways of doing things, and even to solve problems—sometimes people seem to wake up with solutions to problems they could not solve the night before.

It is also thought likely that long-term memory storage is established in the brain during REM sleep (the time when we dream), and that dreams are thus involved in learning (see *The Brain and Senses*, pages 44-47).

Freud's Theory of Where Dreams Come From

Freud thought that our minds are like an iceberg. We are aware only of what is in the top part; the rest remains hidden beneath the surface.

The conscious mind
This is the only part of the mind of which we are aware.

The preconscious mind
This part of our mind contains memories of dreams and thoughts that are temporarily forgotten but can be brought to consciousness if necessary.

The unconscious mind
Freud thought that dreams represent things hidden in our unconscious mind. We never know what is in this part of our mind.

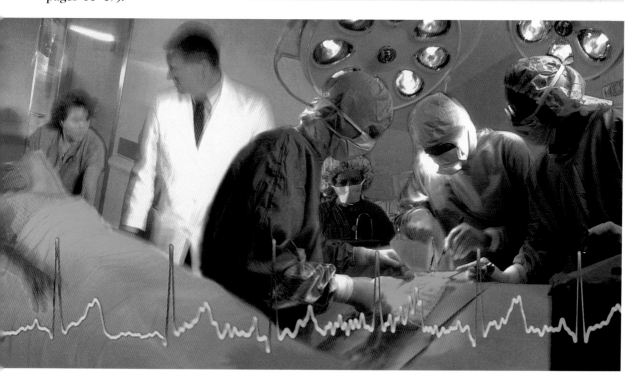

INTRODUCTION

COMMUNICATION IS A basic human activity. It is the interchange of thoughts and ideas by a variety of methods, including words, pictures, and gestures. Every time we send a message to the outside world—however insignificant—it involves a complicated set of skills. Humans learn to communicate through interaction with each other; some scientists believe that this process starts in the womb, even before we are born.

This chapter is about the many different ways that humans use to communicate with each other, and how we learn and employ various methods of communicating as part of the rich and varied pattern of human behavior.

We look, for example, at how language is learned and used (see pages 124–127) and the importance of making conversation and listening (see pages 128–131).

The ways we use to ensure that we get our message across to others, and that we under stand the messages we receive, are covered on pages 132–133 and 136–145. These methods include using touch, body language, scent, advertising, and sign language. The importance of sending the right message is covered in pages 134–135.

Why We Communicate

Proper communication is vital between members of every society. Communication has an important biological purpose that helps ensure our survival. No social animal can survive without communicating. Through the ages, people have developed ever more advanced methods of getting in touch, yet many of the first methods— such as making signs, drawing pictures, and writing words

fact file

Humans and other vertebrate animals have an internal communications network called the nervous system. It consists of the brain and spinal cord, and a mass of nerve fibers that carry messages between the brain and other parts of the body.

There are more phones than people in Washington, D.C.

Combining Skills

These two men (below) are using a combination of the mental skills that allow them to understand the drawing in front of them and the verbal skills that they need to discuss it. Being able to combine a range of skills is a basic need in communication.

Air France

Garuda Indonesia

Air Canada

Air New Zealand

Air Canada

Television

A flood of sound and animated pictures reaches us through television (above). We take in the information that flashes onto the screen and reaches our ears. Is this solitary activity a form of communication, or is communication only possible with another person?

Logos

Airlines spend huge amounts of money on developing an image that identifies them at a glance. Logos like the ones on these aircraft tailfins (above) are repeated on note paper, at check-in desks, and in sales offices to increase people's awareness.

and numbers on paper—still remain as important as ever.

Speech is the oldest and richest form of communication among humans. We use it constantly to express our thoughts and needs.

Vocal sounds enable a new-born baby to tell its mother it is hungry or that it needs comforting. They also allows us to warn others of danger.

As we grow, our communicating skills expand, and we are able to express other needs—including those for material things and companionship. As we become more aware of those around us,

we develop more subtle skills, such as reading people's body language (gestures and facial expressions) and understanding the subtexts (unspoken signals) that help us interact with other people.

Communication lets us learn about the world by listening to our parents, teachers, and others, and enables us to acquire the knowledge and skills passed down from one generation to the next through the spoken and written word.

Without fast, reliable means of communicating—such as telephones, faxes, and via computers—the world of

Poster Power

This Chinese birth-control poster (above) has been designed to make a statement very clearly. The single child, the happy parents, the background, and the wording have been carefully thought out to achieve the maximum effect—in this case, limiting family size.

commerce would not function properly, and keeping in touch with people even a short distance away would be time-consuming. Even our leisure time, increasingly dependent on information technology, would change completely.

LEARNING LANGUAGE

LANGUAGE IS THE most important form of communication between human beings. Acquiring language is a vital learning experience for us all. Without language we cannot heed warnings of danger that might be necessary for our survival or convey our thoughts to other people around us. Although we learn almost all of our language skills when we are young, it is a process that continues throughout our lives.

Babies start developing language skills even before they say their first word. At about four or five months old a baby begins to babble, making a series of simple sounds. Over the next few months these sounds become more complex and varied. By nine or ten months a baby's babbles begin to imitate the rising and falling patterns of normal speech.

Babies begin pointing at about a year old to show they want something, since they cannot use words at this stage.

Gestures and body language are an important part of early communication.

Children usually use their first words at between 12 and 18 months. By the age of two the average child has a vocabulary of about 200 words. As this increases, the child's speech develops grammar—in other words, the child starts to form sentences instead of simply using single words. (Grammar

is the set of rules that determines the way words are used in a particular language.) By using the appropriate words, in the right order, a child learns

Group Learning

Particular skills are needed when people talk in a group. We usually learn these skills at home—during mealtimes, for example (below). Learning when to speak and what to say, in a place where we do not feel under pressure, is good preparation for interacting at school.

Learning to Read

Most children, such as this toddler (right), learn the basics of language from their parents (or other adults). Reading stories to young children lets them get used to the idea that words can be represented by symbols that, in time, they will learn to recognize and read.

to form meaningful sentences. Then a child begins to learn letters of the alphabet and numbers. Starting to scribble, and then to draw pictures, allows a child to record its own ideas and provides writing practice.

As well as learning to speak, a child finds out how to interact with others. It starts to recognize the meanings of expressions on people's faces and their tones of voice. Learning these sorts of signals is an important part of understanding language.

As soon as children can use basic spoken language, they begin to ask questions and try to understand the answers. With this new ability at their disposal, their knowledge of the world begins to build up rapidly. Once they can read, they begin to seek knowledge from computers, books, and other forms of written information.

Learning Difficulties

If a child has a learning disability, such as might be the case if it suffers from Down's syndrome, then the timetable above will not apply. The child's language will develop more slowly, depending on the level of

disability. Language learning will also be delayed if a child does not have enough contact with other people. For example, in extreme cases children have sometimes been kept isolated from normal human contact. When rescued, they have usually been found to be mute (unable or unwilling to speak) but quickly develop speech when normal social contact with humans is established.

Formal Learning

While very young children learn language in an informal way, once they go to school, formal learning starts. For many children this is their first experience of learning to read and write. As their skills increase, formal and informal learning intertwine. A child will read books both in and out of school, for example. As a

Learning Numbers

This boy (above) counts his fingers with great concentration. Numbers are often among the first words a child learns because they have an easily recognizable pattern. Usually the child gets a positive reaction from adults, who are amused and proud of this new skill. This encourages the child to count further.

child's education broadens, its vocabulary increases to cover new areas of study. In addition, children learn to understand not only the actual words spoken but also the subtext (unspoken meaning) that is crucial to all forms of communication.

Even when formal education stops, informal learning continues. Language is not static. It is ever growing and changing, so acquiring it is a continuing, lifelong process.

USING LANGUAGE

LANGUAGE IS ONE of the mind's most powerful tools. It enables us to explain our thoughts and ideas to others and to form and influence opinion. By using a common language, two or more people can learn to cooperate and help each other. But we can only get our message across if we choose our words carefully. If we do not say precisely what we mean, we will be misunderstood.

There are about 5,000 languages spoken in the world today. Trumai, a Venezuelan language, is spoken by only a hundred or so people. Chinese, at the other end of the scale, is spoken by over 1 billion people. English is spoken by about 350 million people around the world.

Each language has its own words and grammar. Spoken language came first. Later on, people developed writing systems to record what was said. Writing developed quite separately in places like the Middle East, South America, and China. One of the earliest systems was cuneiform. It was first used in the Middle East from about 3100 B.C. Early writing consisted of using different sorts of written or drawn symbols to represent words. Later, symbols came to represent the sounds of words, or parts of words (known as syllables).

In our language today we write using letters to show the different sounds of a word. The collection of letters that we use to write all the words in our language is called the alphabet.

The Right Words
The way in which we talk to people depends on our relationship with them. We use informal language to talk to family, friends, and pets. From a young age we learn to use language appropriate to the situation. For example, families use unique phrases and nicknames. We often talk to very young children in simple "baby language."

Talking to Animals
We tend to talk to animals even though we know they cannot understand what we are saying to them! However, this cat (below) understands the child's warm tone of voice, and both it and the child will enjoy the encounter.

We quickly learn that we will be misunderstood—or even ridiculed—if we use these outside our home. Informal language can develop a sense of belonging. Among friends we use particular phrases to indicate a group identity and to communicate our intimacy.

For occasions when we talk or write to strangers or people in authority, like teachers, we adopt a more formal kind of language. This is sometimes very clearly seen in legal documents; many of them use words

sentence is about—for instance, "car" (see below). This sort of word is called a noun or pronoun. A verb describes what the subject does. Words that describe verbs are called adverbs. Adjectives describe the noun or pronoun. Here are the parts above in a sentence: "The yellow (*adjective*) car (*noun*) stops (*verb*) slowly (*adverb*)."

Changing words to alter the meaning is called an inflexion. So, "She drives the car" can become: "She drove the car." In this example the sentence has moved from the present tense to the past tense.

The order that words appear in sentences is important. Changing the order of the same words in a sentence can also change the meaning. Thus, "The boy hits the ball" is different from: "The ball hits the boy." The way words are put together to form phrases and sentences is called syntax.

Using Language Skills

These children (above) are enjoying the experience of the actors communicating with the audience, but they are also communicating back to the actors. The children are combining a variety of language tools, including speaking and listening skills, as well as watching hand and body movements.

and phrases that are hardly ever used in everyday speech.

Grammar

To use language properly we must first understand grammar. Grammar determines the way words are used so that we can be understood.

Sentences must have a subject, which is the thing the

Language and Dialect

Language is the means by which a culture communicates. Any group may have its own language. Within a language there are also dialects—terms, phrases, and pronunciations that are unique to a geographical area. The map (right) charts the English dialects of the East Coast of the United States. This shows how even minor geographical differences can affect language. Many Americans speak English, yet many East Coast communities have their own dialects.

Each language has its own roots. For example, English belongs to the Germanic family of languages. It was originally a dialect known as *Angeles*. Gradually, English absorbed other dialects so that by about 1100 it had become Anglo-Saxon, and by 1500, Modern English. As it has evolved, Modern English has developed into the English language as we now know it.

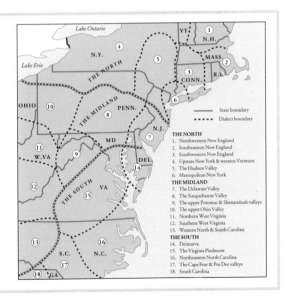

State boundary
Dialect boundary

THE NORTH
1. Northwestern New England
2. Southeastern New England
3. Southwestern New England
4. Upstate New York & western Vermont
5. The Hudson Valley
6. Metropolitan New York

THE MIDLAND
7. The Delaware Valley
8. The Susquehanne Valley
9. The upper Potomac & Shenandoah valleys
10. The upper Ohio Valley
11. Northern West Virginia
12. Southern West Virginia
13. Western North & South Carolina

THE SOUTH
14. Deimarva
15. The Virginia Piedmont
16. Northeastern North Carolina
17. The Cape Fear & Pee Dee valleys
18. South Carolina

MAKING CONVERSATION

IT IS ASSUMED that everyone knows how to make conversation. However, there are often several ways of saying something. A conversation can range from a lively, meaningful discussion to a simple exchange of information. Some people are said to be good at conversation, but why? Is it because they are particularly well informed and can always think of something to say, or are they in fact just very good listeners?

Although we all feel at times that we have "said the wrong thing," most of the time we talk to each other effortlessly, in spite of the fact that we need many different skills to do so.

The aims of a conversation can be many: to give or seek information, to express our ideas or feelings, or to feel emotionally closer to someone. We have millions of conversations throughout our lives, and each one is different.

Making Conversation

Some conversations are very straightforward—like asking the bus driver for a ticket. Other conversations will be more difficult and may require some advance preparation, or at least the use of some ways, to help the flow.

Many of us find it difficult to think of something to say when left alone with someone we do not know well or when trying to start a conversation with someone at a dance or similar social event. How do we break the silence? A very good way to start a conversa-

tion is to ask the other person an open question. This will not only indicate that you are interested in them, but it may also enable you to ask further questions or may lead into other topics, thereby allowing the conversation to develop between you.

In these situations try to ask "open" questions like "How did you get here today?" These require a fuller answer rather than just a single-word answer like "Yes" or "No" and will make it easier for you to think of the next thing to say.

Relaxed Chat

See how relaxed these two women (above) are. They are obviously enjoying chatting with each other. It is clear that they like each other's company.

If you know in advance that you are going to meet someone to discuss a particular topic or get some information from them, it is useful to rehearse the points you want to raise. This will help you come across as a more confident and positive person.

Explaining a Problem
The woman (left) is trying to explain by telephone what is wrong with her car. She has to give clear instructions, since the person to whom she is speaking cannot see the problem.

Talking in a group requires different conversational skills. Timing becomes more important —knowing when to interject with a particular point so that it has the most impact. It is also important to be sensitive to others' views and allow them time to speak.

Listening (see pages 130–131) is an important part of any conversation. People sometimes seem to want to make a specific point regardless of what the other person is saying. If you are fully aware of what the other person is saying to you, your answer will be more appropriate.

Choosing the right language is also vital: chatting to a toddler needs a different set of words and tone of speech from talking to a teacher. Most people switch between the different styles of speech quite easily.

If you watch out for others' expressions as they talk and listen to you, communication will be easier. Body language (see pages 140–141) is often an important part of conversation. It can be used to emphasize the point you are making, or it can give a clue to what others are really thinking. Their words may say one thing, but their expressions and gestures may indicate something different.

This is one of the reasons why telephone conversations can sometimes be difficult, particularly if emotional issues are involved. We subconsciously use our bodies to help express ourselves; on the telephone we must rely on our voices alone.

In Control
The customs official (right) will have tight control of the conversation. She will ask a series of questions that are designed to help her see whether or not the woman is breaking the regulations.

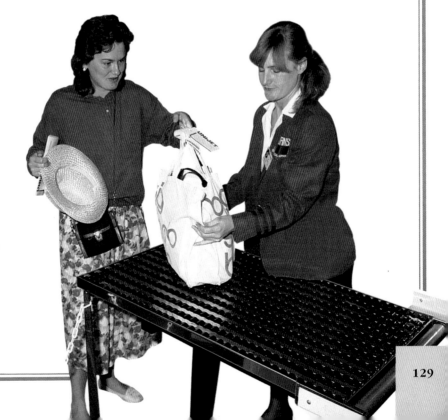

LISTENING

MOST PEOPLE ARE born with the ability to hear what is going on around them. Listening enables us to hear approaching dangers, the sounds of music, and the voices of others as they communicate with us. But listening properly is a skill we have to learn, and being a good listener is something we do not all achieve. In many conversations you must not only be a good speaker but a good listener, too.

Listening is a communication skill that is often underestimated. Yet our first encounter with language comes through listening to the sounds around us when we are babies. From listening to patterns of sound, and then trying to copy them, we learn to speak.

Hearing and listening are not the same. We hear sounds around us all the time—the noise of traffic, people's conversations, and even our own breathing. We may not even be aware of these noises because hearing is a passive activity. Only when sounds carry information that will be useful or

Attentive Listening

This appears to be a serious conversation (right). The younger man appears to be thinking about what he has just been listening to; if he has been listening properly, he will be trying to understand what he hears. He may respond with appropriate questions or may make comments that the other person will then listen to and take the discussion further.

interesting to us do we start to listen to them. For example, we may not be aware of a baby's crying unless we are its mother.

Active Listening

Listening is active; it requires us to make an effort and to concentrate. A team sport, such as football, involves listening to other team members so that the next play can be planned. To catch an airplane we may need to listen to announcements on the public-address system.

Taking note of what is being said in the classroom by teachers is one of the most important forms of listening. During active listening we must think carefully about what is being said and may then need to act on the information.

To Listen or Not To Listen

Our ability to listen for long periods of time is determined by our interest in the subject as well as the way it is delivered by the speaker. A good teacher will often break up a lesson or lecture with small jokes, sudden questions, or other things to keep the pupils listening and hold their interest.

When speaking to someone, it is also important to listen to what the other person is saying and adapt your next response accordingly—rather than just saying what you were going to say anyway. Often, when we are involved in a discussion, we are so concerned to get our points across that we fail to listen properly to what other

Listen Carefully

These pupils (above) take notes so they can recall the content of the lesson. Hearing the words is not enough—they must listen carefully to what the teacher is saying.

people are saying. Good communication involves looking interested and responding to what is being said by making appropriate comments. This is how listening professionals, such as counselors, help build and develop a relationship with their clients.

We must make sure we give others time to have their say, too. As a test, see how long you are able to listen to what a friend has to say without interrupting.

Warning Sounds

We instinctively shout to attract attention when we feel scared or in danger, hoping someone will come to our aid. Sounds that warn us of danger, such as a car horn or a baby's cry, can prevent an accident. The human brain becomes disturbed by constant loud, sharp, or repeated noises, however—they can even cause anger in the listener if they go on for too long. This may be a natural way of ensuring that warning sounds are heeded.

fact file

The composer Beethoven was deaf. The only communication he had with his music was through the vibrations that were created when he played the piano.

Listening to music reduces stress and blood pressure.

From about the age of ten our hearing slowly deteriorates.

GETTING OUR IDEAS ACROSS

Do you ever feel that you are not being listened to or that what you say is being misunderstood? In order to avoid this, you have to find the right time, place, and—more importantly—the most appropriate way to get your ideas across.

Getting our ideas across properly is an essential part of any type of communication. Humans have developed many different ways of doing this. Before we communicate, we first make a series of decisions—both conscious and subconscious—on the best way to say something.

We will first decide on the best form of communication to use. Should we speak or write? Should we do it face-to-face, by telephone, or e-mail, etc.? Then, depending on the type of message we are sending, we will choose a style of delivery. This might be abrupt and to the point if we are complaining about something or friendly and informative if we are talking to a friend.

When speaking face-to-face—or even on the telephone—we also adopt the right body language and facial expression for the occasion (see pages 140–141). We are sometimes unaware of this process going on, but it is an important part of making ourselves understood.

There are many other ways to get our ideas across. For

instance, the clothes we wear, the sorts of music we play, the pictures we hang on our walls, and many of our possessions all help send a message. Usually these visual messages reinforce our written and spoken messages and are used by businesses as well as by individuals.

Crying and Smiling
The tiny baby (above) knows just how to get his ideas across! If he is hungry, tired, or feeling uncomfortable, he instinctively cries so that he will get the attention he wants. The mother is also getting her ideas across by smiling at the baby to help him feel more secure.

The Right Approach

Choosing the right approach can also have very practical reasons. Hailing a taxi, for example, needs a firm approach. A piercing whistle or waving arm are the most likely gestures to attract the driver's attention. At a noisy party the voice has to be pitched at a particular level to be heard and understood. It may even be necessary to keep your conversations short and simple in these circumstances.

In many places hand and arm gestures are still a necessary part of communication. The stock exchange and the race track are just a few examples of places where the hustle and bustle make normal conversation difficult. At sale auctions communicating your bid is done by nodding, raising your hand, or using some similar way of attracting the auctioneer's attention.

An important factor in getting ideas across is to use ways that will be understood by the person to whom you are trying to communicate. Fitting into a new school is often made easier if you are able to quickly learn its traditions, rules, and regulations. Find out if the school has a way of doing or saying things. This will help you communicate better with your teachers and fellow students and enable you to be accepted more readily.

Overcoming Disability

For people with certain disabilities getting ideas across can be very difficult. Their power of speech may be impaired, or

Saturday 7th february my Nana and Poppa came to stay. I went to Debbies Party

Picture Message

Drawing a picture is an easy way for a child to tell a story, with or without words. This child's picture tells the story just as clearly as her words do.

Body Language

These schoolchildren (above) raise their hands so that others know they have an answer to share. They are learning to use their bodies to help get their message across.

they may not be able to write or use other forms of communication such as sign language.

Often people in this situation find ingenious ways to overcome the problem. The British physicist Stephen Hawking has a condition called motor neuron disease, which leaves him unable to operate the muscles that would normally let him speak. Instead, he has a small box attached to his wheelchair that is designed to sound out the words that he cannot physically speak. The resulting mechanical voice means he can still communicate his thoughts.

SENDING THE RIGHT MESSAGE

WE ALL MAKE up our minds about other people based not only on what they say but also on what they wear, their body language, where they live, and what they do. So, how can we be sure of sending the right message?

Humans often misunderstand each other's messages. Sometimes we even deliberately send the wrong message if we want to deceive or provoke people. For example, many adolescents (people between the ages of about 14 and 21) often rebel against the values of older people, such as their parents, by deliberately wearing outrageous clothes or hairstyles in an attempt to shock or get noticed.

Usually, however, we do want to be understood, but it can be hard to send the right message. Sending the right message is important if we want to get the best result. It is vital to present yourself in a positive way in order to achieve a particular goal or aim. (People often clean the house before guests arrive. They do not want to send the message that they do not care if guests enter a dirty house.) Sending the right message can also help you develop your confidence and self-assurance.

How you behave, or appear to behave, can sometimes send out the wrong message about you even when you do not mean it. Being distracted by something during a conversation with a friend can send a message that you are bored or have no interest. Being nervous can sometimes make a person appear distant or even untrustworthy—particularly if eye contact is avoided.

You can avoid sending the wrong message in error by being more self-aware. The more you understand yourself, the clearer will be the impression others have of you.

Clear Message
In this picture (left) uniform dress helps send the message that this is a team of navy personnel. The way they are standing makes the formal message even clearer.

Interviews

You may have been for an interview for a school or club. Being late can send the negative message "I am unreliable." It places you at a disadvantage from the outset. Arriving much too early may give the impression that you are an anxious person.

If you have made a written application, the interviewer may have made certain assumptions about you on the basis of what you wrote. The fact that you have gotten as far as an interview means that the message you presented was probably a positive one.

You can reinforce the message you want to give by the way you dress. Being dressed smartly, even if casually, gives a better impression of you than being dressed in scruffy clothes or wearing dirty shoes. It sends the message that you care enough to make the effort.

Remember that the interviewer is trying to get his or her message across, too. Listen carefully (see pages 130–131)

fact file

It takes four minutes to make a first impression on someone, and 93% of this comes from nonverbal communication. Of this, 55% comes from your clothes and 38% from body language and tone of voice. The other 7% comes from the actual words you use.

Smartly dressed people are often taken more seriously.

to what is being said and give clear answers to any questions. Last, if you are unsuccessful, try to find out why. You could be sending out the wrong message.

At School

School is the ideal place to learn ways of sending the right message. Not only will it help you in your school work, but it will also get you into the habit of good presentation in later life.

Get the most out of your lessons by showing that you are interested. Listen carefully, and join in classroom discussions, etc. You will find learning becomes easier if you do this.

Performance Message

Sending the right message can be enhanced by a mix of things. In this opera scene (above) the costumes, script, scenery, and music all work together to convey the right message so the audience can enjoy the performance.

You can send the right message in your written work, too. Make an effort to present neat, tidy work at all times. It is important to use good grammar (see page 127). Try to increase your vocabulary (choice of words) by using dictionaries and other reference books that will help you find, and spell, the correct words.

VISUAL COMMUNICATION

OUR EYES HAVE a twofold purpose in communication. First, we use them to scan the world and tell the brain what is happening around us, and second, they may show our thoughts and moods to others before we even begin a conversation.

Much of the information we use to figure out the world around us comes through our eyes. Our brains constantly receive visual messages from our eyes. This information is then processed by the brain, and so sense is made of the world (see *The Brain and Senses*, pages 58–63).

It is our sense of sight that helps us distinguish safe from unsafe. For instance, we might recognize that the brown, hairy animal in the street is the dog from next door. We know it is friendly, and there is no need to avoid it. We observe the dog and make a judgment based on what we see. Our other senses, especially hearing and smell, also play a part in this process, but it is usually our eyes that alert us first.

Observation

We use the same sense of sight when we communicate with other people. When we interact with others, we are also observing and making judgments. As we begin a conversation, our eyes take in the situation and show us the moods and feelings of those with whom we are communicating. For example, a teenager comes home late at night after promising his parents that he would be home early. When he comes in, he can probably tell if his parents are angry by looking at the expressions on their faces—or perhaps just the glare in their eyes.

Once conversation has begun, visual clues are still very important. We watch the expressions of others as we talk and listen and try to make sense of the subtext, or underlying message. Are they paying attention to me? Is what I am saying making them angry, sad, or happy? Often we are unaware of the extent to which

Stories without Words

These pictures tell a story: a driver, busy talking, fails to notice a warning sign that a river is ahead. Communication by pictures works in any language, since there is no need for written words. Pictures can be understood anywhere in the world. This approach is useful in advertising, for giving information (such as at airports), or for those who cannot read.

our understanding of what people say comes through what we see.

Other Forms of Visual Communication

As well as using our eyes to find out about the world around us and to gauge the reactions of others when we are speaking to them, visual communication is also used in many other ways.

Before the written word, early humans communicated visually through pictures. In some cultures pictures, as well as the use of signs and symbols, are still vital methods of communication.

Even in those cultures where written language is well developed, art in the form of paintings, posters, and sculpture is an important communicating tool.

In a modern society much of our language is communicated visually through the written word. Much of our learning and recreation comes from reading books and looking at computer screens and printouts.

The Eyes Have It

Thoughtful

The large, expressive eyes of this child could be communicating wonder at something it has seen or a plea to be comforted. Our eyes not only see, they also reflect feelings.

Happy

A cheerful expression often provokes a happy response in the person we are smiling at. Eye communication is also enhanced by the whole facial expression.

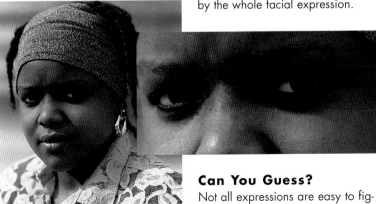

Can You Guess?

Not all expressions are easy to figure out. Are these eyes communicating interest or a slight wariness?

COMMUNICATING BY TOUCH

Touching another living being is a basic way of communicating—we even call communication "keeping in touch." A touch can be formal, such as a handshake, or informal, like a hug. We use touch to express our emotions. It might even be used to cure illness.

Humans have a built-in need for physical contact with others. A newborn baby needs to attach itself to another individual, usually its mother. This is a survival instinct. Most babies feel happiest and most secure when in their mother's or father's arms, experiencing the closeness of the intimate touch of a familiar human being.

As we grow older, we may become more careful about touching other people, especially those we do not know well, in case we cause offence by seeming too familiar.

braille

Braille is a system of writing and printing for blind people. Groups of raised dots represent letters, numerals, or punctuation marks. These are read by touching with the fingertips.

A	B	C	D	E

And	For	Of	!	( )

Sending a Message

Often when people meet, they will shake hands—a gesture that says "I am pleased to meet you." A handshake can also be the final action when sealing a business arrangement, meaning "We agree."

Kissing family members or friends as a form of greeting sends the message "I love you." Courting couples will often put their arms around each other because they cherish the closeness that holding the other person brings. It is also a way

Comforting Hug

Not only is the fair-haired girl in the picture above feeling the comfort of a hug, but the hugger is also comforted. Giving someone a hug makes both of you feel better.

of telling the world that the other person is a partner.

Touching can be informal and at times quite unconscious. Touching a friend who tells you about a family tragedy can be an instinctive move to show support for someone who is

What Touch Tells Us

Touch is important not only for communicating to others but also for giving us information about the world around us. Even if you were blindfolded, it is likely that you could identify each of these two sets of objects on the right. Each would communicate a different weight, shape, and texture. The strength of a handshake can also tell much about another person. Exerting the right amount of pressure is important; too much makes one seem overbearing; too little makes one seem withdrawn.

Pasta

Rocks

having a difficult time. Young children will often hit out at another when they are angry or upset, until they learn better ways of expressing themselves.

Touch is a vital communication tool for the blind or partially sighted: the tap of a stick can warn of obstacles in their path.

Trust Me

These boys (below) are scrapping in the way that the young of many animals do, rolling around together, play fighting, and enjoying the contact that this brings. Touching in this way builds trust.

Blind people can recognize another person by the touch of their hand. Physical contact with other people or animals can be a great comfort in helping them feel less isolated.

When someone loses their sight, the other senses, including the sense of touch, become stronger to help compensate. The braille system (see opposite) enables a blind person to read by feeling pages covered

with raised dots. An experienced person can "read" up to 50 words a minute.

Medicinal Touch

In the medical profession touch is an important part of healing. It would be hard to imagine going to see a dentist or a podiatrist without being touched. Seeing a doctor can make the patient feel anxious: therefore it is important that the doctor uses touch appropriately so that the patient feels reassured.

There has been a growth in therapies that are based on touch (see *Health and Illness*, pages 158–159).

Reflexologists touch the soles of a person's feet in order to diagnose and cure weaknesses and ailments in other parts of the body. Aromatherapy is used to reduce stress by massaging essential oils into the body. Acupuncture uses the touch of needles on pressure points to reduce pain and to cure allergies.

All of these treatments are questioned by some physicians, however, who think there is no proper medical basis to them.

BODY LANGUAGE

WE OFTEN FORGET that when others listen to what we say, they are often watching us as well. The overall impression we make is based partly on the nonverbal way in which we present ourselves. Dress, grooming, accent, tone of voice, and body language (our gestures, posture, and facial expressions) are all part of nonverbal communication. Being aware of body language can help you in your relationships with other people.

Although we often think of animals using body gestures and signals to communicate, humans use them, too. These forms of nonverbal communication are easier to see in a person who shows strong emotions.

If you watch someone receive bad news on the telephone, for example, look at the expression on the person's face, how the body position shifts, or how a hand is run through the hair. People who are hearing something they do not quite understand will usually frown or put their head to one side. See if you can spot any of these visual clues to what someone is hearing before they respond.

Body language is made up of a range of gestures, some more subtle than others. There are, however, some basic signs to look out for.

Observation

Someone who folds their arms or holds an arm across the body is creating a barrier to keep you at bay. Tapping a foot shows nervousness or impatience. Standing up to talk to someone who is sitting can be a sign of a person who wants power.

Being able to understand body language is useful if you want to find out if someone is saying what they really mean. Watching other people's reactions to what you say, or even the way they angle their body toward you when you speak, can also tell you how your information is being received.

To interpret body language successfully, you need to use your powers of observation. Remember that your body

Happy and Relaxed

In this typical restaurant scene (left) both people are smiling and seem relaxed enough to look into each other's eyes. The woman is leaning toward the man, suggesting that she is anxious to please. He has not pulled back totally, showing that he is happy with the situation.

Keep Your Distance
A snapshot (above) that says a thousand contemptuous words. The eyes are saying "Just don't." The hand across the mouth complements the eyes by saying "Don't expect a smile." The arm forms a protective barrier across the body.

language also reflects your own emotional response. Do you clench your fists when you are angry or look away when you feel embarrassed, for example?

People who are comfortable with the company they are in and the conversations they are having will have an open and relaxed stance with good eye contact. If a person likes you, then they will mirror your body language and movements. Their tone of voice will also match yours.

Nervous, bored, or uncomfortable people will have difficulty meeting your eyes. They will look away or at the floor if they are feeling defensive or might also shuffle their feet or cross their arms.

Hiding Feelings
It is possible to change your body language. This is useful when you need to hide your true feelings. For example, it is not unusual to feel nervous walking home alone in the dark. Apart from taking the usual precautions, such as avoiding unlit areas (see *Keeping Safe*, pages 182–183), you can minimize potential danger by a positive attitude. If you feel vulnerable, this can be reflected in the way you walk. If you stride out purposefully with head held high, this not only increases your self-confidence but could also ward off a potential attacker.

This strategy can also be used when you deal with a situation in which you feel you have to prove yourself. Saying to yourself as you are about to walk through a door, "Even though I am nervous, I can do this," can help you appear more comfortable and confident to those you want to impress.

To help you understand body language, watch people walking down the street or shopping in stores. What non-verbal clues can you pick up about them? Look at people in restaurants and try to work out the nature of the relationship between them. The more you look at others, the more you will learn about your own give-away body language.

All Smiles
This waiter (below) is playing his role well. Appearing to be sunny and helpful, he is likely to get more tips. His customers may respond to his smiles in a positive way by being less demanding and having more fun.

LEAVING YOUR MARK

THERE ARE MANY reasons why humans communicate by leaving their mark. Countries and states may fly flags or put up secure borders to tell others that a place belongs to them. Teenagers may want to decorate their rooms in their own style, and artists may sign their work. The urge to leave a mark comes from the need to communicate a sense of individuality and yet to acknowledge that we are not alone.

It is a basic human characteristic to want to leave a mark, and we do it in many ways and for many reasons. From earliest times humans have tried to hold and defend pieces of land that provided them with food, shelter, and other valuable resources.

We still do this today. Countries indicate the borders of their territory on maps and fly flags to communicate to others that the property belongs to them. On a smaller scale, our garden fences and door numbers are another example of territory marking.

fact file

Some territorial markings are highly prized. Famous artists who sign their work are not only marking their territory but also increasing the value of the work.

The Great Wall of China is the longest border ever built.

Each person leaves a unique mark via their fingerprints.

Individuality

Humans also like to leave their mark to express their individuality to others. Walk into two similar houses, and they may feel very different, since each householder tries to stamp his or her own identity by the choice of furniture and pictures and how they are positioned. The clothes we wear, the things we possess—even the way we write our signatures—are designed to allow each of us to leave our individual mark on society.

Many people also leave their mark when they die. Gravestones and memorial gardens are just two ways in which the deceased can be remembered. Others may donate libraries of books or art collections to the public as a way of being remembered after they have died.

For most people, producing children is the most important way of leaving a mark. Each

Steer Clear

This car (above) would not suit the person who does not like to stand out in a crowd! It has been designed to attract attention. Changing the appearance of mass-produced items such as cars is called customizing. It allows the owner to mark his or her property as different from all the others.

Corporate Identity

It is not just individuals who communicate their identity to others; it is often also vitally important to be noticed in business.

Companies may go to great lengths to develop identities that they hope will make them be remembered by clients and customers. Most companies create an individual design for their products and stationery that is recognizable anywhere in the world. This is known as a company logo. They may also have a slogan (a catchy phrase) they hope people will remember. Companies may copyright (protect) their designs, prevent-ing them being used by others.

Hotel groups are an example of corporate identity. The façades (the design of the front of the hotel), the decoration, and even the staff uniforms are often identical. This implies that you will feel secure in the knowledge that the standards are the same worldwide.

Establishing Identity

The girl above has created a personal space for herself. She is at an age when establishing her own identity is important. The choice of posters reflects her interests, not those of her parents or siblings, giving her a chance for self-expression.

child inherits genes from its parents that determine many of the child's characteristics—for example, its appearance and temperament will be similar to its parents. Therefore, although each of us is an individual, we will bear strong resemblances to our parents.

COMMUNICATING BY SCENT

As HUMANS HAVE evolved, we have come to rely less and less on our sense of smell. Our bodies continue to send scented messages to the outside world, but increasingly we go to great lengths to cover these up with deodorants and perfumes.

Most animals, including humans, give off chemicals called pheromones. These substances can only be recognized by other members of the same species.

The release of pheromones in humans is controlled by hormones (see *Body Systems*, pages 30–31). Pheromones are produced by animals when finding a mate, for example. During mating the male releases pheromones that attract the female.

Compared with some other animals, our sense of smell is limited. However, pheromones still play an important part in the mating process. We produce pheromones all the time, but in certain circumstances we produce more. For example, if two people are attracted to each other, they will produce more pheromones—even though the couple will be unaware of this, for they cannot actually smell the odor. Nevertheless, their

Perfumes
Although the sense of smell is less sensitive in humans than it is in many other animals, it still plays an important part in our lives. Many of the perfumes that we use are based on the smells produced by plants such as the lilac (above).

Mutual Respect
Swinging the incense burner toward the congregation is an important part of this religious ceremony (left). It is a way of communicating the respect of the priest for the congregation and their inclusion in the ceremony.

bodies are communicating a liking for each other.

However, some natural body odors that we can smell are considered extremely unattractive. People use deodorants to prevent body odor because smelling of sweat is thought to send the wrong message. Sweat is associated with a lack of washing and therefore sends the message "I don't take care of myself. I don't value myself."

We also apply substances to our bodies to give them a different, more attractive smell. Throughout history perfumed oils have always fetched a high price in recognition of their importance in attracting the opposite sex. Today, the advertising and packaging of a bottle of perfume are also designed to send out the message that this product will make you more attractive.

In the same way, room fresheners and cleaning products are designed to make our homes smell fresh and to get across the message that we are clean living.

Danger Smells

Just as an animal in the wild sniffs the air to smell impending danger, so smell can be a warning sign to humans, too (see *The Brain and Senses,* page 68). We often smell food to make sure that it is still fresh enough to eat. Although our sense of smell is not strong, we can usually detect "bad" smells in this way.

Often the first indication of fire is the distinctive smell of burning. We can even detect dangers like overheating electrical appliances. The clearest sign that a house has a problem with damp or with condensation is a dank and musty smell.

Ailments such as gangrene are accompanied by an acrid smell that sends a powerful warning to the sufferer.

Comfort Smells

In less than two days a newborn baby learns to identify its mother by her body fragrance.

The mother, meanwhile, can identify her baby by smell alone after only 30 minutes. This is probably an example of a primitive survival mechanism, for many animals recognize their young in this way. Possibly our human ancestors did, too.

Entering a home to be greeted by the smell of cooked food makes a house seem more welcoming. Real estate agents know this—they often advise house sellers to have the aroma of fresh bread and coffee in the kitchen, to make the home more appealing to a prospective buyer.

Feast of Smells

It is said that "we eat with our eyes." However, although this food below looks appetizing, it is the sense of smell that sends a message to activate the salivary glands in the mouth and so prepare our digestive system for eating.

INTRODUCTION

THE HUMAN BODY is a delicately balanced piece of biological engineering that is far more complicated than any machine made by humans. Good health is when all our systems work together in harmony. Unfortunately, in such an intricate structure things may go wrong. Sometimes the body can repair itself, but on occasion we must rely on medical science to try to bring us back to full health again.

This section explains the importance of having a healthy body and the steps we can take to maintain our health throughout our lives. It also deals with some of the major causes of illness and how medical science can get us back to full fitness and health again.

Someone who is healthy has a body free from disease and feels fit and well. If you are healthy, you are more able to cope with life, are less likely to fall victim to disease, and can enjoy life more. To take care of your body you should eat a sound, low-fat diet (see pages 148–149), get plenty of exercise (see pages 164–165), ensure that you sleep properly, and keep yourself clean. Regular medical checkups will also help ensure you stay healthy. You should also avoid harmful substances like tobacco and drugs.

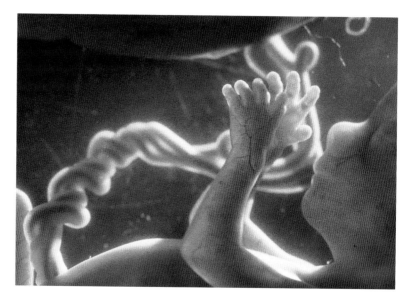

The Unborn Child
The photograph above shows a baby developing in the mother's womb. Checks are made to assess the baby's health before birth, and some medical care may be given while the baby is in the womb.

Causes of Illness and Death
The health of a person depends on many factors—for example, whether or not they were born free from disease, where they live, how they live, their age, and their genetic makeup. In some countries high infant mortality rates are often caused by poor sanitation, poor diet, and a lack of immunization programs (see page 155) to protect young people against diseases.

fact file

Every person, from babies to the elderly, has the same number of muscle fibers. Our physique depends on how well we develop our muscles.

Low back pain causes more lost working days annually than all industrial strikes put together.

All the blood in the body passes through the heart every minute.

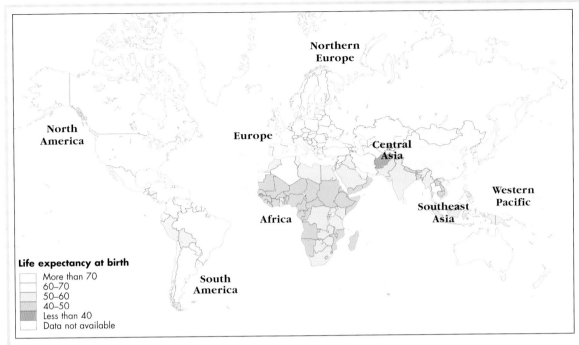

Northern
Europe

North
America

Europe

Central
Asia

Western
Pacific

Southeast
Asia

Africa

South
America

Life expectancy at birth
More than 70
60–70
50–60
40–50
Less than 40
Data not available

Life Expectancy

This map shows that our life expectancy (the average number of years a healthy person can expect to live) is determined largely by which part of the world we live in. In parts of Africa a large proportion of the population will die before the age of 40, mainly from AIDS and malnutrition (lack of proper food). In North America the life expectancy is rising because of a healthier lifestyle and is now well into the seventies. The population of Sweden, in Europe, lives the longest mainly because they eat the least fat and exercise the most. Few people smoke, and alcohol is too expensive to buy.

In the West generally healthier lifestyles, including a better diet and immunization programs, mean that people are more likely to enjoy longer lives. However, young people in wealthier countries are more likely to be injured or killed by accidents (for example, while driving a car), by experimenting with drugs, or through suicide.

Our first 18 years are spent growing. This is when we can catch childhood illnesses like chickenpox and tonsillitis (see pages 160–161). Asthma (see page 161) is also becoming more of a problem because of our increasingly polluted atmosphere and all the artificial additives in food.

Generally, however, it is not until the age of 40 that we are usually at risk of major illnesses like heart attacks, cancer, bronchitis, and strokes. Smoking is the biggest cause of heart disease, along with high-fat, "fast" foods, and heart attacks are the major killer of adults in America. It is therefore important to know about the risks (see pages 151 and 170–171).

It is also in later life that we often experience various organ diseases. AIDS (see page 153) has now become a major killer, particularly in parts of Africa.

The Future

Although medical science is continually improving treatment for a wide range of illnesses, no one can be certain that we will find cures for cancer, stop sudden deaths from heart attacks, invent a vaccination for AIDS, and treat all mental illnesses. However, we will undoubtedly take great steps toward some of these goals in the 21st century.

DIET, NUTRITION, AND WEIGHT CONTROL

OUR FOOD GIVES us the energy we need to live. It enables our organs to function. Food also helps us grow and repair any injuries by providing nutrients for the tissues. Too much food makes us fat, which can cause high blood pressure and heart disease.

To stay healthy, the body needs a wide variety of foods from many sources. This is called a balanced diet, and it consists of the correct amounts of **carbohydrates**—which provide most of the energy—and sufficient **protein** for cell growth and repair.

Vitamins are essential for the maintenance of the body, and **fiber** is needed to help digestion. Unfortunately, most diets also contain too much fat, which leads to excessive weight gain. The amount of food we need can vary tremendously depending on our age and on our daily activity. A young sportsman or sportswoman will require more food than an inactive elderly person, for example.

How Much Is Enough?

Energy from food is measured in calories. The average daily intake for an adult is about 1,500 calories, but children from the age of ten and teenagers need between 2,000–2,500 calories per day—particularly in the form of carbohydrates, proteins, and vitamins. This is because of the rapid growth spurt around puberty.

Unfortunately, young people tend to dislike regular meals and prefer snacks or instant foods—most of which are high in sugars, additives, and fats but are low in protein. It is very easy to exceed the required daily calorie intake when eating these kinds of foods, and any excess will be converted into fat unless regular exercise is done (see page 164).

It is important to start the day with a healthy breakfast, such as fruit juice, a bran cereal, and wholemeal toast. If you intend to have snacks during the day, fruit and nuts are better than high-fat foods like candy. The chart on page 149 shows the daily servings of food for a proper, balanced diet.

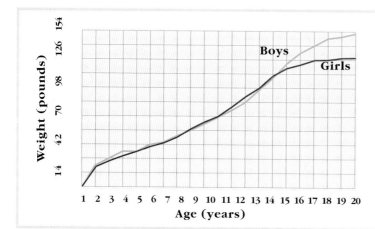

Weight and Age Chart

This chart shows the average gain in weight from infancy to 20 years old for boys (green line) and girls (red line). Although factors such as build affect weight, measurements that fall below these lines indicate the weight is generally too low, while measurements above the lines indicate excessive weight. The chart also shows that after about age 14, boys start to get heavier than girls of the same age.

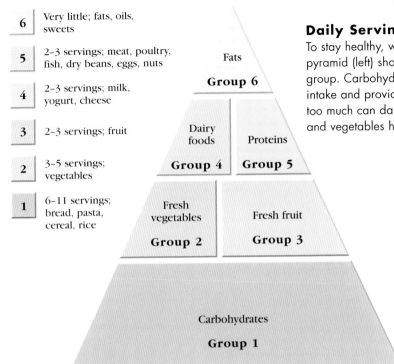

6	Very little; fats, oils, sweets
5	2-3 servings; meat, poultry, fish, dry beans, eggs, nuts
4	2-3 servings; milk, yogurt, cheese
3	2-3 servings; fruit
2	3-5 servings; vegetables
1	6-11 servings; bread, pasta, cereal, rice

Fats
Group 6

Dairy foods
Group 4

Proteins
Group 5

Fresh vegetables
Group 2

Fresh fruit
Group 3

Carbohydrates
Group 1

Daily Servings of Food

To stay healthy, we need a varied, balanced diet. This pyramid (left) shows the daily servings required in each group. Carbohydrates form the biggest part of the daily intake and provide energy. Fats form the smallest, since too much can damage the body. Proteins, milk, fruit, and vegetables help maintain the body's systems.

muscle becomes too weak to pump the blood around the body, and death soon follows.

Excessive dieting to become thin, sometimes encouraged by fashion, can lead to **anorexia nervosa**—a condition in which the sufferer wrongly imagines he or she is overweight and refuses to eat. This is a form of mental illness as well as a physical illness, which may need hospital treatment.

Overweight

If you are overweight, your health is at risk. Overweight children and teenagers become overweight adults, who will then suffer needless health problems throughout their lives. Back problems, arthritis of the ankles, knees, and hips, heart disease, poor circulation, and breathing difficulties are all more likely in obese (very overweight) people.

Hundreds of diets that aim to make weight reduction simple have been devised, but the majority do not work. If you are overweight, the most effective way to lose weight is to reduce your calorie intake by between 500 and 1,000 calories per day. This will still leave some room for the occasional snacks you cannot resist!

Malnutrition

Most of us have seen the tragic pictures on the television of starving children. When the body cannot take its energy from food, it first breaks down the body fat, and then it takes the protein from muscle. Protein deficiency causes fluid retention, which explains the swollen and extended abdomens seen in malnourished children. Eventually the heart

Obesity

This picture (right) shows a lady who has excess fat around her waist and bottom. This weight has to be carried by the hips, knees, and ankles, leading to early wear on these joints. It also puts excess strain on the heart and raises the blood pressure.

HEALTH RISKS

WE MUST TAKE care of our bodies in order to get the best from them. Many of the illnesses affecting people in wealthy countries are the result of their choice of lifestyle. A poor diet, high stress, and lack of exercise, combined with the use of alcohol and tobacco, increase the risk of heart disease and other conditions. Sometimes disablement or even premature death may be the end result.

Lack of exercise is the single most important factor that threatens our health. In our later teenage years we are faced with a choice: we can either maintain the fitness that we enjoyed at school or stop regular exercise, and in so doing let the muscles and joints become weak and inefficient. But as we have seen, exercise improves the body's efficiency and helps prevent many diseases.

The Dangers We Face
The latest studies show that at least one in two people who smoke will die early as a result. While most people believe it can increase the chances of lung cancer, few people know that smoking is linked to other malignant tumors such as those of the stomach and bladder. Nicotine in cigarettes narrows blood vessels, particularly in the legs, and may result in the need to amputate (cut off) the limb.

The abuse of substances such as solvents and illegal drugs can produce a temporary feeling of well-being but carries the risks of death from an overdose, poisoning, addiction, and other health problems.

Alcohol can be harmful, too. It is a drug and

fact file

Smallpox is the first disease to be completely eradicated (wiped out) from the world.

Bacteria were discovered a century before they were found to cause diseases.

The installation of sterile (germ-free) water in Nepal has saved the lives of 900 babies in the past year.

lowers the activity of most body functions. Brain activity is reduced, coordination diminished, and reflexes slowed. Small amounts of wine can be beneficial to the heart, but in excess alcohol raises the blood pressure and weakens the heart

Vaccination
This picture (left) shows a baby being vaccinated against polio, tetanus, and whooping cough. The increase in preventive medicine has caused a dramatic reduction in these diseases.

Fast Foods

Many teenagers regularly eat convenient "fast" food (right). But highly processed foods such as these may have a high fat content and do not, on their own, provide us with a balanced diet.

muscle. Alcoholism eventually produces liver damage that allows toxic substances to build up in the blood and ultimately causes death.

To avoid risks to our health, we must sometimes take special precautions. For example, before traveling to certain tropical countries, it is necessary to be inoculated against diseases such as cholera, yellow fever, and typhoid. It is also important to seek medical advice to avoid getting other local diseases such as malaria. You should also follow advice, for example, about only using water that is safe to drink.

World Progress

People in developed countries are able to eat healthily if they choose and can readily seek medical advice if they contract illnesses. The population of poorer countries is not so lucky, and their health often suffers. However, progress is being made; mass vaccination (see page 155) has eradicated smallpox from the world and greatly reduced other diseases like measles and whooping cough. The number of cases of malaria has also been greatly reduced. AIDS is still the biggest threat, but better sex education is cutting its occurrence.

Lungs
One in three people who smoke more than ten cigarettes per day will develop lung cancer. Nicotine also destroys lung tissue, leading to shortness of breath.

Liver
Excess alcohol destroys liver cells, leading to eventual liver failure and premature death.

Brain
Alcohol suppresses brain function and can eventually lead to a loss of mental powers. Smoking reduces the blood supply to the brain.

Heart
Smoking blocks up the heart's blood vessels, and alcohol reduces the strength of the heart muscle.

Kidneys and bladder
Both smoking and alcohol cause damage—particularly nicotine, which is associated with bladder cancer.

Circulation
Nicotine narrows blood vessels, especially in the legs, leading to gangrene and possible amputation.

Effects of Alcohol and Smoking

Smoking and drinking too much alcohol can damage the body's organs, as can be seen here.

BACTERIA AND VIRUSES

THE HUMAN BODY is constantly infected by organisms, especially bacteria and viruses. Some are beneficial (useful), like the intestinal bacteria that help food digestion, but most are harmful and some are life threatening.

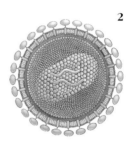
1

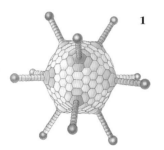

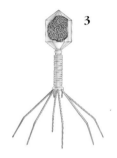
3

Bacteria are single-celled organisms whose shapes very greatly. They float in air and live in water, so infection can occur by breathing them into the throat or lungs or by drinking contaminated water. They are passed easily from person to person either through breathing, sneezing, or coughing close to someone or by touching the infected area.

Bacterial infections produce pus, a thick yellow liquid that contains dead bacterial and body cells. Two common bacterial infections are tonsillitis and conjunctivitis. In tonsillitis the offending bacterium is the streptococcus variety. Conjunctivitis is an infection of the covering of the eye and is highly contagious—especially in young children at school. The eye looks red and oozes pus that makes the eye sticky. The offending bacterium is the staphylococcus variety.

Many Virus Shapes

Some of the many different virus shapes are shown above. The adenovirus, which infects throats and noses, with its characteristic spikes (1). The AIDS virus, with its strong covering of surface protein (2). A bacteriophage (a virus that attacks bacteria) with tail fibers (3).

Bacteria Cells

Most bacteria have a strong cell wall within which is genetic material, but there is no distinct nucleus. An outer capsule usually envelops the cell wall. Some bacteria have a flagellum, or tail, for swimming. Under the microscope each type of bacteria is different. The four shown here are: spirilla from syphilis (1), vibrio from cholera (2), rod-shaped bacilli from dysentery (3), and spherical streptococci from tonsillitis (4).

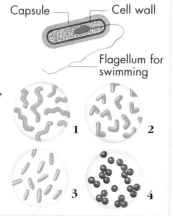
Capsule — Cell wall
Flagellum for swimming
1 2
3 4

More serious diseases that are caused by bacteria include dysentery, pneumonia, syphilis, and bacterial meningitis.

Antibiotics kill bacteria by destroying their outer membranes. Worryingly, antibiotics are prescribed so often these days, often for ailments like viruses that are best left to the body's own defenses to fight, that the bacteria are developing resistance to these drugs.

Viral Illnesses

Viruses are the smallest disease-causing agents. Billions of them can cover a pinhead, and they can cause many illnesses, including colds, polio, influenza, and measles. The common cold is caused by up to 100 different viruses, which is why it is so difficult to find a cure. Polio has been almost wiped out in most developed countries by vaccination, however.

Antibiotics cannot kill viruses. Instead, the body must produce specific antibodies to combat each virus. Viruses are unable to reproduce by themselves and need to invade a host. They break into the host cell and use its nutrients to multiply. When the host cell is full, it bursts open, releasing the viral cells. The body's defenses can deal with some viruses, like colds, but others, including AIDS, are too strong for the immune system (see page 155) to destroy.

Effects of the AIDS Virus

Infected people may have no symptoms for many years, but at a certain stage these symptoms will occur (right).

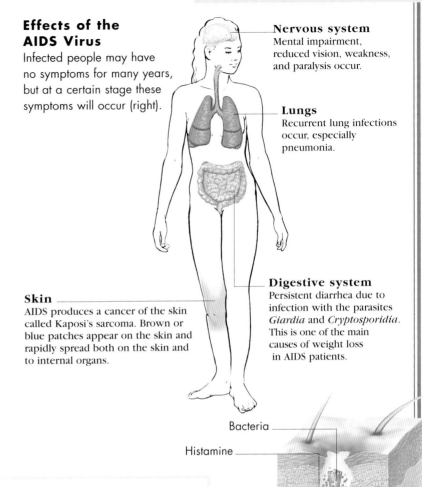

Nervous system
Mental impairment, reduced vision, weakness, and paralysis occur.

Lungs
Recurrent lung infections occur, especially pneumonia.

Digestive system
Persistent diarrhea due to infection with the parasites *Giardia* and *Cryptosporidia*. This is one of the main causes of weight loss in AIDS patients.

Skin
AIDS produces a cancer of the skin called Kaposi's sarcoma. Brown or blue patches appear on the skin and rapidly spread both on the skin and to internal organs.

Bacteria

Histamine

White blood cell

Blood vessel

How Bacteria Damage Cells

This illustration (1) shows toxins (poisonous agents) being released by bacteria. These enter the body cells and alter some of its chemical reactions. In the illness diphtheria the toxins damage the heart muscle by inhibiting protein manufacture.

This illustration (2) shows that some toxins can make blood clot in small blood vessels. Damage to the cell walls can also make blood leak out. An example of this is the meningococcus bacteria that causes meningitis.

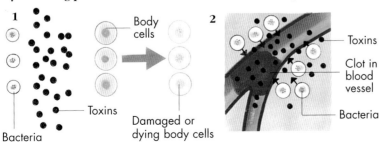

1
Body cells

Toxins

Damaged or dying body cells

Bacteria

2
Toxins

Clot in blood vessel

Bacteria

Infected Wounds

A wound infected by bacteria (above). The body cells release a substance called histamine to cause inflammation and trap the bacteria. Blood vessels widen and allow white blood cells to pass through their walls into the tissues where they destroy the bacteria.

BODY DEFENSES AND IMMUNIZATION

UNWANTED INVADERS ARE all around us. They are bacteria, viruses, and other living things that are too small to be seen by the naked eye. Once inside us, however, they can multiply and spread unless they are destroyed by our body defenses.

Microscopic organisms float in the air and land constantly on our skin, clothes, food, drinks, and other objects. Many of them are harmless, but some can cause infections. These infections may range from a cold or sore throat, which can soon pass, to life-threatening diseases such as pneumonia.

The body has several external defenses against invading organisms. The main one is the **skin** (see *Body Systems*, page 9). Most germs are unable to penetrate healthy skin.

White Blood Cells

Invaders sometimes do breach the external defenses and reach the blood and other internal body parts. When this happens, white blood cells (see *Body Systems*, pages 18–19) go into action as the first line of defense. The white blood cells

Natural Defenses

Even the parts of the body that are not covered by the external skin layer are still well protected from invading organisms (right).

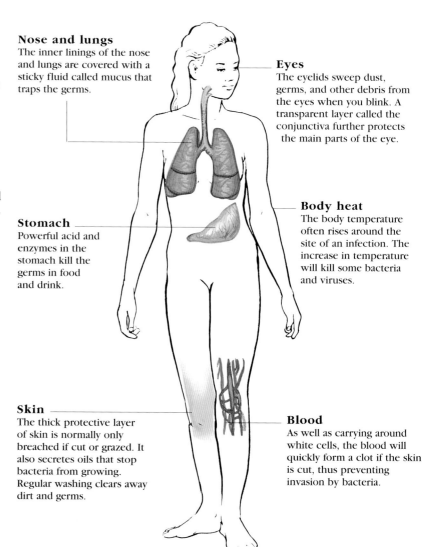

Nose and lungs
The inner linings of the nose and lungs are covered with a sticky fluid called mucus that traps the germs.

Eyes
The eyelids sweep dust, germs, and other debris from the eyes when you blink. A transparent layer called the conjunctiva further protects the main parts of the eye.

Stomach
Powerful acid and enzymes in the stomach kill the germs in food and drink.

Body heat
The body temperature often rises around the site of an infection. The increase in temperature will kill some bacteria and viruses.

Skin
The thick protective layer of skin is normally only breached if cut or grazed. It also secretes oils that stop bacteria from growing. Regular washing clears away dirt and germs.

Blood
As well as carrying around white cells, the blood will quickly form a clot if the skin is cut, thus preventing invasion by bacteria.

known as **macrophages** and **granulocytes** engulf and eat germs whole.

The body also has about 1 trillion other white cells known as **lymphocytes**. They are produced in the bone marrow—which is the jellylike substance in the middle of large bones—and by the spleen, located just below the left rib cage. Lymphocytes make body proteins called **antibodies** that attach themselves to the germs like a key fitting into a lock. They then kill or disable them. As the battle rages, white blood cells travel and multiply in the blood and lymph fluid.

Immunization

The body's defenses can be triggered into fighting a particular type of invader by injecting it with a harmless amount of the organism, known as a **vaccine**. This makes the body produce antibodies. The introduction of bacteria or viruses into the body in this way is called vaccination, or immunization.

Large-scale immunization of millions of people against polio, tetanus, whooping cough, mumps, and measles has greatly reduced the incidence of these diseases. Smallpox has now been completely eliminated from the world by a program of intensive immunization by world health organizations.

After the immune defense system has gone through the process of destroying the germ, the antibodies it has formed against it remain, and the body is said to be immunized. These

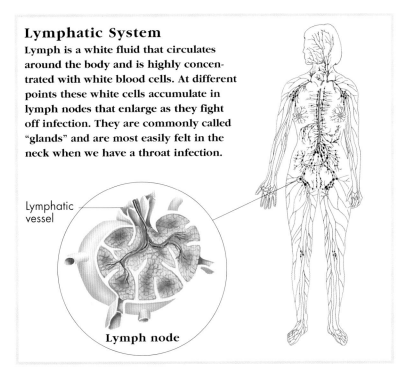

Lymphatic System

Lymph is a white fluid that circulates around the body and is highly concentrated with white blood cells. At different points these white cells accumulate in lymph nodes that enlarge as they fight off infection. They are commonly called "glands" and are most easily felt in the neck when we have a throat infection.

Lymphatic vessel

Lymph node

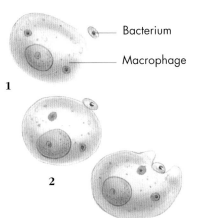

1

2

3

Bacterium

Macrophage

Destruction of Bacteria

The sequence (left) show how an invading, hostile bacterium (plural: bacteria) is attacked by a white blood cell known as a macrophage. The bacterium initially sticks to the surface of the macrophage and is then engulfed (surrounded) and finally destroyed.

antibodies are then ready to destroy the germ if it ever invades again in the future. All babies are now given a course of vaccinations starting a few months after birth, and booster doses are given throughout childhood.

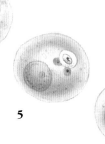

4

5

6

EXAMINATION AND TREATMENT

PRECISE DIAGNOSIS OF a disease and accurate treatment are essential to return us to full health. Examinations, tests, and specialized investigations like X-rays are used to reveal the nature of the illness, and then treatment such as drugs or surgery can begin.

When a doctor is training in medical school, great emphasis is placed on the initial examination of the patient. An accurate description of the symptoms (the outward signs of the illness) usually helps in reaching a diagnosis. (The diagnosis is the decision reached by a doctor about which illness the patient is suffering from.) Some of the signs—called diagnostic signs—that doctors look for are described below.

fact file

The first satisfactory anesthetic (pain killer) to be used was ether. It was given to a patient by an American doctor in 1846 in an operation to remove a tumor.

The first peacetime blood bank was set up in Chicago in 1937.

One of the oldest drugs in use comes from the foxglove plant.

Diagnostic Signs

In younger people, listening to the chest may reveal a wheeze that can indicate asthma. When the patient breathes out, the doctor will listen for a high-pitched whine associated with shortness of breath. Examination of the throat can reveal unhealthy tonsils, which can be the reason for recurring infections. Feeling the abdomen with the flat of the hand will reveal any enlargement of the spleen or kidneys; and if

Examining the Chest

The picture on the right shows a doctor listening to the chest of a young child. Although the child cannot explain his illness, listening with a stethoscope can make the diagnosis of a chest infection.

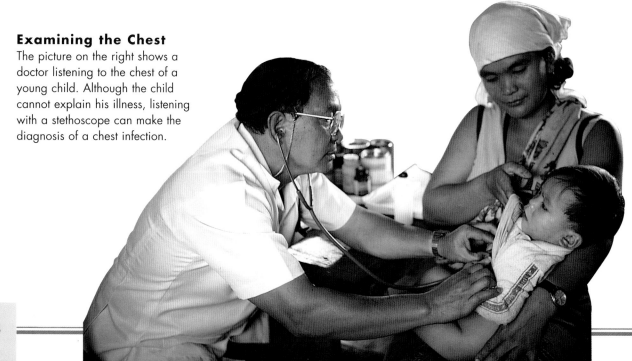

appendicitis (swollen appendix) is suspected, there will be extreme tenderness low on the right side.

Listening to the sound of the heart with a stethoscope uncovers any murmurs that may have been present from birth. These may be harmless or suggest a hole in the heart (see page 171).

Testing the urine under the microscope may reveal infection. The presence of sugar in the urine indicates that the patient may be suffering from **diabetes**—a condition in which the body is unable to control blood sugar levels.

Seeing Into the Body

Ever since X-rays were first introduced in 1895 to capture a likeness of the bones of the human hand, scientists have been steadily developing methods for looking inside the body. However, the X-ray still remains the most frequently used method, since it is quick, cheap, and effective. It does have limitations, however, since it does not reveal the deeper parts of the body and cannot be used in pregnancy because the fetus may be damaged.

Ultrasound was the first development following the discovery of X-rays. Sound waves are bounced off the internal structures of the body, and the echoes are picked up by a scanner. It is especially useful in detecting objects in liquid—for example, gallstones mixed in bile within the gall bladder (see *Body Systems*, page 26). Ultrasound is perfect for

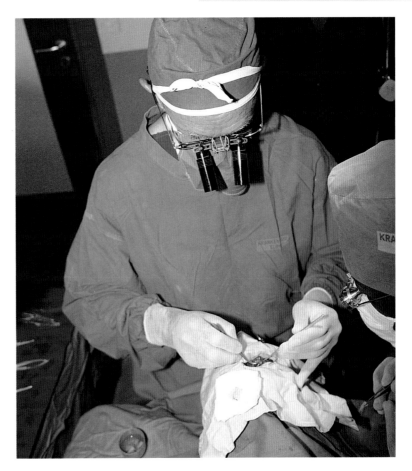

measuring the growth of a baby in the womb and provides the expectant parents with an unusual photograph of their unborn baby.

CAT (computerized axial tomography) scans are more sophisticated than ultrasound. In this method X-rays are passed through the body, and a computer records the number of rays absorbed by the different tissues. Cancerous tumors have a particularly high uptake and show quite clearly on a CAT scan.

Unfortunately, the risk from exposure to X-rays with these

Eye Operation

In the photograph above an eye surgeon is operating to remove a cataract—a clouding of the lens that prevents it from focusing light onto the back of the retina in the eye. By putting in a new, artificial lens, the doctor can restore the patient's sight to normal.

scans cannot be ignored, so they have mainly been replaced by NMR (nuclear magnetic resonance) scans. These work in the same way except that harmless radio waves are used instead of X-rays.

DRUGS AND NATURAL REMEDIES

MODERN MEDICINE CAN now cure many serious illnesses that in the past were often fatal. Treatment usually involves administering carefully developed drugs. However, all medicines have side effects, so many people prefer to be treated by natural methods.

The number of drugs available to medical science is enormous, and every year new ones are developed. Drugs such as aspirin relieve pain by reducing the stimulus from the source of the pain to the brain. Others, like morphine, reduce the brain's ability to feel pain. Steroids work by reducing inflammation and are used to relieve joint swellings and in asthma and skin problems.

fact file

Every father in China is taught the basic principles of acupuncture in order to treat his children. Instead of needles he uses a finger to press on the acupuncture point.

Over 80 million antibiotics are prescribed every year around the world. Over one-third are derived from penicillin.

If antibiotics were freely available throughout developing countries, it is estimated that life expectancy would rise by 20 years.

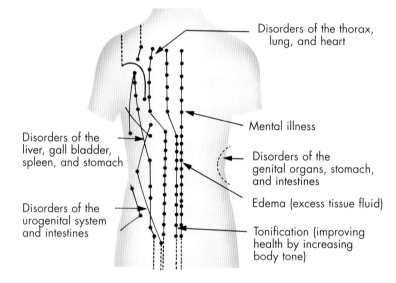

Disorders of the thorax, lung, and heart

Mental illness

Disorders of the genital organs, stomach, and intestines

Edema (excess tissue fluid)

Tonification (improving health by increasing body tone)

Disorders of the liver, gall bladder, spleen, and stomach

Disorders of the urogenital system and intestines

One of the greatest discoveries was the antibiotics that kill bacteria. Penicillin was the first antibiotic, discovered by Alexander Fleming. Many other antibiotics are now available for curing infections. Before antibiotics infections often spread, especially in wounds, leading to blood poisoning and gangrene (tissue death). The latter often led to amputation or death but is now virtually nonexistent due to antibiotics.

Unfortunately, every drug has side effects: some people are allergic to penicillin and develop

The Acupuncture Map
The illustration above shows the main energy lines, or meridians, of various organs, mapped out on the back. The dots indicate the acupuncture points where needles are inserted to cure the illness.

a rash; aspirin can cause internal bleeding; and steroids produce weight gain. These unwanted side effects mean alternative medicine is increasing in popularity, although not all physicians believe in the value of such treatments.

Reflexology

Reflexology is an ancient method of healing that involves the use of massage and pressure on different parts of the feet (see photograph far right). These parts are thought to be linked to various regions of the body, as shown by the diagram on the right. If a patient has a pain in a particular part of the body, the reflexologist will work on the part of the foot that corresponds to the area of pain to try and release the "energy blocks" that are causing the pain and thus cure the illness.

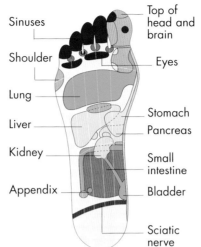

Sinuses
Shoulder
Lung
Liver
Kidney
Appendix
Top of head and brain
Eyes
Stomach
Pancreas
Small intestine
Bladder
Sciatic nerve

Acupuncture

Half the world's population is treated by acupuncture. In China, Japan, Singapore, Malaya, and Sri Lanka it is the preferred treatment. Acupuncturists believe that energy called *chi* flows through our bodies. It enters via our feet or hands and flows upward in vertical lines, or meridians, each of which passes through a major organ.

When an illness occurs, it is said that there is an interruption to the flow of *chi* through that organ. The acupuncturist locates key points along the meridian and inserts small, sterile needles into them. Extra *chi* is drawn into the body by rotating the needle rapidly between thumb and forefinger, thus restoring the energy balance.

More modern theories of how acupuncture works say that the needles stop the nerve transmitting pain, or that they stimulate pain-relieving substances called endorphins.

Homeopathic and Herbal Medicine

Homeopathy, like vaccination, works by introducing a minute amount of a substance into the body. This stimulates the body to produce a cure when it is attacked by the illness. For example, in polio vaccination a minute amount of polio is given so that the body produces antibodies (see page 155) that will destroy any future polio virus. Homeopathic preparations stimulate the body in the same way but are given in tablet form. An example is ipecac, which in large doses induces vomiting but in dilute form allows the body to produce a reaction to stop a sickness.

Herbal medicine uses the natural chemicals present in some plants to provide the treatment. Many of the modern drugs of today are derived from plants. An example is digitalis, which is used for treating heart failure. It is extracted from foxgloves.

Herbal Medicine

Herbalism—using plant extracts to cure illnesses—is the oldest form of medicine and is still practiced widely today. Shown below are four of the plants commonly used. Herbal medicine is used for a range of conditions such as coughs, colds, stomach upsets, and arthritis.

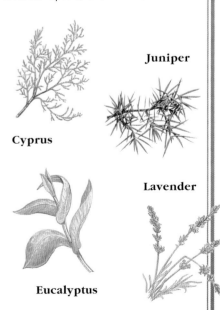

Juniper

Cyprus

Lavender

Eucalyptus

CHILDHOOD ILLNESSES

WHEN WE ARE young, we are not always able to tell an adult what is wrong with us when we feel ill. But a child with a painful ear infection may cry or scream, and a baby with a virus infection may develop a telltale, bright-red rash, for example. Most of the illnesses that affect very young children are diagnosed by careful examination and with the doctor looking for symptoms (outward signs) to help make a diagnosis.

Most of the illnesses that children in developed countries get are not serious, since immunization programs (see page 155) now protect them against dangerous diseases such as diphtheria (see page 173). However, these diseases still cause suffering in countries without effective immunization programs.

Sore throats and stuffy noses are the commonest illnesses in children, and infections can be passed quickly from one person to another. The first lines of defense against these kinds of infections are two types of glandular tissue—the tonsils and the adenoids—at the back of the throat. When faced with invading organisms, they swell and become inflamed.

Operations to remove these glands used to be common-place, but removing them leaves the back of the throat unprotected. Now, they are usually only removed if they are causing discomfort.

Fevers of Childhood

A number of illnesses occur only once in a lifetime; an

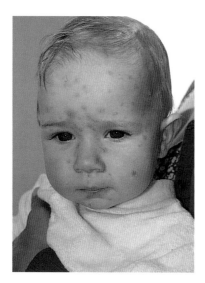

Chickenpox

This is a virus infection, appearing 14 to 21 days after contact. Often there are no symptoms until the first spot appears. These last for 7 to 10 days and look like tiny blisters on a red base (above). They can appear anywhere and are intensely itchy as they burst and dry up. The patient is infectious for one week.

attack by the disease makes the body's immune system produce antibodies that provide protection against further attacks (see page 155). These

Measles

This virus infection occurs 7 to 14 days after contact. The child has a runny nose, red eyes, and a cough. Small white spots appear in the mouth. A blotchy red rash occurs, initially on the face, but then on the rest of the body (above). It lasts for 4 to 5 days. When it has faded, the patient is free of infection.

initial attacks usually happen when we are young and so are called childhood fevers. They include **chickenpox**, **mumps**, **measles**, **German measles**, scarlet fever, diphtheria, and whooping cough. Chickenpox and measles are described on page 160. Mumps is a painful disease that causes swelling in the salivary glands at the angle of the jaw, often making the whole neck appear swollen.

German measles, or rubella, is a milder illness than measles. The patient does not normally feel particularly ill. A pale pink rash—rather like sunburn—appears, starting behind the ears. German measles can be dangerous to mothers in the first months of pregnancy, for if passed to the unborn baby, the child can suffer deafness and heart defects as a result.

Scarlet fever is much less common today. At the beginning of the century it was responsible for the deaths of many children. It causes a severe fever and rash.

Diphtheria and whooping cough (see page 173) are both dangerous bacterial illnesses that are now rare in many parts of the world due to vaccination.

Asthma

Asthma occurs in one in four children, and symptoms include wheezing and shortness of breath. The condition is increasing as our atmosphere becomes more polluted by chemicals. Other causes include house dust, pollen, cold air, and even exercise. All these irritate the breathing tubes, causing the delicate muscles in the lungs to go into spasm (tighten), thus narrowing the air passages.

The condition is treated by using an inhaler in which a small amount of a drug is breathed directly into the lungs. Some inhalers prevent an attack, and others relieve the symptoms of an attack. Usually, children grow out of asthma by the age of seven, although it can persist through teenage years.

Other Illnesses

Diarrhea and vomiting are symptoms of gastroenteritis—a bacterial infection of the intestine. It can cause fluid to be lost from both ends of the body. Young children can quickly become dehydrated (short of body fluids), and a doctor will take steps to replace the lost fluids in addition to treating the cause of the illness. Warning signs of gastroenteritis include a listless child totally disinterested in his or her surroundings.

Meningitis is an uncommon, but dangerous, condition in which the linings of the brain and spinal cord—known as the meninges—become infected (see page 177).

Eczema is a dry, flaky rash that may become cracked and inflamed. It is common over joints and in skin creases.
Fungal infections may appear as scaly, circular patches. They may be localized or widespread.

Hemophilia

Before treatment was available, hemophilia caused high death rates in childhood. Hemophilia is a condition in which one of the chemicals needed for blood clotting— known as Factor 8—is missing. Its absence means that cuts do not readily stop bleeding, and any bruise or injury can cause bleeding internally. The condition is hereditary and is caused by a chromosome abnormality. The diagram on the right show how some people may inherit the condition while others are only carriers. Treatment is by infusing Factor 8 into the bloodstream when bleeding occurs.

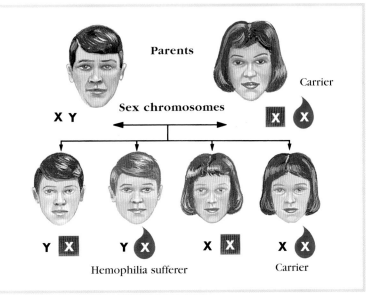

Parents

Carrier

X Y   Sex chromosomes   X X

Y X   Y X   X X   X X

Hemophilia sufferer   Carrier

INJURIES AND HEALING

THE BODY HAS an amazing ability to keep itself in good condition by carrying out running repairs. Bruises, scrapes, and scratches are quickly healed, and only in the case of more serious injuries is medical intervention needed.

Many of the most common injuries involve damage to the skin, the bones, and associated tissues such as the tendons and the ligaments. Injuries to organs such as the eyes, the brain, and the liver are usually more serious.

Cuts

The most familiar injury is a cut in which bleeding occurs from the wound. As soon as cells are damaged in this way, the blood releases a substance called fibrinogen that combines with platelets in the blood (see *Body Systems*, pages 18–19). These turn the fibrinogen into fibrin. Fibrin acts like a net or mesh, covering the wound and holding the platelets in the mesh so they prevent further blood loss. A clot is quickly formed that fills the gap, seals the wound, and stops further leakage. This keeps germs and other

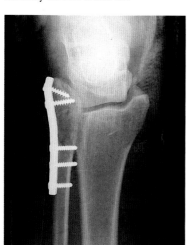

Internal Fixation

The X-ray above shows an unstable fracture of an ankle joint. To allow it to heal, a metal plate has been placed over the two bone ends and five screws inserted into the bone. They will be removed after several weeks when the bones have knitted firmly together.

Bone Healing

Initially, when a bone breaks, a blood clot forms between the bones at the fracture (break) site. This quickly turns into callus, or new bone tissue. Although callus has the appearance of bone, it is very brittle. The callus surrounds the break, so the bone appears thickened if seen on an X-ray. Bone cells called osteoblasts then turn the callus into actual bone. This slowly hardens and reshapes itself, so that after a few weeks all swelling and thickening disappears. Normally a fracture mends in four to six weeks.

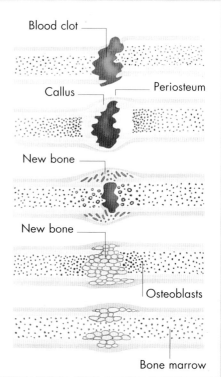

Blood clot

Callus

Periosteum

New bone

New bone

Osteoblasts

Bone marrow

particles from entering the body and allows healing to start. The fibrin in the clot contracts, drawing the edges of the wound together and hardening to produce a scab. By the time the scab drops off, normal skin has re-formed underneath.

Blood Transfusions

Sometimes emergency treatment is needed to prevent blood loss. It is done by pressing directly on the wound (see *Keeping Safe*, page 202).

In the emergency room stitches or clips will be used to hold the wound edges together to stop the bleeding. If the blood loss is too great, then a transfusion is needed. During a transfusion blood from another person is given to the patient through one of his or her veins.

We each belong to a particular blood group— either A, B, AB, or O—and great care is needed to ensure we only receive blood of the same type; otherwise, clots or lumps may form within the blood vessels. Hospitals need daily supplies of blood for accident victims. New blood donors are always welcome.

Fractures

A broken bone can heal itself if the ends are held together, and no stresses and strains are placed on the bone for a time. This can be achieved either with a plaster cast or a splint from the outside, or by attaching metal or plastic supports inside the body with screws and glues. If the bone ends

have moved apart, they must first be put into position under a general anesthetic. Bones take several weeks to heal, and one of the most effective treatments is the use of an external fixator. In the case of a fractured shinbone steel rods are screwed through the bone above and below the break, and they are joined outside the skin. The strength of the steel takes the weight, so the injured person can walk only a few days later. The rods are removed when the bone is fully healed.

In multiple fractures several types of fixators and metal plates may be used together.

Other Tissue and Organ Regeneration

Damaged muscle can regenerate because the tissue is able to form new fibers. The surfaces of the lungs, the digestive system, and urinary system also heal well. Kidneys heal only very slowly. Liver cells can also regenerate if the liver is damaged by disease or accidentally.

Mature brain cells cannot be replaced. However, nerve cells outside the brain or spinal cord can regenerate and reconnect.

Repair of Cuts

The stages in the healing of a cut (right). Platelets and red cells from the blood combine with fibrinogen from the damaged cells to form a clot. Over the next few days the clot dries and hardens to form a scab. This stays in place until new cells have formed underneath, and the scab then drops off naturally.

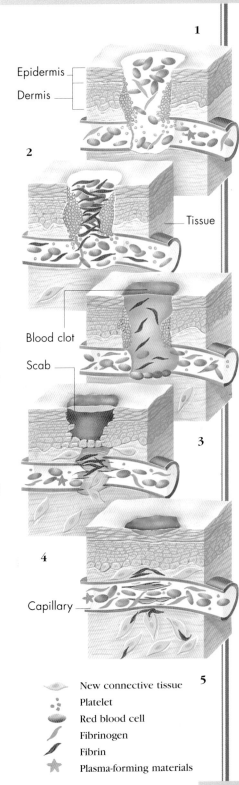

1

Epidermis
Dermis

2

Tissue

Blood clot

Scab

3

4

Capillary

5

New connective tissue
Platelet
Red blood cell
Fibrinogen
Fibrin
Plasma-forming materials

EXERCISE

PHYSICAL ACTIVITY HELPS us all. It improves the quality of our daily lives and delays the inevitable decline of our bodies as we grow older. Exercise keeps our muscles strong. It protects our joints and helps prevent the development of heart and lung disease in later life. Psychological benefits go hand in hand with physical fitness, increasing our self-confidence and well-being. We smile more and are generally much happier.

Children are naturally active and eager to play games and run around, but we tend to exercise less as we grow older. However, if we develop an interest in sports when we are young, we are more likely to continue to enjoy physical activities when we are older. The sports we enjoy in school can often be pursued outside by joining clubs and sports centers.

Benefits of Exercise

Exercise speeds up the body's chemical activity and burns off excess fat. Physically active people have fewer fatal heart attacks, their blood pressure is lower, and blood cholesterol levels fall. This is important, because although the effects may not be apparent until later in life, many heart-related problems—such as buildups of cholesterol—actually begin when we are young. Exercise also improves blood-clotting mechanisms (see pages 162–163), helping wounds heal more quickly. Simple fitness programs can prevent wear on the joints as we get old.

Which Exercise?

If you just want to improve your health in general, then the simpler exercises are sufficient. Walking for 30 minutes a day, or 60 minutes three times weekly, will increase your heart efficiency by 20 percent and drop your blood pressure by 10 points (see page 169).

If you also include some swimming and cycling, then the pumping volume of the heart will improve by 30 percent, and the fall in blood pressure will be about 20 points.

For younger sportsmen and sportswomen much greater health benefits can be achieved by pushing your body close to the limit. Team sports, like football and basketball, help do this, although individual fitness

Swimming

The swimmer shown on the right benefits by increasing her body strength, speed, and stamina. Lung volume increases dramatically with the increased use of the breathing muscles, and her physical appearance will benefit through maintaining her correct body weight.

work is also required. While an average pulse rate is 70 beats per minute, regular hard training may reduce it to 30 beats per minute. This means the heart has reached an efficiency over 100 percent greater than in an average person.

Medical Risks

Deaths from exercise occasionally occur but are very rare. Usually they occur in people who exercise when already ill with a viral infection or in those with known heart problems

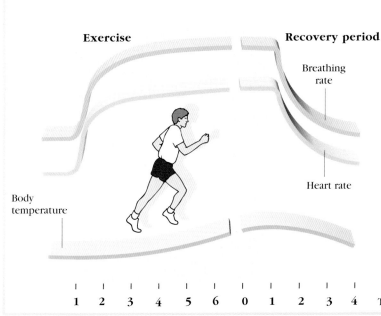

Exercise

Recovery period

Breathing rate

Heart rate

Body temperature

| 1 2 3 4 5 6 0 1 2 3 4 | Time (minutes)

As We Exercise

The runner on the left will increase his heart and breathing rates as he exercises. At the same time, his body temperature rises slightly with the heat generated. The heart rate may exceed 200 beats per minute and the breathing rate more than 40 breaths per minute. As fitness improves, these levels become much lower. Recovery time is also an important indicator of fitness, since fit hearts and lungs recover quicker, reaching their resting rates within five minutes.

who push themselves too hard. Perspective is important: only 4 in 100,000 are at risk of death playing football, whereas 40 in 100,000 are at risk who do no exercise, and a massive 500 in 100,000 people risk death from cigarette smoking.

Brain
Exercise makes us feel well and improves our appearance. Self-image and self-confidence both grow, and we become more outgoing. Memory failure as we grow older is also reduced.

Heart
The heart is made mainly of muscle, and as we exercise, this muscle strengthens, thus pumping the blood more efficiently. This reduces the risk of heart attacks and improves circulation.

Skin
The appearance of the skin is improved by exercise. The increased activity stimulates the sebaceous and sweat glands, making the skin more moist and supple and prevents aging.

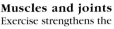

Effects of Exercise

Exercise has a beneficial effect on many organs and tissues within the body, as can be seen here.

Muscles and joints
Exercise strengthens the muscles. These then move our joints more efficiently and protect them from early wear and tear.

Circulation
Exercise improves the circulation to all parts of the body, but especially to the legs, where the normal blood flow is relatively poor. Blood cholesterol levels fall, thus preventing blocking of the major blood vessels.

SPORTS INJURIES

TODAY, MORE AND more people are playing sports—not just at school but in leisure time, too. It is inevitable, therefore, that the number of sports injuries will increase. The type and seriousness depend on the particular sport. Direct contact in football may produce broken bones, while track athletes might suffer muscle and ligament tears. People in sports such as boxing may suffer bruising and injuries to the internal organs.

Young people are usually less likely than adults to sustain contact injuries in sports, since their bones are stronger, and their ligaments are more supple. However, young people also engage in many activities where injuries are common. These include skateboarding, rollerblading, and biking. A fall can result in cuts, scrapes, or more serious bone and muscle injuries.

A bone may break as a result of a direct blow or a twisting force being applied to it. If the bone is displaced, then a splint (support) needs to be applied. This injury commonly occurs in the arm or leg, which, instead of being straight, will bend at an odd angle. An X-ray at a hospital confirms the break.

More frequent than bony breaks are muscle tears. They may be partial or complete. Complete muscle tears may occur in the upper arm, particularly in basketball or baseball players. The end of the biceps muscle is torn from the bone, and bending the elbow makes the unattached end of the muscle appear as a lump halfway down the upper arm.

In partial tears there is a sudden pain in the affected area. In running sports—including football and track—the muscles of the thigh and calf are most at risk. It is impossible to play on any longer, and the affected area becomes swollen.

Every joint in the body is held in place by ligaments. They do not move like muscles but are purely supportive. The knee joint, for example, is held in position by the knee ligaments. If one of these tears, then the knee immediately becomes unstable, causing pain and swelling.

Fractures

Different bone breaks, or fractures, are shown right. In the simple fracture the bone ends are undisplaced. A greenstick break occurs when the bone bends but only partially breaks. In a compound fracture the bone punctures the skin, and there is risk of infection. In impacted breaks the bone ends are driven together, and in comminuted fractures the bone ends splinter.

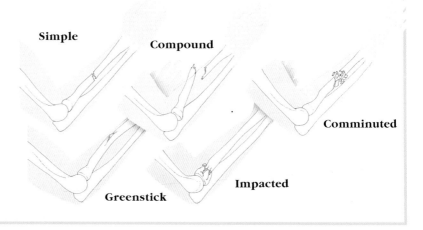

Simple Compound Comminuted Greenstick Impacted

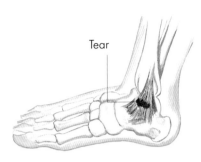

Tear

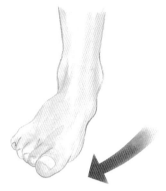

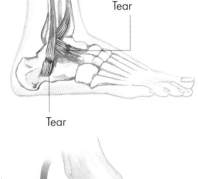

Tear

Tear

Tear

Treatment

If you suffer a broken bone, it will usually be repaired using a plaster cast or a splint (see page 163).

Muscle and ligament injuries recover much sooner than bone damage, especially if the correct, immediate treatment is given. Treatment for these injuries is likely to be as follows.

When muscles tear, there is some bleeding inside, and any further movement may make it worse. Thus rest will be prescribed for the first day Ice will be applied to cool the tissues, stop the bleeding, and reduce the swelling. It should always be applied through a towel to prevent the skin from burning. The sooner ice is applied following the injury, the less the tear will swell.

Compression will be applied by firmly—but not too tightly—

Ankle Ligament Tears

The ankle ligaments are torn by twisting the foot sideways (above left) or turning the foot over (above right). The joint becomes very swollen and unstable. Correct taping is essential so that the ligament can mend.

bandaging the affected part. Again, this action helps reduce the swelling. Finally, elevation will be needed. The injured limb will be raised to allow free drainage by gravity of the tissue swelling.

Once the initial pain and swelling have gone, then the injured part can be treated by a physiotherapist who will use manipulation and exercises to slowly bring the muscle or ligament back to full strength.

Knee Ligament Tears

This athlete (right) has torn his cruciate ligament. A splint is applied to support the knee while the ligament heals. Sometimes an operation is needed to repair it.

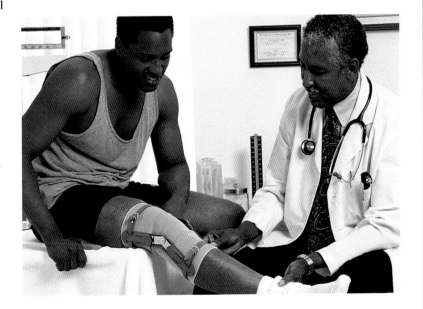

CIRCULATORY SYSTEM DISEASES

THE BODY HAS a highly complicated system of blood vessels, enabling the blood to carry oxygen and food to the tissues while at the same time removing waste products. This intricate network is also prone to disease and malfunction from time to time.

In addition to the heart (see pages 170-171), other parts of the cardiovascular system can become diseased. Healthy blood is bright red in color because it is packed with millions of red blood cells (see *Body Systems*, pages 18-19). They transport the oxygen that diffuses into the blood

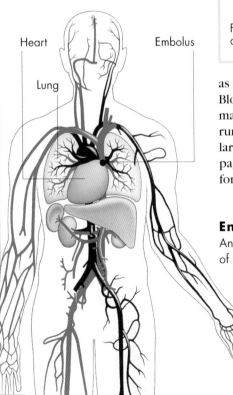

Heart

Lung

Embolus

Blocked Arteries

An artery that is damaged by fatty deposits of cholesterol (1) may cause the blood to form fibrin. The fibrin traps blood platelets, forming a clot (2) that can block the artery.

1

Artery wall

Fatty deposits

Platelets

Fatty deposits

Fibrin strands

Clot blocking artery

2

as it passes through the lungs. Blood is produced by the bone marrow—the jellylike substance running down the middle of the larger bones (see *Body Systems*, page 8). Each blood cell lives for about 80 days, so the

Embolism

An embolism is caused when part of a clot (an embolus) breaks off and passes to another part of the body. One particular site for clots to form is on a damaged heart valve (left). The embolus may pass up to the brain and cause a stroke.

marrow is continually making new blood cells. Occasionally, the marrow stops making enough cells, and the blood then becomes pale and inefficient at carrying oxygen. This is the condition called **anemia** and is due to a reduction in hemoglobin, the oxygen-carrying molecule found in red blood cells. As a result, the sufferer may have shortness of breath, caused by less oxygen being available.

A serious loss of blood due to injury will also cause a reduction in red blood cells, and a blood transfusion (see page 163) may be needed to restore the normal blood volume in the body.

Other Blood Diseases

Blood also contains white blood cells that help fight off any infection that may get into your body when you breathe or eat, or through a cut in the skin.

If infection does occur, then the number of white blood cells increases to help combat the disease (see page 155).

Serious infections can also occur when there are fewer white cells to protect us from infection. This is a condition known as **aplastic anemia**.

On the other hand, the marrow may become overactive and produce too many blood cells. A huge rise in the white blood cell count is seen in the disease called **leukemia** (cancer in the blood).

Other Conditions

The blood vessels themselves may become damaged. The condition called **varicose veins** occurs (usually later in life) when the walls of the leg veins weaken. It may be caused by standing for long periods of

time; the veins get stretched through gravity, making them appear blue and knobbly.

If you sit with your legs crossed for long periods or have a period of bed rest—perhaps after an operation—then the blood flow through the deeper leg veins becomes sluggish, and the blood may even clot. This is known as a **thrombosis**. Tablets must be taken to thin the blood. Otherwise, a small piece of the clot, called an embolus, may break off and pass to the lungs, causing severe chest pain and shortness of breath.

Occasionally, the wall of an artery may become weak and bulge outward to produce an **aneurysm** (see page 176). An operation may be needed to strengthen the wall, since there is a risk that it may burst.

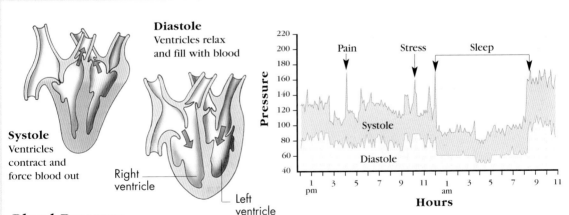

Diastole
Ventricles relax and fill with blood

Systole
Ventricles contract and force blood out

Right ventricle

Left ventricle

Blood Pressure

Blood pressure is a measure of how hard your heart has to pump to send the blood around your body. Two numbers are used to express this pressure: an upper one, known as systole, that is the pressure as the heart squeezes the blood out; and a lower figure, known as diastole, as the heart relaxes and refills between beats. A normal blood pressure reading is about 120 over 80, or 120/80.

Elevated blood pressure is called hypertension and may be caused by stress or smoking. The chart above shows how, over a 24-hour period, various factors affect blood pressure.

HEART DISEASES

ALTHOUGH HEART DISEASE is not usually a condition that affects normal, healthy young people, it is an illness that sometimes has its origins in the bad eating and general lifestyle habits of one's early life. It is also important to note that heart conditions often run in the family. Therefore it is worth taking special care if your parents, or their parents, have had a history of heart disease.

Any disease or disorder that stops the heart from working properly is potentially life threatening. Some heart conditions affect young people particularly (see below), but the majority are seen more usually in older people—especially in those who smoke, are overweight, get little or no exercise, have a high-fat diet, or have high blood pressure. However, even for those at risk, advances in surgical techniques, including heart bypass surgery and artificial pacemakers (electrical devices that take over the job of stimulating the heart to contract), have greatly increased life expectancy.

Heart Disease in Young People

Some people are born with heart diseases. Occasionally, the major arteries leading from the heart are the wrong way around. This leads to oxygen starvation. About one in every two hundred babies is born with a wrongly shaped heart valve, which means that the heart does not function properly, or with a hole in the septum (the wall between the two main heart chambers; see page 171). This condition is normally corrected by surgery later in life.

A disease of young people called rheumatic fever can also affect the heart. When it occurs, it often does so in

Coronary Thrombosis

A coronary thrombosis is caused by a blood clot blocking one of the coronary arteries supplying blood to the heart muscles (right).

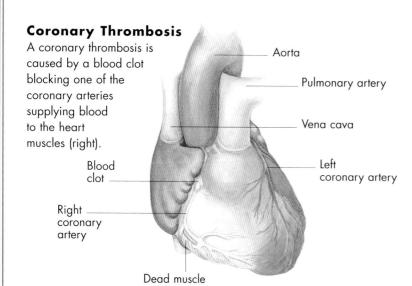

Aorta

Pulmonary artery

Vena cava

Blood clot

Left coronary artery

Right coronary artery

Dead muscle

Blocked Artery

A healthy artery has a wide internal channel, or lumen (1). In heart disease fats called cholesterol, and calcium, form within the blood vessels as a result of eating excessive fat and smoking cigarettes. This leads to narrowing (2), and eventually a clot may form, blocking the artery completely.

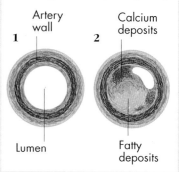

Artery wall

Calcium deposits

1

2

Lumen

Fatty deposits

someone who has had a sore throat caused by a bacterial streptococcus infection. The disease can cause the heart tissue to become inflamed and damaged. For example, it may leave the heart valves (see *Body Systems*, pages 16–17) scarred and unable to work properly. This may strain the heart, causing it to fail years later.

Coronary Thrombosis

A coronary thrombosis, or heart attack, occurs when the blood supply to the heart muscles is interrupted. Without food and energy these muscles cannot function, and some may die. The pumping action of the heart then falters. In major attacks the heart may stop completely, cutting off oxygen to the rest of the body, including the brain. Death then follows in a few minutes.

The blood supplying the heart muscles flows through the coronary arteries, and heart disease is often caused when they get clogged with fatty deposits. This initially causes a chest pain called **angina**. Eventually a blood clot may form, blocking the artery. Heart attacks are also caused by factors like stress (see page 179.)

Treatment

For minor attacks drugs that improve the heart's pumping action may be sufficient, combined with removal of the risk factors. This includes reducing fat in our diet, doing regular exercise, and avoiding smoking. In more serious attacks an operation may be needed, either an angioplasty (in which a small balloon is inserted into the artery to break up the clot and the fatty deposit known as plaque) or a heart bypass. In the latter a piece of vein from the leg is used to bypass the blocked artery, thus restoring

Hole in the Heart

Occasionally babies are born with a hole (gap) between the two main heart chambers. This allows some blood to pass through the heart without first going to the lungs to receive oxygen. The baby may have a blue color and be short of breath. An operation to close the hole may be necessary.

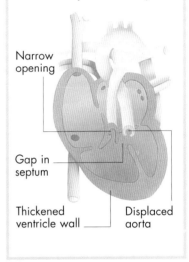

Narrow opening

Gap in septum

Thickened ventricle wall

Displaced aorta

the blood flow. In some instances the electrical system of the heart may be damaged, and an artificial pacemaker is then inserted to ensure the heartbeat is regular.

Worldwide Coronary Heart Disease

This chart (left) shows the number of deaths from heart disease in different countries. The healthier the diet, the lower the death rate. In the U.S. deaths have been cut dramatically by reducing the amount of fat that is eaten. In general, men are nearly three times more likely to have heart disease than women.

Finland

Northern Ireland

Scotland

England and Wales

United States

Canada

Norway

Austria

Italy

Female | Male

Spain

Japan

Deaths (per 100,000)

200   400   600   800

OTHER ORGAN CONDITIONS

THE MAJOR PARTS of the body are called organs. Most organs, like the heart, brain, liver, lungs, and kidneys, are vitally important in helping keep us alive. Any serious malfunction in a major organ requires urgent medical treatment.

To maintain a healthy body, it is important that all our organs are working properly, and we have already seen how diet and lifestyle can help achieve this. Sometimes, however, our organs can deteriorate or fail through illness, old age, or as the result of accidents.

The Eyes

The eyes are protected by a thin, invisible film called the conjunctiva (see *The Brain and Senses*, page 59) that stops dust and grit from damaging them. They can become infected by bacteria, causing **conjunctivitis** (see page 152). The eyes then become red and swollen, and require antibiotic drops to heal them.

Light passes through a natural lens in the eye before being focused onto the retina, at the back of the eye. In some older people the lens becomes opaque, forming a **cataract**, and the light bounces off it instead of passing through. The

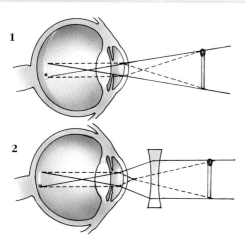

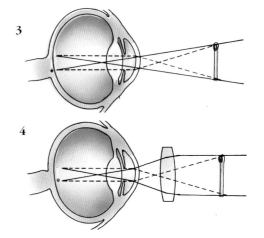

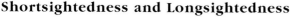

Shortsightedness and Longsightedness

Both shortsightedness and longsightedness are caused by inefficient muscles controlling the shape of the lens in the eye or by the shape of the eyeball. Shortsightedness, or myopia, is a condition in which the lens incorrectly focuses the image in front of the retina (1). A concave lens will correct this by diverging the light rays before they enter the eye (2). Longsightedness, or hyperopia (3), is the opposite. In this condition the light has not focused by the time it reaches the retina. A convex lens will correct this by converging the light rays so they focus onto the retina (4).

damaged lens can be replaced with a clear, artificial one. If the lens does not focus the light correctly, **short-** or **longsight-edness** develops. Glasses or contact lenses correct this.

A sharp blow to the head can sometimes detach part of the retina, causing partial loss of sight. The retina then needs to be reattached using a laser.

The Kidney

The kidney's main function is to filter waste products out of the blood and produce urine to wash them from the body. Sometimes this urine becomes infected, producing **cystitis**, in which there is a constant desire to urinate but to do so is very painful.

Far more agonizing, however, is when the urine becomes so concentrated that a kidney stone forms and blocks one of the outlet tubes. This produces a condition called **renal colic** and requires very strong painkillers. If the kidneys become very diseased, then the blood has to be filtered artificially on a machine, a process called dialysis. This must be done three times a week.

Stomach Ulcer

Stomach acid helps break down the food we eat. If the acid level becomes too high, usually from too much fat or smoking, it eats away at the stomach lining. Eventually a small ulcer (sore) can form that is painful and may bleed. Modern drugs will heal the ulcer, and surgery is now rarely needed.

1 Pleurisy
An infection of the lung's covering, causing severe pain on breathing.

2 Pneumonia
A lung infection producing a high temperature and a strong cough.

3 Bronchitis
Due to infected breathing tubes, producing shortness of breath, a tight cough, and wheezing.

4 Tuberculosis
A severe bacterial infection causing widespread destruction of the lungs.

5 Emphysema
Due to the elasticity of the lungs having been lost, usually by smoking, causing increasing shortness of breath.

6 Asthma
Common in young people, it produces a strong wheeze and nighttime cough.

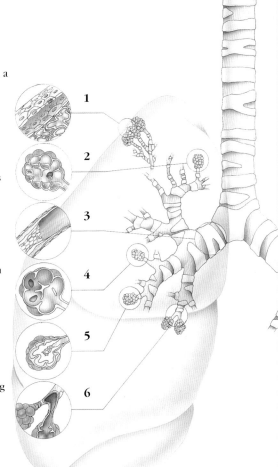

Some Lung Diseases

Shown above are some of the diseases that can affect the lungs. Two other lung diseases that were once common in children are diphtheria and whooping cough. They are both caused by bacteria. Diphtheria killed many children before a vaccination was available. The bacteria cause a blockage in the throat, preventing air from reaching the lungs. Diphtheria also produces a toxin that causes weakness and sickness. Whooping cough affects the air passages, causing a severe cough and making it difficult for the sufferer to breathe.

CANCERS

ONE IN FIVE people in Western countries dies from cancer. Avoidance of the various risk factors can prevent some of these cancers from ever developing. Lung cancer from cigarette smoking is the biggest killer, but other factors like diet are important, too. Happily, more and more cancers are being successfully treated, either through operations, by radiotherapy, or with chemotherapy—where a combination of drugs is used.

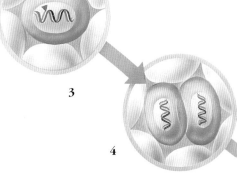

1   2

3

4

Cancers occur when the cells in the body start to grow too rapidly. Cell division is normally carefully controlled by the body and is a natural process during growth and when replacing cells lost through injury or disease.

When this self-control is lost, however, the rapid increase in the number of cells forms a lump, known as a tumor. Some tumors are not a cause for concern, since they stay in one place in the body. They are described as benign. A wart on the skin is benign; it is quite harmless, even though it can slowly grow larger.

Other tumors are cancerous because as they grow, cells can break away and travel around the body in the blood supply. These cells are deposited in other organs and form new tumors. If untreated, the continuing growth of the tumors eventually causes overwhelming damage to the body, leading to death. Many tumors spread to the liver and produce a yellow

skin color known as jaundice.

Poisonous chemicals can produce cancer. Nicotine inhaled into the lungs from cigarette smoke will cause lung cancer. Radioactive fallout from nuclear weapons or from accidents at nuclear power plants like Chernobyl in the former USSR in 1986 can cause leukemia, which is cancer in the blood.

As the fashion for vacations in the sun and acquiring a tan has grown, so has the number of people developing skin cancer. A malignant melanoma is the most dangerous type and particularly affects people between the age of 20 and 40. Those with a fair skin are most at risk because they have fewer natural skin pigments to protect the skin from harmful ultraviolet rays.

However, many cancers develop for no apparent reason. Different infections with viruses have been blamed, and cancers

Cancer Development

When a cancerous substance like cigarette smoke enters the cells, a chemical called an enzyme is produced to destroy it. Occasionally these enzymes fail to do their job, and the cancer starts to develop. Within the cells there is initially very rapid growth of the cancer. If the outer lining of the cell remains intact, then the tumor remains benign; but if the lining breaks, the cancer can spill out into the bloodstream. White blood cells may destroy the cancer cells while in the blood; but if they fail, then the cells will be deposited into distant parts of the body, and new tumors will grow (stages 1–8, above).

Radiotherapy
This picture (right) shows a woman with a skin cancer on her forehead being treated by radiotherapy. The rays are placed very precisely onto the tumor to avoid damage to the surrounding skin. Note the protective lead covering on her eyes.

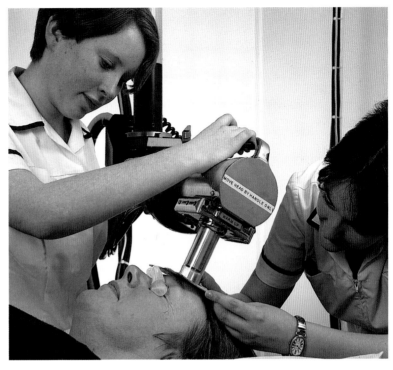

often seem to follow a period of extreme stress, which is known to weaken the body defenses.

Cancer Treatment
The three main weapons for treating cancer are **surgery**, **chemotherapy**, and **radiotherapy**. For treatment to be successful, every single cancer cell must be destroyed; otherwise, the tumor will start to grow again. The surgical operation can be simple, like cutting out a lump in the skin, or more complicated, such as removing a complete lung or breast.

If it is impossible to remove the tumor, or if it has spread to other parts of the body, chemotherapy (a treatment that uses powerful drugs to kill the cancer) may be used. In some cancers, like leukemia in the blood or Hodgkin's disease that affects the lymph glands,

chemotherapy alone may effect a cure. In other cases a combination of treatments may be needed.

In radiotherapy X-rays or neutrons are beamed at the tumor, destroying cancer cells without damaging the surrounding healthy tissues. Certain types of skin and brain cancers are treated by radiotherapy.

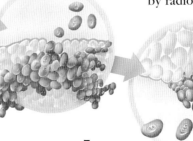

5

6

7

8

BRAIN AND NERVOUS DISORDERS

THE BRAIN IS the body's control center. It enables us to think and feel. The brain also controls our movements by passing messages down millions of nerves to make our muscles contract. Diseases of the brain or nerves can seriously damage these functions.

Inside the brain are more than 25 billion nerve cells, yet it weighs only about 3 pounds (1.3 kg). It is far more complex than the most modern computer, since it is able to carry out so many different functions at the same time (see *The Brain and Senses*).

For example, if you are in a dangerous situation, not only do you feel fear, but also your breathing rate increases, your heart speeds up, and you break out in a sweat. At the same time, the muscles in your legs move to make you run away. All these actions are initiated by the brain, which sends impulses down the complex system of nerves supplying the whole of the body (see *Body Systems*, pages 14–15).

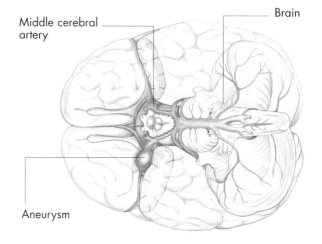

Middle cerebral artery

Brain

Aneurysm

Brain Disorders

The brain is well protected by the bones of the skull, but they may fracture if struck by a hard blow. **Concussion** follows; it is an injury to the brain tissue leading to prolonged dizziness and headaches. In severe injury one of the blood vessels beneath the skull may burst, creating pressure on the brain that can only be relieved by immediate surgery. This type of injury is often suffered by boxers after a punch to the head. It is called an **extradural hemorrhage**.

Although the brain only accounts for 2 percent of body weight, it requires 20 percent of the body's blood supply. Each part of the brain is designed to do a particular task, so if the blood supply is reduced or cut off, then that action will be affected. General narrowing of the arteries occurs as we grow older—and more rapidly if we eat excess fat. If an artery to the brain

Aneurysm

An aneurysm (above) is a weakness in the middle cerebral artery that bulges outward and can rupture. It may be present at birth or may be caused by disease or injury. Inserting a clip on the artery can repair the damage if the initial bleeding is not too severe.

blocks completely, then we suffer a **stroke**. This commonly causes paralysis of movement down one side of the body. Eating little fat, doing regular exercise, reducing stress, and controlling high blood pressure can help prevent strokes.

Occasionally, an episode of uncontrolled, chaotic activity in the brain produces unconsciousness and involuntary movements. This is known as **epilepsy**. The cause is usually unknown but may follow a head injury. An electrical tracing of the brain known as an EEG (electroencephalogram) will show that an epileptic fit has occurred. Epilepsy is treated by drugs.

Nerve Disorders

Messages pass to and from the brain down the spinal cord (see *Body Systems*, page 14). If the spinal cord is cut, all function will be lost below that point. Serious damage to the spinal cord may occur following traffic accidents and occasionally with sports injuries.

Protecting and surrounding the brain and spinal cord are the meninges (see *The Brain*

Blood vessels

Areas of dead brain tissue

Blocked blood vessel

Dementia

This condition causes a loss of mental powers and memory. It is caused when brain cells degenerate (die) with age or when a blockage (such as a clot) occurs in a blood vessel carrying blood to the brain, causing brain cells to die (above and right).

and Senses, page 40). An infection of the meninges is called **meningitis**. It is a potentially dangerous bacterial condition and is characterized by high fever and severe neck stiffness. Meningitis often affects teenagers. Diagnosis is confirmed by a lumbar puncture. A small amount of fluid is taken from around the meninges in the back region. The bacteria can then be identified and antibiotic treatment started.

Multiple Sclerosis

Nerve fibers are protected by a fatty covering called a myelin sheath. The myelin sheath helps the passage of nerve impulses. In some young people enemy cells called macrophages can damage these sheaths. The nerves are then exposed, which reduces their ability to pass impulses. Symptoms include blurred vision, partial paralysis, and clumsiness. These episodes may last a few weeks, but the nerves can recover, and the illness may sometimes be followed by months, or even years, of relief from symptoms. Damage also occurs in the brain, and the diagnosis can be confirmed with a brain scan that shows white dots indicating damaged myelin sheaths. Modern drugs, including beta interferon, slow the rate of destruction and help nerves recover partly.

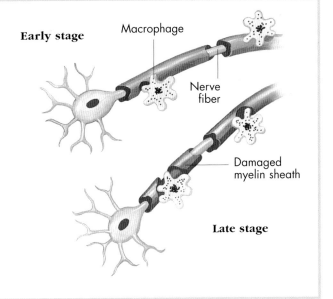

Early stage

Macrophage

Nerve fiber

Damaged myelin sheath

Late stage

STRESS DISORDERS

WHEN SOMETHING WORRIES us or makes us nervous, we say we are under stress. Stress is the body's reaction to demanding situations. During stress our heart rate and blood pressure rise, and our muscles become tense. Stress is caused by many factors, such as constant noise, a poor diet, physical exhaustion, or problems at home or at school. When stress occurs repeatedly, it can eventually damage our bodies and lead to illness.

How do you know if you are under stress? There are some classic signs associated with stress that may help you decide. If you are constantly worried about something, if you feel near tears most of the time, if you are always fidgeting and biting your nails, if you find it hard to concentrate, if you snap at people, and if your normal sleep pattern is disturbed, then you may be suffering from stress.

What Damage Can Stress Do?

Whatever the causes of stress, the body's response is the same. The bloodstream is flooded with epinephrine (see *Body Systems*, page 31), blood pressure rises, muscles flex, and the body feels tense. When stress lasts for a long time without being resolved, the body becomes overloaded, leading to permanent high blood pressure, digestive problems such as ulcers, and chronic headaches.

The natural body defenses (see page 155) become weakened, so catching an infection is more likely. In the long term there is also a risk of heart disease (see pages 170–171). It is also thought that we are more susceptible to certain cancers when our body resistance is lower due to stress.

Stress commonly disturbs our sleep pattern, leading to a spiral of declining health. The loss of sleep can take several forms: an inability to sleep, fitful and disturbed sleep, early wakening with immediate anxiety, and the

High-level Stress
A typically stressed executive shouting into the telephone and becoming extremely agitated (left). At this time there is an increase in his epinephrine output, leading to a rise in his heart rate and blood pressure.

fact file

Stress occurs in 96% of people in America after the age of 11. Maximum peaks are at age 16 to 18 during exams and between 25 and 35 when seeking promotion at work.

Your pulse rate may double at times of stress—from a resting average of 70 beats per minute to around 150.

Driving can be a cause of stress. Changing lanes frequently in traffic jams is a classic sign.

wrong level of sleep, which produces tiredness and even more stress. We need to reach a certain depth of sleep called REM sleep (see *The Brain and Senses*, pages 56–57) that maintains our emotional and mental stability. In times of stress this level is rarely reached.

Stress can also lead to mental depression. Young people especially are more likely to commit suicide when under stress—problems with relationships, bullying, and worries about examinations can sometimes lead to feelings of hopelessness and total despair.

Dealing with Stress

Removing the reason for stress may also remove the physical illness caused by it. Sometimes we can change the situation that causes our stress by thinking differently about problems or thinking more positively (see *The Mind and Psychology*, pages 118–119). In cases of extreme stress it is important to talk to someone to help us understand our feelings better (see *The Mind and Psychology*, pages 108–109).

If stress is a constant part of someone's life, then a relaxing pastime may help that person unwind. Physical exercise is a good form of relaxation, too, since it gets rid of pent-up energy, releases aggression, and encourages self-confidence. Runners who cover long distances in training each week have been found to reduce their anxiety and become more emotionally stable. Small amounts of stress can be beneficial. The epinephrine produced during challenging pastimes like surfing improves the condition of the heart and muscles.

How Stress Damages the Body

Stress causes reactions in the body. Some are designed to prepare the body for action, but prolonged stress can cause damage (below).

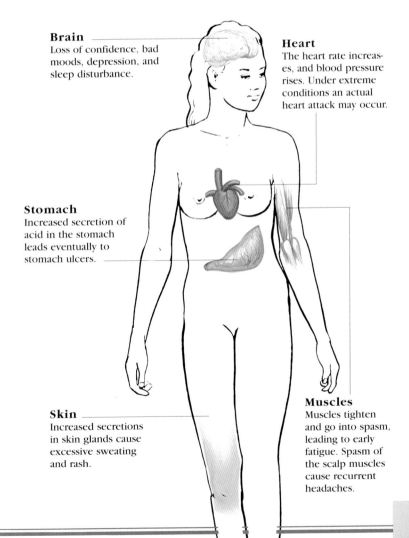

Brain
Loss of confidence, bad moods, depression, and sleep disturbance.

Heart
The heart rate increases, and blood pressure rises. Under extreme conditions an actual heart attack may occur.

Stomach
Increased secretion of acid in the stomach leads eventually to stomach ulcers.

Skin
Increased secretions in skin glands cause excessive sweating and rash.

Muscles
Muscles tighten and go into spasm, leading to early fatigue. Spasm of the scalp muscles cause recurrent headaches.

INTRODUCTION

KEEPING SAFE MEANS avoiding dangers in our everyday lives. Sometimes, we can do this by being sensible and thoughtful and knowing about possibly dangerous situations that we might encounter. Keeping safe is also about protecting and caring for others, and this may also involve the use of the rescue and first-aid techniques described in this chapter that could even save a life.

This chapter describes many of the methods you can use to ensure you keep safe, healthy, and out of danger at home, at school, or when traveling.

It also provides valuable information about how to care for others by giving simple first aid or by helping them get comfortable when they are unwell or injured. There is also advice here about how you can learn more about first aid—it could even help you save a life.

Keeping safe means many different things. First, it means knowing which situations are likely to be dangerous and how to avoid them. This often requires nothing more than using common sense and thinking through the consequences of your actions before you do something. (For instance, it might be better to avoid swimming in a river until you have checked out the strength of the current or asked someone who is knowledgeable about the area if it is safe to swim there.)

Second, it means knowing how to deal with unexpected problems if they do occur—

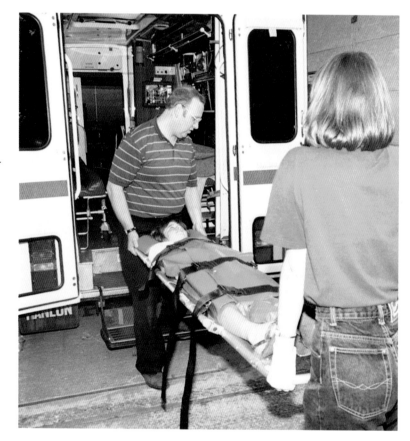

and that includes knowing how to get the right sort of help. This chapter will show you many of the things you can do to keep safe in what otherwise might become potentially dangerous situations.

Special Training
People who join the volunteer emergency services are highly trained in all aspects of first aid and life-saving. These volunteers (above) are learning to use ambulance equipment.

We begin by looking at personal safety (pages 182–183) and then go on to consider safety in the home and yard (pages 184–185), including the safety of other family members like younger brothers and sisters. The many ways we use to travel—both at home and abroad—can sometimes be potentially hazardous, and advice is also given on how to travel safely and on how to maintain bicycles (see pages 186–187).

Being safe at school involves knowing about rules designed for safety as well as knowing how to avoid harmful substances (see pages 188–189). Many of the harmful substances we may be offered, and the effects that they can have on our bodies, are also described.

Between pages 190 and 195 we look at the various places we visit, including when we are on vacation. There is advice about keeping safe in cities, on country walks and trips, and when near water—including how to avoid dangerous animals. Pages 196 and 197 describe what to do in emergencies and, most importantly, how to get help.

Finally, pages 200–209 describe a range of common illnesses, injuries, and aches and pains, and give advice on how they can be treated.

Learning First Aid

There are some very simple first-aid tips described in this chapter that you can easily apply yourself—such as how to make someone who has a toothache more comfortable. However, there are others—like giving a victim mouth-to-mouth resuscitation—that are included to show what an experienced first aider will do in an emergency situation. Do not attempt any technique if you feel unsure how to apply it properly.

If you are interested in learning more about first aid so that you can provide life-saving care if necessary, there are organizations that offer training. Having sound, thorough knowledge of such techniques is invaluable.

Safety in Sports

Some very physical contact sports, like football (right) and ice hockey, could cause injury if the players were not protected with padding and helmets. It is always advisable to wear the recommended clothing in any sport.

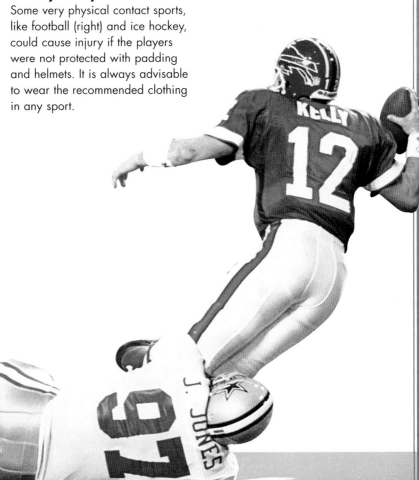

PERSONAL SAFETY

YOUR PERSONAL SAFETY is your own responsibility. We learn much about being safe from our parents or other caregivers when we are young, but as we grow older, we face situations in which we must sometimes look after ourselves. Some of the more specific issues about safety are to be found in other parts of this chapter, but here we deal with the basic aspects of keeping safe in everyday life.

Throughout this chapter there is advice and information about ways to keep safe when you are in particular places or doing particular things, or when you are faced with emergencies or unforeseen situations. Here, however, we look at ways in which you can help ensure your personal safety as you go about your everyday life. We also look at ways in which you can help protect your personal belongings.

Playing Safely

If you cannot play in the safety of a yard, the park, or in the house, let your parents or caregivers know where you are going. Do not play near roads or railways. You should also avoid places like old quarries (which can be dangerous due to the possibility of falling rocks or may be filled with deep water) and old buildings (which may be unsafe or may be frequented by drug users). Rivers and lakes can also be dangerous (see pages 192–193).

If you find any unusual objects while playing—canisters or unmarked bottles of liquid, for example—do not touch them, but inform your parents, caregivers, or the police.

Do not tease farm animals—which may feel threatened and attack you—or dogs, particularly if they are guarding property by standing at a gate, for example.

Avoiding Crime

You can do a lot to avoid crimes such as muggings by keeping away from places like poorly lit sidestreets and neighborhoods that are known to be

Avoiding Fights

Sometimes arguments or misunderstandings between people develop into fights (left). Do not involve yourself in other people's fights; just keep away. If you see someone being attacked or robbed, however, call the police.

checklist

Some personal safety tips:

- Always tell someone where you are going and when you expect to return.
- Make sure you have your house keys and enough money to get home.
- Always refuse drugs.
- Avoid going with strangers.
- Be sure you know how to make an emergency telephone call.
- Don't carry valuables.
- Keep handbags and the like securely closed.
- Try to look confident.
- Remember that some places are best avoided. Don't wander off alone and get lost.

dangerous. It is also advisable not to carry more money than you need. Do not put all your money or valuables in one pocket or bag. If you put coats or bags down in cafes or shops, keep an eye on them at all times. If you have a personal stereo, put it away out of sight when it is not in use.

Staying in touch is a good way to keep safe. As well as letting your parents or caregivers know where you are going, it is sensible to contact them to let them know you are safe and well—this is particularly important if you are traveling abroad (see page 187). It is also worthwhile informing them of any changes in your plans.

Looking Confident

At events like pop festivals (above) or in crowded streets, where you are mixing closely with a large number of people, try to look confident and relaxed. Keep jewelry, money, and items like personal stereos out of sight.

Your Health

Keeping your health safe is important, too, and the chapter *Health and Illness* provides much advice about exercise, diet, and other health issues. Smog and other forms of pollution affect us more and more today, and if we can, we should try to avoid unhealthy places as well as unhealthy lifestyles.

SAFETY IN THE HOME AND YARD

ALTHOUGH OUR HOME is usually the place we feel safest, every year many thousands of accidents occur in the home or the yard—especially to young children and old people. Many of these accidents can be avoided if you are aware of the potential dangers.

Accidents usually happen because someone has been careless or has used something in a way it was not intended to be used. A little thought can prevent many mishaps from occurring. Family members should look after each other, and you should try to ensure older family members or younger sisters or brothers are not in danger. If an accident

Gun Safety

Guns intended for hunting or target shooting should only be used outdoors or on specially designed firing ranges by experienced or authorized persons. All guns should be locked away securely in gun cabinets when not in use. They should never be left loaded. Never point a gun at anyone as a joke or pull the trigger unless you are using the gun in an authorized manner. You should never take guns into schools or other public places. There are laws concerning the purchase and use of guns that vary from state to state. Your local police department or gun dealer will have details.

occurs at home, it may be you who must assist the victim or get help (see pages 196–197 and 200–209 in particular).

Falls account for many accidents in the home, so make sure toys and other items are not left where people might trip over them. If you spill liquids, wipe them up, since slippery floors can be dangerous.

Most households use substances that can cause poisoning. There may be bleach, detergents, solvents, and cleaners. Read the safety labels on the containers, and never allow

Helping Your Family

You can help the older members of your family—especially if they are infirm or confined to a wheelchair (above)—by making sure, for example, that everyday items they use are within easy reach.

these substances to enter the body (see page 185). Leave the substances in their original containers—never transfer them to a drink bottle. Any substance no longer required should be disposed of properly. Medicines must also only be used in accordance with the instructions provided. Keep all medicines away from young children.

If you smell gas in the home, do not turn any lights on or attempt to light the gas; open the window, and turn the gas off or get help. Fire can be a major hazard, and you should read the advice given on pages 198–199 concerning fire safety.

In the Yard

Playing in the yard can be safe and fun if you remember a few rules. In the same way that you should not leave things lying around the house, do not leave garden tools, bicycles, or other items where they can cause an accident. Put things in their proper place when you have finished with them.

If you are allowed to use guns in the yard, make sure you fire them only at proper targets. Never use guns in a way that might injure other people, and never leave guns where young children can touch them.

Every year there are tragic and unnecessary deaths caused by children becoming locked inside discarded household items like freezers. These objects are dangerous and should not be used for play. Any unwanted household items such as these, as well as old furniture, bottles, and so on should be taken to the dump by a responsible adult.

Some plants are also poisonous. A few of the most common dangerous plants are shown below.

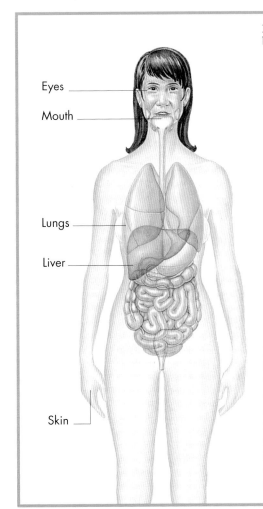

Eyes

Mouth

Lungs

Liver

Skin

Poisonous flowers, berries, seeds, bulbs, and roots

Iris

Belladonna

Lupine

Holly

Mistletoe

Yew

Poisonous fungi

Fly agaric

Death cap

Poisons

Poisons can enter the body in a number of different ways. They can enter through the eyes; through the airway when we breathe; they can be injected; they can enter when an animal such as a snake bites; they can be swallowed; or in the case of some chemicals, they can be absorbed through the skin. Poisons may attack organs such as the liver or the lungs. Many cases of poisoning are the result of eating poisonous plants like those shown above. Do not put any plants in your mouth, and only touch those you know are safe.

TRAVEL SENSE

KEEPING SAFE WHEN we travel means observing a few simple rules. If you are walking, take extra care when near roads. If you are using a vehicle on public roads, be sure to observe the rules and bylaws. You must also ensure that your method of transport— whether it is a bicycle or a car—is in good working order. Do not use rollerblades, skateboards, and so on where they could be a danger to others.

One of the journeys you will take most often is the one to and from school. It may involve you walking all the way or walking to catch the school bus or a train. Remember that you are traveling at the same time as commuters, shoppers, and other travelers—many of whom will be in their cars rushing to their destinations. Take extra care at these busy times. Observe the traffic, and watch out for fast-approaching vehicles. If possible, cross streets at specially marked places, and obey "Walk" and "Don't Walk" signs.

Crossing the Road
Busy roads like this highway (above) jammed with rush-hour traffic need extra care. Only cross where it is safe to do so—such as by a bridge or an underpass.

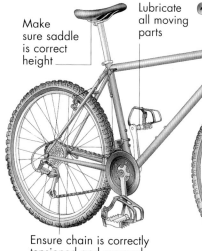

Make sure saddle is correct height

Lubricate all moving parts

Check brake pads are free from dirt and not worn

Ensure chain is correctly tensioned and greased

Bicycle Maintenance
Keep your bicycle in a safe and roadworthy condition by following the maintenance instructions left. Make sure lights are working correctly.

Check tire condition and pressures and remove stones, etc.

If you use any sort of vehicle for travel, it should be maintained properly. On page 186 there is advice about how to maintain your bicycle, but even rollerblades, skateboards, and the like need to be looked after. Straps and fasteners need to be in good condition, and wheels and other moving parts must work efficiently. Not only will this make it safer for traveling, but it will also increase your enjoyment.

Cars need to be maintained correctly and driven safely. Brakes, steering, lights, and windshield wipers in particular must be in good working order. Seat belts and other safety devices like airbags should also be in good condition. Keep windshields clean.

Always drive carefully, particularly in places where people are likely to be around. Observe all speed limits, traffic signs, and other bylaws. If in doubt, get information from an experienced driver first.

Travel Abroad

When you travel abroad, there are many other things to remember. First, you may need a passport, visa, or other form of documentation to allow you to enter a foreign country. You must not stay in the country beyond the authorized date without getting official permission.

If you are going to spend any money, you may need some currency of the country you are visiting. It can be obtained from banks, currency exchanges, and so on. Many credit and charge cards can be used in foreign countries, too.

Some countries have laws controlling the kinds of things you can bring into, or out of, them. There may also be restrictions on the quantities of such items. This information is usually given on immigration forms or on posters at airports, ports, or border crossings.

You may also need to provide medical certificates giving proof of inoculation against certain diseases before you are allowed to enter some countries (see *Health and Illness*, page 151). If in doubt, seek advice from your doctor, from the travel company arranging your trip, or from the embassies of the countries you intend to visit.

Finally, never take drugs (see pages 188–189) into or out of a foreign country or accept any offers of drugs. Apart from the dangers from the drugs themselves, many countries—for example, some Asian countries—impose very severe penalties on anyone breaking their strict drug laws.

Using Skateboards

These boys (below) look confident on their skateboards, but it is advisable to wear helmets, gloves, and knee and elbow pads in case of a fall—particularly if you are an inexperienced skateboarder.

187

HARMFUL SUBSTANCES

HARMFUL SUBSTANCES CAN be found in many places—in the back yard, in the garage, and even in the home. They include cleaning products, paint, fuels, and medicine. Many of these substances can cause damage to your health if used incorrectly or if swallowed or allowed to come into contact with other parts of the body. Other harmful substances include nonmedicinal, illegal drugs.

Cleaning products used in the home include ammonia and lye, which are poisonous and corrosive. Acids, such as sulfuric acid used in car batteries, are also corrosive. All of them should be stored in clearly labeled containers out of reach of small children.

Paints, as well as paint thinner and paint remover, are also poisonous. Fuels, such as gasoline, kerosene, and bottled gas, are highly flammable (likely to catch fire) as well as poisonous. They should be stored in a cool, safe place—such as a shed—away from the risk of fire.

Most medicines can be harmful if taken in large doses or by people for whom they were not prescribed. Even mild painkillers, such as aspirin and acetaminophen, can be dangerous. Aspirin should not be taken by anyone under the age of 12, even in small doses.

Illegal Drugs

Another hazard is the abuse of nonmedicinal drugs in our society. Some, such as alcohol and tobacco, may be legally bought once you have reached a certain age. They are taken regularly by large numbers of people. But they are addictive and can cause serious illness, including heart disease and cancer (see *Health and Illness*, page 151). Even caffeine, found in coffee, tea, and cola drinks, can be harmful if taken in excess.

Alcohol is one of a class of drugs known as depressants. Others include barbiturates and tranquilizers. They have the effect of increasing the user's confidence and overcoming shyness. In large doses they

Young Drug Users

Drug dealers, or pushers, know that taking some kinds of drugs can become habit-forming, or addictive, so they sell drugs to young people in order to get them addicted or "hooked" on drugs (above). In this way they gain new customers and a regular source of illegal money.

can impair judgment and can cause drowsiness or sleep.

The opposite effects are caused by stimulant drugs. They include amphetamine and cocaine. They increase the heartbeat, giving a feeling of increased energy called a "high." Prolonged use can lead to physical and mental problems.

Narcotics include heroin and its derivatives. They cause drowsiness and a feeling of being remote from the real world. They depress breathing, and an overdose can kill. There are also various drugs, such as LSD, called hallucinogens. They distort the user's senses. Drugs like cocaine, heroine, and LSD are illegal in many countries. There can also be severe penalties for being caught in possession of drugs (see page 187).

Drug Addiction

All of the drugs described above can rapidly lead to addiction. The user becomes physically dependent on the drug. Psychological dependence may also occur, in which the user needs regular doses of a drug in order to cope with everyday life. In either case, once a user is "hooked," it is extremely difficult to stop using the drug. Stopping may lead to distressing physical and mental withdrawal symptoms that range from depression and nightmares to attempting suicide (taking one's own life).

Some drugs can be especially dangerous because they contain harmful additives. There is also the risk of infection from diseases such as AIDS or hepatitis with drugs that are injected. Sharing needles can transfer disease-causing viruses.

The only guaranteed way to prevent drug addiction is to never start taking drugs. This can be difficult if other people around you are drinking or smoking or indulging in hard drugs. Fortunately, when most people become aware of how drugs can ruin lives, they have the good sense not to start.

Commonly Used Drugs

Caffeine—It is a stimulant drug found in coffee, tea, and cola drinks. Overuse of such drinks can cause excitement or sleeplessness.

Tobacco—It contains nicotine and tarry substances that can cause cancer, heart disease, and other illnesses. Its long-term use can eventually cause death.

Alcohol—Present in alcoholic drinks, it is a poison and a depressant. It makes people drunk and can be addictive. It can cause death.

Cannabis—It is made from the hemp plant (marijuana) and may be smoked as "dope" or eaten. It produces relaxation and talkativeness. It is not addictive, although long-term use may cause psychological dependence and problems with the lungs and the respiratory system.

Solvents—These are substances used in adhesives and aerosols that are abused by people sniffing them. They are fast-acting and extremely dangerous. They can cause death.

Amphetamines—Usually taken as tablets, and called "speed" or "bennies," these are stimulants, causing excitement and loss of appetite. Long-term use can cause depression and mental illness. A common type of amphetamine is "ecstacy" (see below).

Cocaine—Known as "coke" or "snow," it is usually sniffed in the form of a white powder. It causes brief feelings of power and well-being, but long-term use causes loss of appetite, sleeplessness, and mental problems. Its modern derivative is called "crack."

Opiates—These include opium, morphine, and heroin, or "smack." They are all derived from the milk of the opium poppy. Heroin comes in powder form and may be white, gray, brown, or beige. It may be sniffed, smoked, taken orally, or injected. Opiates produce a feeling of well-being and a relief from physical pain. Repeated use results in physical and psychological dependency. Large quantities can cause coma and death.

Hallucinogens—These are mind-changing drugs and include LSD or "acid." Mescaline and "magic mushrooms" contain similar drugs. They cause "trips," in which the user enters an unreal world, which can be pleasant or terrifying, and can cause the user to behave in an unpredictable manner. Long-term use can cause mental problems.

Designer drugs—These are drugs deliberately designed to produce mood-changing effects. They include "ecstacy," or "E," which can cause a happy feeling leading to hunger and mental problems. Just one tablet has been known to cause sudden death.

HIKING AND WALKING

EXPLORING THE GREAT outdoors is fun, but it is always sensible to take a few precautions before going on a trip. Plan your route carefully, and let others know where you are going and what time you intend to return. Make sure that you have some knowledge of the area you are going to, such as the type of terrain and the likely weather. Take plenty of food and the necessary equipment, and wear the right clothing.

Before setting off on any trip—whether it is a hike near your home or an exploration of somewhere new on vacation—the following advice will help you stay safe and enable you to get the maximum enjoyment from the trip.

First, plan your route. If you know the area well, you probably won't need a map; but if you are venturing somewhere new, it is sensible to take a map showing footpaths, potentially dangerous areas like marshes, and other important features.

Make sure you know how to read a map before you set out. You should also know how to use a compass. Compass needles point to north, so you will always know the direction in

Well Prepared

These two young people (right) are well prepared for a walk in the countryside. Their strong outdoor shoes will enable them to cope with rough ground. Each carries a large backpack containing extra clothing, food, and equipment that might be needed in the unlikely event of getting lost.

checklist

Here is a list of the essential items you will need for a trip:
- Warm, waterproof clothing, strong footwear, gloves, and a hat.
- Sunglasses.
- Sunblock.
- First-aid kit.
- Plastic sheet.
- Plenty of food and water.
- Flashlight.
- Whistle—to alert people if you get lost.
- Map.
- Compass.
- Backpack.

If you are planning a longer trip, you will also need:
- Tent.
- Sleeping bag.
- Cooking stove and fuel.
- Matches.
- Cooking utensils.
- Extra food and water.

Finding Your Way

It is easy to get lost in woodlands (right). Keep to paths if there are any. A map or a compass is especially useful to help you find your way. Look out for any features—such as streams—that will help you remember the route you want to take. If you are following the same route back, mark the route with stones or piles of twigs at intervals.

especially if you intend to be out after dark. You will need to wear the right clothing, and take some food, water, and safety equipment. The checklist on the left lists the most important items to take on a trip. If the activity is quite challenging, make sure you are fit enough to undertake it.

Check the weather before you set off—newspapers, television, and radio all provide weather forecasts, and there are numbers you can call, too. If the forecast is for poor weather, consider postponing your trip until things improve. When you are out and about, keep a watchful eye on the weather. Different types of clouds,

changes in wind direction and humidity—even natural signs like sheltering animals—can indicate bad weather to come.

There are various sorts of emergencies that can occur on a trip—such as an injury or an illness, a sudden change in the weather, or you are lost. Pages 194–197 and 200–209 explain what steps to take if you are in an emergency situation.

which you are traveling. When using a map, place the compass on the map, and turn the map until the north–south line marked on the map lines up with the compass needle. This will show you which way around to hold the map. There are also other ways to find your way around; you can read about some of them in books on hiking and exploring the countryside.

Starting Off

Whenever you set off on a trip, always tell someone where you are going and when you expect to return. If you can, go with older, experienced people—

Emergency Stretcher

Blankets or quilts can be used to make a stretcher, but it will need at least four people to carry it. Roll the edges in to make a tube that can be used as handles. Now gently lift the injured person (right), and move to the required spot. Remember to lower the victim carefully, so that his or her head does not hit the ground.

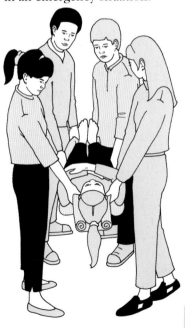

WATER SAFETY

WATER ACTIVITIES ARE usually safe and fun, but it should be remembered that water can also be hazardous. Deep water, currents, tides, offshore winds, and even some aquatic animals can all play their part in creating dangers not only for the unwary swimmer but for anybody using the water for recreation or work. Even strong swimmers can soon find themselves in difficulties—especially when the water is very cold.

Everyone should learn about keeping safe in the water. Events can occur very rapidly in water; one minute you are rowing a boat offshore, and the next it has overturned and you are being taken out to sea by the tide. Suddenly entering cold water may cause uncontrollable gasping that can lead to water inhalation, a sudden rise in blood pressure, an inability to swim, or hypothermia.

Beach Awareness

Look out for flags and other notices on beaches that tell you when and where it is safe to go in the water. Be sure that the wind and tides are right for sports such as windsurfing, surfing, and bodyboarding (below).

Swimmers should be aware of their own abilities and never get out of their depth unless they can swim well. They should heed all warning signs about tides, etc. Small children must be supervised at all times and never be allowed to float off on inflatable rings or rafts.

Surfers, windsurfers, and other water-sports enthusiasts can usually swim well, too, but they can still get into difficulties if currents or tides take them out to sea. A cold wind can affect tired muscles, making it hard to control a sailboard or even to climb back onto it.

If you intend to explore rockpools, it is advisable to start at the lowest part of the beach and work your way back up to the top. This will prevent you from becoming cut off by the incoming tide. If you find

Pulling from Water

To avoid going into the water yourself, try to find a stick or piece of rope with which you can reach the victim. Lie on the bank as close to the edge as possible, and reach out as shown above.

Shark
Attacks by sharks (left) are extremely rare, but you should always heed shark-warning notices on beaches.

Alligator
Attacks by alligators (below) and other similar reptiles are also very uncommon, but don't go swimming in swamplands where they are present.

Dangerous Animals

Although attacks on swimmers by aquatic animals make headlines, they are rare occurrences. Most injuries happen when swimmers get stung by a stingray or a jellyfish, for example. At certain times of year sharks are found in some waters, and in tropical regions some types of cone shells are known to be highly venomous. It is also best to seek advice before swimming in waters that may support snakes or other dangerous reptiles.

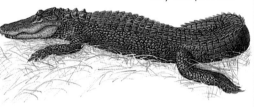

anything unusual on the beach, such as canisters washed ashore from a ship, inform the Coast Guard at once. Do not touch anything; it may be dangerous.

Safety on Rivers and Lakes
Many of the rules about safety at sea apply equally to fresh water. If you are in a boat, it is advisable to wear a life jacket even if you can swim. Learn the meanings of the various marker buoys and flags that are used. They indicate, for example, which way to proceed on certain waterways. To ignore them can mean entering unsafe waters or becoming involved in a collision with another vessel.

If you are on foot, beware of steeply shelving banks or marshy areas. Test the depth with a stick first if you are unsure. Always tell someone where you are going if you intend to go near water.

Drowning
Death by drowning usually occurs because air cannot enter the lungs. This happens when there is water in the lungs, but drowning can also be caused by throat muscles going into spasm.

Someone who has nearly drowned should always receive medical attention. Even if the casualty recovers well, there is a further risk of a condition known as secondary drowning (this is when the air passages begin to swell).

Rescue from Water
If it is necessary to rescue someone from the water, try to do it from the safety of dry land; do not put yourself at risk while trying to save someone else. Reach out with your hand, a stick, or branch, or throw a rope. If you are trained as a life-saver or if the victim is unconscious, you may have to enter the water to reach him or her. It is safer to wade than to swim. If you cannot reach someone safely, get help immediately.

Treating Drowning
First lay the victim on his or her back. Make sure that nothing is blocking the mouth or throat. Remove wet clothing, and shield the victim from the wind to prevent the body from being chilled further. Place the victim in the recovery position (see page 201), remembering to keep the head low so that water drains from the mouth. Get help so the victim can be taken quickly to a hospital.

FINDING SHELTER FROM THE WEATHER

SOMETIMES ACCIDENTS AND injuries can occur during a hike or ramble, or even when just playing, but the most likely hazard is getting lost or encountering bad weather. In these instances it may be necessary to find shelter until things improve or someone finds you.

Even the best-planned trips can go wrong. You, or perhaps someone who is accompanying you, may get injured by falling or being bitten by an animal, for example. This may make it impossible for you to continue your journey.

Sometimes, particularly in mountainous places, the weather can change suddenly. It can become much colder—perhaps causing snow to fall—or storms, high winds, mist, and rain can make it hard to find your way. In all these situations you may need to shelter until help arrives or you feel well enough to go on.

There are some important rules to follow when you decide to take shelter. **1. Inspection.** Check yourself for injuries such as cuts and bruises, and then check your equipment and clothing to prevent further problems. For example, clothing may need repairing to reduce exposure to the elements. **2. Protection.** Keep yourself warm and dry or out of the sun and wind by building some sort of shelter or by using any available buildings or natural features

like caves. Use backsacks, etc. to provide extra protection. **3. Location.** Find a way of letting rescuers know where you are by leaving something conspicuous for them to see. **4. Food and water**. If rescue seems more than 24 hours away, try to find natural food such as blackberries. Do not eat anything that you cannot be sure is safe. **5. Keep calm**.

Sheltering from the Cold

Try to find some shelter so you do not get wet if it rains

Beware Lightning

In an electrical storm, lightning tends to discharge its electricity on objects that project against the landscape. Isolated trees like these (above) are not the safest place to shelter in a storm, therefore. If you have to shelter under an isolated tree, make sure that you stand several feet away from it and do not touch it.

or snows. If you get wet, you will become even colder. Huddle close to companions to retain warmth. Wind can lower

Surviving Outdoors

If you are lost or unable to return due to bad weather, stay where you are, and try to find somewhere warm and dry to shelter until you are rescued or conditions improve. Put on as many layers of clothing as you can, and place your feet in your backpack. Try to find something to sit on so that you are not in contact with the damp ground. Keep your limbs close to your body—this will help retain body heat. Eat some food, and take a warm drink if possible. A plastic sheet with air holes will keep out the cold wind.

something waterproof on top. Or sit with your arms, head, and knees tucked in tightly. If you shelter from a storm, choose dense woods, cliff overhangs, or hollows in the ground. Do not stand under single trees, on hill tops, near power lines, or in small, isolated buildings. If you shelter by trees, do not touch them but sit crouched as described above.

Finally, note any features or landmarks that may help you find your way back or that could provide shelter if needed. And remember that rescue is just a matter of time.

temperatures even more, so always try to get out of the wind. The diagram above shows how to keep warm. If you are caught in a snow storm, and there is no shelter from buildings, etc. it is best to lie in a hollow if you can, so that you are out of the driving wind.

Sheltering from Storms

Storms can blow up suddenly, and it can be dangerous to be caught in one, since you could be struck by lightning. If you are caught in the open, lie face downward on the ground with

Good Shelter

When you are out on a hike, make a mental note of any structures, like this birdwatching blind (right), that you come across. Or if you have a map, make a mark on it to show the location. If you need to shelter, it may be worth retracing your route to get back to such a place.

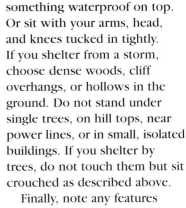

EMERGENCIES AND GETTING HELP

THE CHIEF THING to remember in an emergency is to get professional help as soon as possible. While waiting for the emergency services to arrive, make the victim comfortable, and prevent him or her from coming to further harm.

An emergency can happen anywhere—in the home, at school, or when traveling. If someone becomes ill or has an accident and is seriously injured, call an ambulance. If there is a fire, call the fire department. And if you see someone getting into difficulties while sailing or swimming in the sea, get in touch with the Coast Guard or alert a lifeguard if there is one patroling the beach. If you are not sure which emergency service

Heat Exhaustion

If too much water is lost from the body, the victim suffers heat exhaustion. Move him or her to a cool place. Lay the victim down with the legs raised, and help rehydration by giving plenty of water to drink (right).

Heatstroke

Overexposure to heat results in heatstroke. Remove some of the victim's clothes, and pour cold water onto the victim. Then call for a doctor (below).

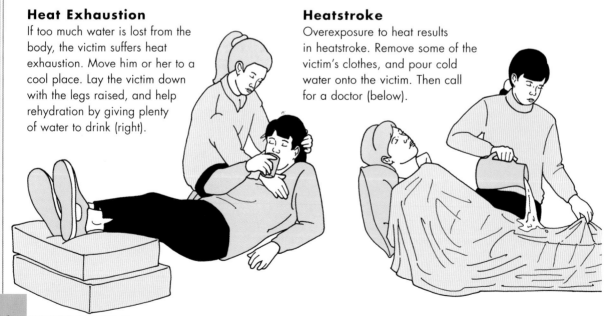

Road Accidents

People injured in a road accident (left) generally need help from the emergency services such as paramedics and, if someone is trapped, the fire department. If you see an accident, make an emergency call to get help as shown below. If there are victims who are out of the vehicle, you may be able to comfort them, but do not put yourself in danger.

The Professionals

Ambulance crews and paramedics (right) are trained to deal with victims of accidents and other emergencies. They know how to give medical treatment and how to move an injured person without the risk of causing further injury.

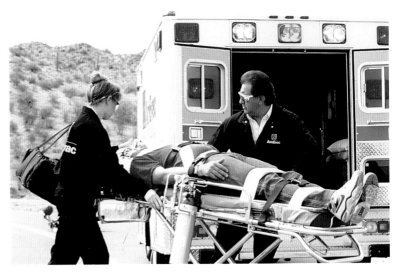

to call, just call the police; they will then contact the necessary emergency services. There is more information about keeping safe in the above situations to be found in other parts of this chapter.

Many emergencies need the help of paramedics or other professionals. If there is a qualified first-aider on the scene, ask what you can do to help. You may be asked to call for help (see below) or may be asked to help keep curious people from crowding around and getting in the first-aider's way.

Making Emergency Calls

Unless you have a mobile telephone, quickly find a public phone. Dial 911 (this is a toll-free call). An operator will ask which service you need (for example, police, fire service, or ambulance service). Keep calm and talk clearly. When you have been connected to the emergency service, they will need some information:
• Your telephone number.
• The location of the incident (building, road name, number).

• The type of incident (road traffic accident, fire, etc.).
• The number of victims.
• The condition of the victims.
• Any hazards (such as damaged power lines, gasoline on the road, etc.).
Do not disconnect the call to the emergency services unless they tell you to do so.

Hypothermia

Hypothermia occurs when the body temperature drops. It can happen indoors in poorly heated conditions as well as outdoors. It is common in old people and sometimes infants. The signs are shivering, looking pale, feeling cold to the touch, and looking drowsy. If indoors, wrap the victim in a blanket (right) and give them a warm drink and some chocolate. Outdoors, hypothermia can be caused by exposure, wet or windy conditions, illness, and alcohol. Wrap the victim in a blanket or something warm, and try to get him or her somewhere warmer.

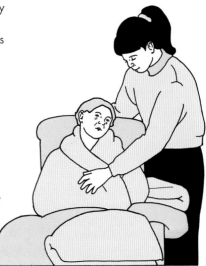

FIRE SAFETY

FIRES ARE ALWAYS potentially dangerous situations. A small fire can often spread quickly and become a major inferno, causing property damage, injury, and even death. Never put yourself in danger when trying to extinguish a fire or help a victim. If you cannot put a fire out quickly, you must leave the area as fast as possible and then telephone the emergency services, giving as much information as you can.

Fires can start for a variety of different reasons, including faulty electrical appliances, sparks from fires, and cooking accidents. All fires need three basic components: **ignition** (such as a spark); **fuel** (such as gasoline, fabric, wood, or paper); and **oxygen** (present in the air). Every year about 2.5 million fires are reported to fire departments in the United States. It is important to know how to prevent fires, how to avoid danger if there is a fire, how to help a victim, and how to get the emergency services.

Local fire departments inspect public buildings regularly to check for fire hazards, and firefighters give demonstrations at schools to teach about fire dangers. Your school will rehearse what to do in case of fire by holding fire drills. Make sure you know the fire drill, the exits you should leave the buildings by and the assembly points, and listen to any special instructions you are given.

General Fire Safety
Many fires are avoidable if a few safety rules are followed:

Fire Extinguishers
There are several different types of fire extinguishers available, and each is designed to be used on a particular sort of fire. Carbon dioxide extinguishers (1) are for use only on fires involving flammable liquids or gases and electricity. Dry powder extinguishers (2) are for general purpose use. They smother flames. Soda-acid extinguishers (3) squirt water onto fires involving materials such as wood and paper. They must not be used on electrical fires. The fire triangle (left) shows the three components necessary for a fire to start. Fire extinguishers attack one or more of these components, putting the fire out.

• Never play with fire or matches.
• Always keep a guard around an open-hearth fire, and make sure it is safe to leave unattended.
• Make sure nothing is so close to a fire that it could ignite.
• Do not stand too close to bonfires or fireworks.
• Avoid hot fat catching fire in the kitchen.

• Do not use faulty electrical appliances.

If There Is a Fire
If a fire alarm sounds at school or in a public place you should observe the fire drill and leave the area immediately. In public places follow signs for fire exits if you hear fire alarms. Do not use elevators or escalators; use

Smoke and Fumes

If you become trapped in a burning building, find a room with a window and close the door. Place a blanket or coat against the bottom of the door to stop the smoke from entering. Open the window and call for help (below). If you go through a smoke-filled room to escape, keep low to the floor since there is more oxygen, and it is also cooler at ground level.

Fire-safe House

Many homes now also have fire-prevention devices built in (below).

stairs. If a fire occurs at other times and you cannot put it out easily, you should again leave the area immediately and call the emergency services (see pages 196–197). *Never put yourself at risk when trying to put out a fire*. If you have to leave a building, alert everyone else in the building first, if safe to do so. Close all doors behind you. Look for fire exits and meeting points; wait in this area until it is safe for you to leave.

Dealing with Fire

If the fire is small, it may be possible for you to extinguish it. Fires involving wood, such as campfires and bonfires, can be put out using plenty of water. Never pour water onto an electrical fire—use a fire extinguisher designed for the purpose. Fires involving hot oil, such as a burning frying pan, can be put out using a fireproof blanket or a towel drenched in water.

Turn off any cooking appliances before putting out the fire.

In a confined space a fire will use up oxygen as it burns. Never enter a smoke-filled building or open a door leading to a fire or smoke, since there may not be sufficient oxygen to breathe. There may also be dangerous fumes from burning materials.

Helping Fire Victims

If someone has been overcome by smoke or fumes, try to get him or her into fresh air so that breathing becomes easier. It may be possible for you to douse them or their clothes with cold water if they are smouldering or burning. Lay the victim down with the burns uppermost before you do this. Minor burns can be treated by following the advice given on page 203.

If you know how, use the technique described on page 201 to restore breathing if necessary. As soon as you can, get help by calling the emergency services.

Flame-proof fabrics
Do not ignite when in contact with fire

Sprinkler
Automatically squirts water onto a fire once it has started

Fire alarm
Alerts the fire-fighting services

Smoke detector
Emits a piercing alarm to alert you

Fire-proof doors
Close automatically and prevent fire from spreading

Fire escape
Allows you to leave safely

Fire extinguisher
Fights fires

BREATHING PROBLEMS

WHEN WE BREATHE through either our nose or mouth, air enters our windpipe and travels down to the lungs. This happens automatically, so we do not have to think about it. Problems arise when something obstructs the airway, and we are unable to take in air. The body will try automatically to remove the obstruction by coughing. Sometimes, however, we need help to clear the obstruction.

Breathing problems can be caused by a number of things. There may be an object—such as candy—stuck in a person's throat that is blocking the airway and causing the victim to choke. Breathing difficulties may also be caused by panic attacks (see *The Mind and Psychology*, page 117) or asthma (see page 201 and *Health and Illness*, page 161).

Breathing problems can be very serious, so get help immediately if someone is showing any of the signs listed in the checklist below or is unconscious.

checklist

Look out for the following signs of someone with breathing problems:

- **Victim has difficulty speaking and breathing.**
- **Victim may be grasping at his or her neck.**
- **Victim's skin may be a blue-gray color due to a lack of oxygen.**
- **Victim may point at his or her throat to indicate problem.**

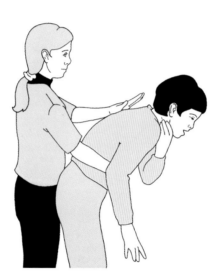

Choking

Choking requires quick action, since the victim may collapse and stop breathing. Choking in adults is usually caused by food that has not been chewed or swallowed correctly, although fluids can sometimes cause choking as well.

A child can choke very easily, and care should be taken to make sure that small children do not put objects in their mouths that could block the airway. For the same reason it is also important that children do not have food in their mouths when running and playing.

Choking Child

If someone seems to be choking get him or her to bend forward as shown (above left), and then give five sharp slaps between the shoulder blades with your open hand while asking the victim to cough. If this treatment fails to remove the object, make a fist with one of your hands and hold it against the victim's abdomen just below the ribs as shown above. Now hold the fist with your other hand. Press into the victim's abdomen and pull up sharply four or five times to remove the object. The victim must then go to see a doctor or go to hospital to be checked out.

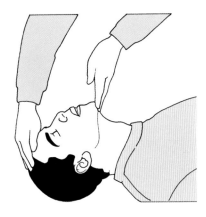

Opening the Airway

Help the victim by lifting his or her chin and tilting the head, which pulls the tongue away from the throat and opens the airway (above). Kneel beside the person about level with his or her shoulder. Place two fingers under the point of the chin with one hand, and place the other hand on their forehead. Gently tilt the head back (above). If you think the victim has hurt his or her neck, you must handle the head very carefully.

Hyperventilation

If someone becomes anxious or has a panic attack, they may start breathing too fast and too deeply. This increases the oxygen in the circulatory system and can cause dizziness, fainting, trembling, and cramps. You can help restore normal breathing for the victim by taking him or her to a quiet place and asking them to breath into, and out of, a paper bag. This lets the victim breathe air that he or she has just breathed out, which has less oxygen in it.

Asthma

This condition is becoming increasingly common in young people. It makes the muscles in the air passages contract, reducing the airway and making it difficult to breathe. Asthma attacks can be triggered by dust, pollen, food allergies, tablets, smoke, or animals.

Asthma victims usually

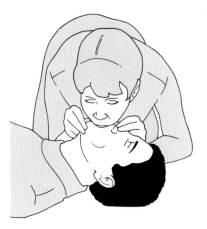

Mouth-to-mouth Resuscitation

This is how this life-saving technique is done (above). After the airway is opened, the soft part of the victim's nose is pinched closed. Then the first-aider takes a deep breath, places his or her lips over the victim's mouth, and blows for two seconds. The victim's chest is allowed to fall for four seconds before the sequence is repeated. If a pulse is felt, mouth-to-mouth resuscitation is continued at a rate of ten breaths per minute. Then the pulse is checked again. At this stage the paramedics will be called for. If there is no pulse, the paramedics will use other procedures to get the victim to begin breathing.

control the condition with their own medication. Keep the person calm and comfortable. Help him or her take the medication and encourage the victim to breath deeply and slowly. This should ease the breathing after about five minutes. If it is the person's first attack, he or she gets worse, or the medication has no effect, call for medical help.

Recovery Position

Open and check the airway. If you can see anything stuck in the throat, try to carefully remove it. Check the victim's pockets and remove any fragile or bulky objects. Now carefully turn the victim onto his or her side to lie as shown below. The foot of one leg should be level with the knee of the other leg. Notice how the hand on the same side as the bent leg is placed under the victim's cheek. Once the victim is in this position, tilt the head back slightly to open the airway again.

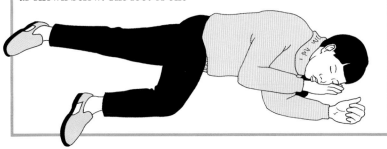

CUTS, SCRAPES, SCALDS, AND BURNS

THERE ARE SOME common injuries that most of us get from time to time. Fortunately, most of them are not serious, and the advice here will help ease the condition. More serious wounds, or pains that persist, should be checked out by a doctor as soon as possible.

When the skin is broken because of a wound, blood is lost from the body. This is known as external bleeding. If the skin does not get broken but blood is still lost from vessels, it is known as internal bleeding.

Nosebleeds

Nosebleeds can be caused by blood vessels in the nose being ruptured, usually by a blow or as a result of high blood pressure.

Nosebleeds

Get the victim to sit down and lean forward so that the blood is not swallowed. Ask the victim to pinch the soft part of his or her nose, which will help the blood clot. After ten minutes, release the pressure from the nose. If bleeding starts again, apply pressure for a further ten minutes.

Mouth Bleeds

Bleeding from the mouth can result from a cut to the tongue, lips, or lining of the mouth, which can be caused by the victim's own teeth or a blow to the mouth. As with nosebleeds, get the victim to sit down and lean forward so that the blood drains from the mouth. Place a pad over the wound, and press for ten minutes.

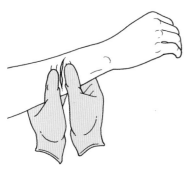

Severe Bleeding

Squeeze the wound edges together to minimize the blood loss (above). Place the limb higher than the heart to also reduce the blood loss. Place a pad lightly over the wound and secure in place with a bandage. Get the victim to a hospital as soon as possible.

To stop a nosebleed, apply the technique described above. When the nosebleed has stopped, tell the victim not to pick, blow, or squeeze their nose for 24 hours.

Mouth Bleeds

Bleeding from the mouth can result from a cut to the tongue, lips, or the lining of the mouth. These can be caused by the person's own teeth, a blow to the mouth, or something sharp being put in the mouth.

Head Wounds

Head wounds are very serious, since the brain can become damaged. The skin may also tear, causing a wound and loss of blood. The victim must go to hospital for treatment.

Embedded Objects

An embedded object can result from an accident in the home or garden. It can include pieces of glass (from falling into a door), sharp twigs and branches, or even tools in the garden.

Cooling a Burn

As soon as possible, cool the burn with cold running water for at least ten minutes (above). This will stop the burn extending through the body and will ease the pain. Try to lay the victim down and raise his or her legs to minimize the shock.

Do not try to remove the object, but seek medical help as soon as possible.

Severe Bleeding

Wounds to the trunk (chest), abdomen (below the chest), or legs can cause serious bleeding since they are large areas with a rich blood supply. Follow the instructions on page 202 to deal with severe bleeding, and also call for help.

Burns

When someone has been burned, try to find out what caused it. You may need to tell the hospital so that they can give the correct treatment.

If the victim's airway has been affected, it may cause breathing difficulties. If this is the case, a first-aider may need to give mouth-to-mouth resuscitation (see page 201).

Types of Burn

A **superficial burn** is the least serious burn. It usually affects only the outermost skin area.

A **partial-thickness burn** usually causes blisters when it burns the skin.

A **full-thickness burn** is the most severe type. It burns the underlying nerve, fat, and muscle tissues.

How Burns and Scalds Are Caused

• Scald—hot liquids, fat, and steam.
• Dry burn—cigarettes and rope burns.
• Electrical burn—low- or high-voltage currents, power cables, and lightning strikes.
• Cold burn—liquid oxygen or nitrogen and frostbite.
• Chemical burn—paint stripper, bleach, acid, and alkali.
• Radiation burn—X-rays and sunshine.

checklist

• Do not place yourself in danger when helping a burn victim.
• Do not remove any sticking clothing since this will remove the skin as well.
• Do not touch the affected area with your hands.
• Do not break blisters.
• Do not apply creams or lotions to the burned area since they will have to be removed at a hospital.

Treating Burns and Scalds

All treatment for burns and scalds by the first-aider is aimed at stopping the burning, reducing infection, and relieving pain. The most effective treatment for the first-aider is to quickly cool the burn with plenty of cold water (see above), dress the burn if necessary, and get the victim to a hospital for further treatment.

Improvised Bandages

If you do not have a first-aid kit available, you can make an improvised bandage (1–3, right). Do not use fluffy materials, but use items such as pillowcases, scarves, and dish towels. Your aim is to stop the bleeding; when the injured person gets to a hospital, all dressings will be removed so that the wound can be treated.

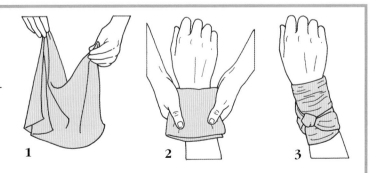

1   2   3

MUSCLE AND BONE INJURIES

MUSCLE INJURIES CAN range from sprains and pulls to more serious tearing of the tissues. Ligaments and tendons can also get sprained or torn. Bone injuries normally result in a breakage, or fracture, that may require surgery in order to help reset the bone.

Muscles are attached to bones by tendons. The joints are supported by sheaths of connective tissue called ligaments (see *Body Systems*, pages 10–11). Because muscles and bones are connected, an injury to one can sometimes cause an injury to the other.

Sprains

A sprain is an injury to the ligament (the tissue that supports bones around joints) caused by a sudden wrenching movement at the joint. It can be caused, for example, when the ankle is twisted by landing awk-wardly (see *Health and Illness*, page 167). The ligament is often torn in such an injury.

Tendons (as well as the muscles themselves) can also be torn, causing internal bleeding.

Strains

A strain can occur when the muscle is overstretched. It can again cause internal bleeding. This injury is commonly caused when you exercise while your muscles are cold—for example, if you sprint hard before warming up first.

The treatment for sprains and strains is the same. The injured part is placed in a position that is comfortable for the person. A cold compress—a towel soaked in cold water and then wrung out—or an ice pack (crushed

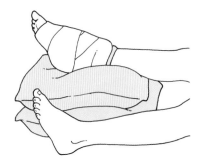

Sprains and Strains

The victim's limb is raised to reduce swelling, using either an item of furniture or the first-aider's knee for support. The affected area is cooled with an ice pack (a pack of frozen vegetables makes a useful emergency ice pack) for ten minutes and then removed. The area is then surrounded with soft padding and secured with a bandage (above). The limb is kept raised while a doctor checks out the injury.

Broken Bones

If someone has an open fracture, a first-aider will cover the wound with a dressing and apply gentle pressure to help prevent bleeding (left). If the victim has a closed fracture, the limb will be held still to stop further injury. In both cases the person should be taken to a hospital quickly.

ice wrapped in a cloth) is placed over the injured area, and the injured limb is raised. This will reduce bruising and swelling and ease the pain. If the sprain or strain is severe, the casualty must go to a hospital. If it is a minor injury, the victim will be advised to rest and to see their doctor (see also *Health and Illness*, page 167).

Broken Bones

Even though bones are tough and resilient, they can be fractured (broken) by a heavy blow or dislocated (pulled from their sockets) by a violent twist. If the bone breaks through the skin, it is called an open, or compound, fracture. If the skin remains intact, it is called a closed fracture (see *Health and Illness,* page 166).

If you think someone has a broken limb, do not move the victim or the broken limb unnecessarily, since this may cause further injury and may be very painful. Steady and support the injured limb with either your hand or, if the broken limb is an arm, by placing it in a sling (see right). This will help protect it and keep it still. Get help as soon as possible.

Dressings and Bandages

Dressings are prepacked, sterile materials that are placed onto wounds such as cuts and scrapes (see pages 202–203) to help prevent blood loss and to keep the wound free from infection. They consist of a piece of gauze attached to a bandage and are available in many sizes. Wherever possible, a dressing is used to cover a wound in order to prevent infection and reduce blood loss.

The main purpose of a bandage is to hold a dressing in place. It can also be used to control bleeding and to help reduce swelling.

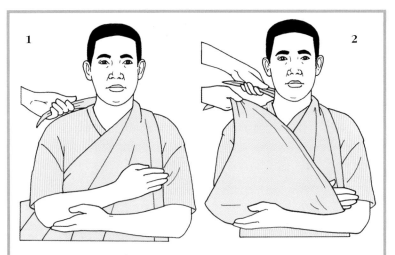

Putting on a Sling

The victim's injured arm is placed across his or her chest in the most comfortable position, and it is supported with the other hand. One end of a large bandage is slid underneath the injured arm and opened out;

the top end is brought over the shoulder (1). The lower end of the bandage is brought up and over the shoulder and tied with a reef knot on the injured side (2). Both ends of the bandage are tucked under the knot.

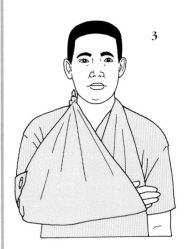

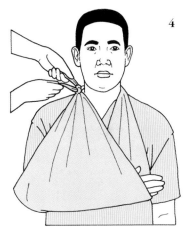

The part of the bandage near the elbow should be pinned to the front using a safety pin (3). This will secure the elbow in place and acts as a corner for the sling. If the first aider does not have a safety pin, the flap can be tucked

into the corner of the sling. The circulation should be checked regularly. If necessary, the sling should be undone and tied in a more comfortable position (4). The arm should not be moved around too much while doing this.

BITES AND STINGS

INSECTS AND OTHER animals do not usually attack unless provoked, injured, or placed in a situation that frightens them—such as being cornered or accidentally stepped on. Most of the time they try to avoid humans if they can. Bites and stings often occur when we are on vacation or when out in the countryside, but in some areas snakes and spiders in particular can be found in the home.

Most animal stings cause discomfort, but they can often be treated with simple first aid. Animal bites are usually more serious, however, and may carry with them the added danger of infections entering the body.

Rattlesnake

Adder

Snake Bites

There are many poisonous snakes in the warmer parts of the world. The United States has several dangerous species— such as the rattlesnake, the harlequin coral snake, and the water moccasin—and you must be extra careful when entering

fact file

The world's most poisonous creature is the box jelly—a kind of jellyfish. The box jelly lives in the waters off the coast of Australia.

The rattlesnake rattles the scales on the end of its tail as a warning to keep away.

A bee can sting only once; a wasp can sting many times.

an area where they might live. Most snake bites occur because someone has frightened a snake or accidentally stepped on it. If you see a snake, just leave it undisturbed and move away.

If someone has been bitten, try to reassure the victim and keep him or her calm while you get help. An overexcited victim's heart rate will speed up, circulating the poison more quickly.

Other Animal Bites

If an animal bites, the teeth can cause deep puncture wounds that will carry germs into the body. This can cause a reaction

Snake Bites

Try to reassure the victim and keep him or her calm. Lay the victim down so that the bite area is lower than the heart—this will prevent the poison from circulating so quickly. Get help as soon as possible. Two poisonous snakes that are sometimes encountered are shown left.

known as anaphylactic shock.

Anaphylactic shock is a condition in which the victim suffers a major allergic reaction to a poison. Their blood pressure will fall, and breathing will become difficult. The skin will appear to be red and blotchy, and the neck and face may swell. A person showing these symptoms must be taken to a hospital quickly, so you should get help as soon as possible.

Insect Stings

When wasps, bees, and hornets sting, the affected area will become painful, red, and swollen. It is rarely dangerous, but anaphylactic shock may develop (see above), which is very serious. If the person has

Spider Bites

Some spiders, such as the black widow (right), are extremely poisonous. If someone has been bitten by a spider, follow the instructions opposite for treating snake bites.

Marine Animal Stings

If someone has been stung by a poisonous fish, jellyfish, or Portuguese man-of-war (left), sit them down, reassure them, and wash the affected area with vinegar, if available, or with sea water. This will help reduce the effect of the venom. Cases of severe stinging should be treated by a doctor.

suffered multiple stings, the throat and airway may become swollen, and help must be sought as soon as possible.

The stings of other animals—such as some scorpions—may be more serious because the poison is very strong, and medical help should be sought if someone is stung.

Marine Animal Stings

Marine animals such as the Portuguese man-of-war, sea anemones, and jellyfish pass on their venom through stinging cells on their tentacles. If you see jellyfish or similar creatures floating in the sea, get out of the water. Wear something on your feet when wading in rock pools to avoid being stung by sea anemones.

First Aid for Bites

Bleeding wounds are usually first cleaned and covered with a dressing that is secured in place with a bandage (below). If you are bitten by an animal, such as a dog, you should go to a hospital for a tetanus injection in order to prevent a blood infection.

Treating Stings

If the sting is still in the wound, try to wash it away with water. Someone may be able to remove the sting by grasping it with tweezers just below the poison sac (see detail) and then carefully pulling it out.

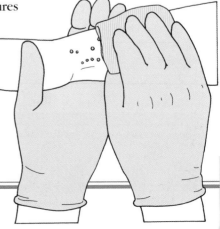

MISCELLANEOUS AILMENTS

THERE ARE SOME minor conditions that many of us suffer from occasionally. It is usually a straightforward matter to ease the discomfort of these common aches and pains. Medical help should always be sought if any ailments continue to cause pain.

Miscellaneous ailments describe the various conditions that many of us suffer from occasionally. Often these conditions can develop quickly and can be unpleasant, although many may be prevented from becoming worse if treated quickly. These are the most common ones.

Toothache

Most people can tolerate a mild toothache, but sometimes a tooth can be very painful. This can be caused by a decaying tooth or an infection in the gums. The condition can be made worse by either hot or cold drinks, eating food, or brushing your teeth too hard.

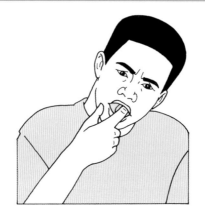

Toothache

To ease the pain of a toothache, place a warm hot-water bottle, wrapped in a towel, on the victim's face. Place the person in the position most comfortable for him or her. As soon as possible, arrange an appointment to see a dentist. Holding a piece of absorbent cotton soaked in clove oil against the tooth (left) may help.

Cramps

This condition is often very painful and is caused by the muscles going suddenly into

Cramps

To relieve bouts of cramps, gently massage the area and slowly stretch the muscle after each spasm has passed. Repeat until the cramp has disappeared. For foot cramps, first get the victim to put his or her weight on the front of the foot until the spasm has passed.

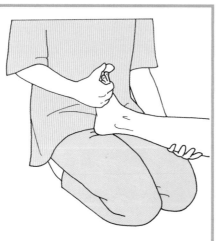

fact file

Our normal body temperature is 98.6°F (37°C). Certain conditions, such as earache, may cause a rise in body temperature. Call a doctor if it rises above 104°F (40°C).

Some conditions, such as headaches, can be symptoms of more serious illnesses such as influenza, poisoning, or meningitis.

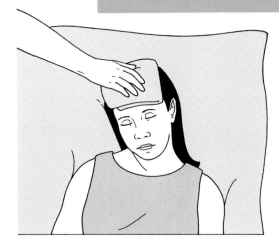

Earache

If the pain is severe, the victim should see a doctor as soon as possible. If the pain is mild, place the person in a comfortable position. Ease the pain by placing a warm hot-water bottle, wrapped in a towel, on his or her ear (above). If the pain persists, call a doctor.

Headache

Help the victim to sit or lie down in a quiet room with no loud distractions, and apply a cold compress (above). If possible, keep lighting low, and make sure the person has plenty of fresh air. If the pain does not go away, seek medical advice as soon as possible.

a spasm (in other words, they contract involuntarily). This may occur when the person is asleep, but can happen after exercise when salt and fluids are lost through sweating.

Earache

Earache can be caused by colds, influenza, an infection such as a boil, or by something in the ear. The condition can cause partial or total hearing loss.

Headache

Headaches can be caused by colds, stuffy or smoke-filled atmospheres, stress, tiredness, alcohol, or drugs. Headaches also sometimes occur as a result of something more serious, such as a head injury. If the victim has had a fall or a blow to the head, he or she should see a doctor as soon as possible.

There are other conditions that will need medical help immediately. They are when the pain is severe, when it occurred quickly and for no reason, when the person also suffers a stiff neck, or when the person suffers from loss of feeling to a limb or even unconsciousness.

Hiccups

The easiest way to cure a bout of hiccups is to get the victim to place a paper bag over the nose and mouth and ask him or her to breath normally (right). This will result in the person breathing in air that has just been breathed out, which will contain higher carbon dioxide levels than fresh air.

Hiccups

This is caused by the diaphragm (the sheet of muscle above the abdomen) going into a spasm. This causes the windpipe to partially close, causing the repeated hiccups. The problem usually lasts only a few minutes.

GLOSSARY

Abdomen The part of the body between the diaphragm and the pelvis. It contains the digestive organs.

Absorption The uptake of a fluid or gas by a cell across the cell membrane.

Accident An unexpected or unplanned event that may result in damage or harm.

Accommodation The process by which the eye lens changes shape to focus images sharply on the retina.

Acupuncture An ancient medical treatment that involves inserting needles into the body at specific points.

Adenosine triphosphate (ATP) The energy-carrying molecule present in all cells. It is formed by the breakdown of glucose molecules during respiration.

Adolescence The period of life between puberty and early adulthood during which a person experiences physical, emotional, and cognitive changes. It usually starts between the ages of 12 and 14 and goes on until the early 20s.

Aggression Outward physical violence toward people or property; the severity of the violence can be measured by the amount of destruction or by the intention behind it.

Alphabet A collection of written symbols—for example, letters—that can be variously arranged to form all the words of a language.

Amino acid An organic, water-soluble molecule. Amino acids combine to form proteins.

Amphetamine A type of drug that is sometimes used as a stimulant.

Amygdaloid body One of the parts of the brain that controls basic body functions to aid survival.

Anaphylactic shock A dangerous condition in which the victim suffers a major allergic reaction to a substance; it can be triggered by certain drugs, poisons, or foods. Symptoms include a drop in blood pressure, a blotchy skin, and difficulty in breathing.

Anxiety An unpleasant feeling of apprehension that can vary in intensity from uneasiness to dread.

Anxiety reaction An instinctive reaction in response to anger or fear that physically arouses the body, preparing it for action.

Arousal The physical state of our body when it is ready for action.

Artery A thick-walled, muscular blood vessel carrying blood from the heart to other parts of the body.

Assumption Something that is taken as fact before it is proven to be true or false.

Asthma A narrowing of the breathing tubes, or bronchi, in the lungs, causing wheezing, coughs, and shortness of breath.

Attachment A long-lasting bond of affection between two people—for example, between a parent and a child—as a result of intensive interaction over a period of time.

Axon The long, threadlike part of a nerve cell that carries impulses to other cells.

Barbiturate A chemical compound that, under medical supervision, can be used for sedation or to encourage sleep.

Behavior The actions that we carry out. Behavior can be learned through practice, like riding a bicycle, or can be instinctive, like running from danger.

Bereavement process A series of stages that everyone passes through in order to come to terms with a loss; also known as the grieving process.

Birth control The prevention of pregnancy by various means.

Bite A cut, puncture, or wound to the body caused by the teeth or jaws of another animal.

Blind spot The part of the retina at the end of the optic nerve that contains no light-sensitive cells.

Blood pressure The pressure exerted by blood pushing against the walls of vessels. Blood pressure is determined by rate and force of heart beats.

Body clock The internal biological mechanisms that control and regulate the natural cycles and changes within the body.

Body language The gestures and movements of the body by which a person communicates nonverbally to others.

Bond A strong emotional attachment to someone or something.

Brain stem The lower portion of the brain; responsible for controlling activities such as breathing and digestion.

Brain The large mass of interconnected nerve cells located in the skull that controls the body's systems and enables us to have conscious thought.

Brain wave The electrical activity of the brain cells, which can be shown as a pattern of waves.

Bronchus Either of the two branches of the windpipe leading into the lungs.

Bullying The act of an individual or group physically, verbally, or emotionally abusing another.

Burn An injury to the tissues in a part of the body, such as the skin or muscles, caused by heat, extreme cold, or by coming into contact with certain chemicals.

Canister A sealed container— usually a type of drum or can— containing a substance.

Capillary One of the minute blood vessels linking the arterial blood system to the venous blood system.

Carbohydrate An important energy-providing food substance. Sugars such as glucose are carbohydrates.

Caregiver An individual who makes a significant contribution toward the care of a child.

Cartilage A type of smooth connective tissue covering the ends of most bones.

Caudate nucleus A group of brain cells that assists in the control of body movements.

Cell The basic functional and structural unit of the body.

Central traits The main features, or characteristics, of a person's personality.

Centriole One of the paired, cylinder-shaped structures in a cell that assist in cell division.

Cerebellum The part of the brain that coordinates muscular movements.

Cerebral hemisphere One of the two halves of the cerebrum.

Cerebrum The largest part of the brain; responsible for our thoughts and conscious actions.

Choking A potentially serious condition in which the wind-pipe is blocked—for example, by food— and the victim coughs violently to try to clear the obstruction.

Chromosome One of the threadlike structures containing DNA that is present in the nucleus of all cells. Sperm and egg cells have 23 chromosomes each; all other cells have 46 chromosomes.

Classical learning Learning that occurs without the use of rewards to reinforce the activity.

Cochlea The coiled structure in the inner ear that turns sound waves into nerve impulses that are then carried to the brain.

Cognitive development The development of intellectual knowledge and reasoning skills.

Color vision The ability to recognize different wavelengths of visible light and to combine them to produce colored images.

Conception Fertilization; the start of pregnancy.

Cone One of the light-sensitive receptor cells in the retina responsible for color vision.

Conscious mind (in Freud's theory) The part of our mind that contains the things of which we are aware.

Contact sport Any sport that involves physical contact with one or more opponents.

Convalescence The period of recovery following ill health.

Cornea The transparent part of the sclera at the front of the eyeball.

Corrosive substance A chemical that can cause burning when in contact with the body; corrosive chemicals include some acids and alkalis.

Cortex The highly folded outer part of the cerebrum.

Cranial bone Any one of the bones that make up the skull.

Cultural norms The unwritten rules and values of a society that determine which types of behavior are acceptable, and which are unacceptable.

Cytoplasm All the organelles and their surrounding fluid in a cell, apart from the nucleus.

Defense mechanism An alternative way of thinking about things in order to protect ourselves from unpleasant emotions or thoughts that would damage our self-esteem.

Depressant A substance that lowers the level of one or more of the body's activities.

Depression A lasting mood of deep sadness; it is often accompanied by feelings of worthlessness and hopelessness.

Detergent A substance used for cleaning purposes; some detergents can be poisonous.

Development The sequence of changes over the full life span of an individual.

Developmental stage Any period of development during which certain characteristic patterns of behavior appear.

Dialect The form of language spoken in a particular part of a country.

Digestion The process of breaking down food into molecules small enough to be absorbed by cells.

Disappointment Distress resulting from being unable to fulfill one's expectations or desires.

Discomfort An unpleasant feeling or mild pain.

DNA (deoxyribonucleic acid) A large molecule containing, in a chemically coded form, all the information needed to build and maintain a living organism. DNA is organized into chromosomes.

Drug When given under medical supervision, a drug is a chemical substance used for preventing or curing a disease or illness. Some drugs are used illegally to produce feelings such as relaxation or excitement in the user.

Duodenum The first part of the small intestine.

Ear The organ responsible for hearing; consisting of the outer ear, the middle ear, and the inner ear.

Eardrum The sheet of tissue at the inner end of the auditory canal that vibrates in response to sound waves; also called the tympanum.

Early childhood The period of childhood from birth until the age of around six.

Ego (in Freud's theory) The realistic part of our personality that prompts us to behave in socially acceptable ways.

Embedded object A foreign object that is fixed firmly in the body and either protruding out from it or projecting into it.

Embryo The early stage of a baby from fertilization to the eighth week of pregnancy.

Emergency A dangerous situation that requires sudden and urgent action.

Emotion An experience of an intense feeling. Emotions result from the physical sensations we have in reaction to a person or an event.

Emotional development The process of understanding one's own, and other people's, emotions.

Empathy Sharing of an emotional experience with another person.

Environment The place in which we live; our physical and social surroundings.

Envy A desire for things possessed by others.

Enzyme A chemical substance in the body that helps speed up the rate of a process, such as digestion.

Epidermis The outer layer of the skin, composed of stratified epithelial cells.

Exhaustion The condition in which a person is lacking completely in mental or physical energy.

Extended family Relatives who are not part of the nuclear family (the parents and their children).

Extinguish To put out (for example, a fire).

Extroversion The display of outgoing, attention-seeking, or sociable behavior by a person.

Eye The organ responsible for vision.

Facial expression The movements of the face, such as smiling or frowning, that show how one feels.

Fallopian tube One of the two tubes along which eggs pass from an ovary to the uterus.

Fat An important energy-providing food substance.

Fertilization The fusion of a sperm and an egg, following sexual intercourse.

Fetus A developing baby from the eighth week until birth. Before the eighth week, it is an embryo.

First aid The act of giving immediate medical assistance to a victim before the arrival of a doctor or other qualified persons.

Flammable substance One that is easily set on fire.

Fovea The part of the macula (in the retina) that has the greatest concentration of cones.

Frontal lobe Part of the cerebrum, at the front of the brain, concerned with thinking and reasoning.

Gasping Taking short, sudden breaths; the condition is often caused by physical or mental shock.

Gender stereotyping The belief that someone will think or behave in a certain way because of their sex.

Gender The sex of a person: male or female.

Gene A segment of DNA that carries the instructions for producing a particular feature.

Genetic code A chemical code that instructs a cell to make proteins in a particular way.

Genetic modification The artificial alteration of the genes (the inherited units that determine the nature of all living things).

Gesticulate To make expressive movements with the hands and arms.

Gesture A movement or an action that helps show what is meant or felt.

Glucose A sugar that is the major energy source for all cells.

Goal Something that we are trying to achieve; an aim.

Grammar The set of rules that determines the way words are used in a particular language.

Gray matter The regions of the brain and spinal cord that are made of neuron cell bodies.

Grief An intense emotion associated with the loss of someone with whom a deep emotional bond has been established.

Grieving process A series of stages that everyone passes through in order to come to terms with a loss.

Group behavior The way in which individuals behave when part of a group.

Gun cabinet A strong, securely locked cabinet used for the safe storage of weapons and ammunition.

Hallucinogen A chemical or drug that causes illusions in the mind.

Halo effect The assumption that someone with one or two positive or negative characteristics also has other positive or negative characteristics.

Hazardous substance Any substance that is harmful if it comes into contact with the body.

Heat exhaustion A condition caused by the body losing too much water.

Heatstroke A condition caused by overexposure to high temperatures.

Hemoglobin The oxygen-carrying substance found in red blood cells.

Hierarchy Any system that ranks objects, events, people, or concepts in a graded order—for example, in order of importance.

Hormone A chemical secreted by an endocrine gland that helps control the way the body works.

Hyperventilation A condition in which the victim breathes at a quick and very deep rate, causing too much oxygen to enter the body.

Hypothalamus A small structure at the base of the brain that controls the pituitary gland.

Hypothermia A condition in which the body temperature drops to a dangerously low level, and the victim becomes very cold.

Id (in Freud's theory) The selfish part of our personality, driven by unconscious instincts demanding immediate satisfaction.

Ideal self An idea about how we would like to be, which we aim to achieve.

Impression management The presentation of a particular image of a person in order to influence the impression others have of that person.

Incus One of the three tiny bones of the middle ear.

Individuality The characteristics that make each person unique. A display of strength of character.

Infection An invasion of the body by foreign organisms such as bacteria or viruses, causing disease or illness.

Inflexion A change in the form of a word—for example, from present to past tense—in order to alter its meaning.

Inhalation The act of breathing in, or inhaling.

Instinct An unlearned piece of behavior that aids survival.

Intelligence A combination of human mental abilities including thinking, reasoning, understanding, and memory, together with the speed they can be carried out.

Intelligence test A psychological test designed to measure a person's intelligence.

Interaction The action or behavior of a person in a social situation that results in a response or change of behavior in another person.

Intermingling The mixing together of objects.

Internalization The process whereby what we learn from our family and the society we live in becomes a part of what we are.

Introversion The display of withdrawn, avoiding behavior by a person.

IQ (intelligence quotient) A way of expressing a person's intelligence in certain tests.

Iris The pigmented (colored), muscular diaphragm that controls the amount of light entering the eye.

Jealousy A feeling of envy or resentment against an individual or group.

Language Communication in which people use sounds, gestures, signs, and symbols in a uniform manner to express their thoughts and feelings to others.

Larynx The structure at the top of the trachea that contains the vocal cords; also called the voice box.

Late childhood The period of childhood from the age of around 11 until the age of around 16.

Lateral thinking Thinking about a problem in unusual or unconventional ways.

Learned helplessness The condition in which a person feels unable to escape unpleasant situations and so does not try.

Learning The acquisition of knowledge or a skill through experience or instruction.

Lens The transparent structure in the eye, behind the iris, that changes shape to focus light rays onto the retina.

Ligament Fibrous tissue that supports bones, especially at joints.

Literacy The ability to read and write.

Long-term memory The part of the memory that remembers events for long periods of time.

Lymphatic system A network of vessels and glandular swellings (lymph nodes) containing white blood cells, which help fight infection by foreign agents.

Macula The central part of the retina.

Malleus One of the three tiny bones of the middle ear.

Marker buoy An anchored float that is used to give information to vessels traveling on water; for example, warning of submerged rocks or dangerous currents.

Medicine Any substance that is used to treat a disease or cure an illness. Many medicines can be dangerous if they are used incorrectly.

Melanin A dark coloring present in skin and hair.

Memory The ability of the brain to store experiences of past events and to then recall (remember) them.

Meninges The three protective membranes (layers of tissue) around the brain and spinal cord.

Meningitis An infection of the meninges—the membranes that surround the brain and spinal cord—leading to a high fever and neck stiffness.

Metabolism The body's combined physical and chemical processes.

Midbrain A part of the brain stem containing nerve fibers mainly involved with muscular movements.

Middle childhood The period of childhood from the age of around six until the age of around 11.

Mineral One of the substances in the diet that is used as a raw material to build the body.

Mitochondrion One of the tiny organelles within cells. These sausage-shaped miniorgans are the site of energy production during cellular respiration.

Mitosis The division of a cell

nucleus to produce two identical daughter cells.

Motor neuron disease A disease of the central nervous system.

Mouth-to-mouth resuscitation A form of first-aid treatment in which the first-aider breathes into the victim's mouth or nose in order to put oxygen into the lungs.

Mugging An attack on a person with the intention to rob.

Narcotic Any of the class of drugs known as opiates that can dull the senses, relieve pain, or induce drowsiness. An overdose can lead to death.

Nature The characteristics of people that are assumed to be inherited and not learned through experience.

Nephron One of the filtering units of a kidney.

Neuron A nerve cell. Most neurons consist of a cell body with its nucleus together with short, connecting dendrites, and a long, filamentlike axon.

Nonverbal Communication not carried out by use of words; unspoken.

Nucleus The part of a cell that contains the genetic material.

Nurture The influence of our surroundings on our growth and behavior, including the things we learn through experience.

Nutrition The means by which the body gets the chemicals, in the form of food, that it needs in order to live and grow. Vitamins and minerals are important nutrients.

Occipital lobe Part of the cerebrum, at the back of the brain, concerned with vision.

Olfactory bulb A mass of gray matter at the end of the olfactory nerve.

Olfactory nerve One of the two nerves associated with the sense of smell that run from the nose to the brain.

Operant learning Learning that usually involves the use of rewards to reinforce the activity; also called instrumental learning.

Optic nerve One of the two nerves associated with vision that run from the retina to the brain.

Optical illusion A picture or object that confuses the brain by making it misinterpret the information.

Organelle A specialized structure, or miniorgan, in a living cell.

Ovary The reproductive organ in females that produces eggs.

Oviduct A fallopian tube.

Ovulation The monthly release of an egg from the ovary.

Ovum An egg cell.

Palate The roof of the mouth.

Panic attack An unexpected feeling of intense fear, accompanied by unpleasant physical symptoms.

Paramedic A professionally trained person who is qualified to give first aid and medical treatment when necessary.

Parietal lobe Part of the

cerebrum, at each side of the brain, concerned with touch, temperature, and pain.

Peer A person of the same rank or status as another person.

Peer group Any group in which members have more or less equal status. The term is most often used to describe children's or adolescent's groups.

Pelvis The structure made up of the sacrum, the coccyx, and the two hip bones (ilia); also refers to the soft body parts in that region.

Personal constructs The individual set of ideas or beliefs that we each develop to help us direct our actions.

Personality The set of features, or characteristics, that makes each person unique and likely to respond in situations in consistent ways.

Personality types The theory that there are different kinds of personality, each with particular characteristics, and that people can be grouped together according to their type of personality.

pH A measurement of the acidity or alkalinity of a solution.

Pharynx The passage from the back of the nose and mouth leading to the esophagus; the throat.

Pheromone A chemical substance secreted by many living creatures that produces a stimulus in others of the same species.

Phobia An intense fear of an object or situation from which there is no actual danger.

Pigment Natural coloring, such as that found in skin and hair.

Pituitary gland A gland underneath the brain that secretes hormones to control the activities of other glands.

Placenta The organ that attaches a developing embryo to the uterus and allows the embryo to receive nourishment from the mother.

Plasma The liquid part of blood.

Platelet A tiny cell fragment in the blood that helps it clot.

Poison Any substance that can cause illness or death.

Pollution The poisoning of the natural environment.

Preconscious (subconscious) mind The part of our mind that contains memories of thoughts and dreams temporarily forgotten, but which are easily brought into consciousness.

Preschool The period of childhood before entering formal education—usually refers to the years up to the age of about five.

Primacy effect The tendency for the first information we see or hear about someone to have the biggest effect on our overall impression of them.

Psychological Relating to the mind and the way we behave.

Psychology The scientific study of the human mind.

Puberty The beginning of sexual maturity (the ability to produce offspring). It usually comes between the ages of 10 and 14 for girls and 12 and 16 for boys.

Pulse The throbbing that can be felt in an artery as the heart contracts.

Quarry The site of an excavation in the ground, especially to extract rocks and other minerals.

Recovery position The safe position in which to place a victim who is unconscious; it maintains the airway by keeping the head low and allowing the chest to move freely.

Red blood cell A cell responsible for transporting oxygen around the body; also known as an erythrocyte.

Reflex An action that cannot be controlled by thought.

Reflexologist A person trained to treat illnesses by using massage and applying pressure to different parts of the feet.

Rehydration A form of treatment in which a victim is given sufficient water to restore body fluids after he or she has been dehydrated (has lost fluids from the body).

REM (rapid-eye-movement) sleep A period within sleep when the eyes move rapidly behind the closed eyelids.

Remembering Recalling events from the memory to the conscious mind.

Respiration The biochemical process in which food molecules are broken down to release energy in the form of ATP; also refers to the process whereby oxygen enters the bloodstream and carbon dioxide is removed.

Retina The light-sensitive layer that lines the inside of the eyeball.

Rod One of the cells in the retina that are sensitive to low levels of light.

Role Any pattern of behavior involving certain rights, obligations, and duties that an individual is expected, trained, or encouraged to perform in a social situation.

Safety The condition in which a person is free from harm or danger.

Salivary glands Small glands in the mouth that produce saliva needed for digestion.

Schemata The overall set of memories and ideas about events, objects, and people that direct our actions.

Self-actualization The fulfillment of a person's potential and abilities.

Self-awareness An awareness of one's self and what one is like.

Self-esteem A person's sense of what he or she is worth.

Self-identity The view we have of who we are.

Self-image The view we have of ourselves and what we can do.

Self-monitoring The act of consciously watching, or being aware of, our own behavior.

Self-presentation The way that we try to present a particular image of ourselves to others depending on who they are and what we think is expected of us.

Separation anxiety A fear, common among one-year-olds

especially, of separation from one's mother.

Short-term memory The part of the memory that remembers events for short periods of time.

Sibling A brother or sister.

Sibling rivalry A term used to describe the competitive and often aggressive interactions that often occur between siblings.

Sign language A system of gestures used in place of speech by those incapable of speaking or hearing for any reason and between people lacking a common spoken language.

Social development The development of the ability to interact and form relationships.

Social learning Learning by observing and imitating the actions or behavior of others.

Social pressure The pressure social groups can apply to individuals to make them behave in a particular way.

Social rules Rules we learn that determine the way we behave in different social situations.

Socialization The process whereby an individual acquires the knowledge, values, and social skills to enable him or her to become part of society.

Spasm A condition in which some of the muscles contract involuntarily for a period of time—for example, when a person suffers from cramp.

Sperm The male sex cells, produced in the testes. Sperm are carried in seminal fluid.

Spinal cord A thick bundle of nerve cells that extends from the base of the brain to the base of the back.

Spine The column of 33 bones that provides the main skeletal support; also called the vertebral column or backbone.

Stapes One of the three tiny bones of the middle ear.

Stimulant A substance that raises the level of one or more of the body's activities.

Sting A small puncture hole made in the skin by an animal such as a wasp, or a plant such as a stinging nettle, with the intention of injecting a poison into the body.

Stress A state of physical and mental tension produced by environmental pressures.

Subliminal At a level of the mind of which the senses are not aware.

Superego (in Freud's theory) The part of our personality that contains our beliefs about what is right and wrong.

Synapse The junction between two nerve cells.

Syntax The rules of grammar that determine the way in which words are put together to form phrases and sentences.

Taste bud A group of cells, mainly on the tongue, that detect flavors.

Temporal lobe Part of the cerebrum, at each side of the brain, concerned with hearing and memory storage.

Testis One of the two male sex glands producing sperm and male sex hormones. Plural: testes

Thalamus A part of the brain that acts as a relay center, passing sensory impulses to other parts of the brain.

Thorax The part of the body between the neck and the abdomen.

Tranquilizer A drug that has a calming effect on the body.

Unconscious mind (in Freud's theory) The inaccessible part of our mind that contains things that are too upsetting or worrying to allow into our conscious mind.

Ureter One of two tubes carrying urine from the kidneys to bladder.

Uterus The saclike organ in which the embryo develops.

Vein A vessel that carries blood from the body to the heart.

Venom The poisonous fluid that some animals inject into their victims by stinging or biting them.

Venomous Possessing venom.

Vertebra One of the 33 interconnecting bones that make up the spine. Plural: vertebrae.

Vitamin A vital nutrient.

Vocabulary All the words in a language or known to a particular person.

White blood cell A colorless blood cell that is part of the body's defenses and helps give immunity to disease.

White matter The regions of the brain and spinal cord that are made of nerve filaments, or axons.

MORE INFORMATION

BOOKS

Nick Arnold, *Disgusting Digestion (Horrible Science Series)*, Scholastic Hippo (Coventry, 1998).

Nick Arnold and Tony De Saulles (illustrator), *The Body Owner's Handbook (Horrible Science Series)*, Scholastic Hippo (Coventry, 2002).

Carol Ballard, *Bones / The Digestive System / Heart and Blood / Hormones / Lungs / The Reproductive System (Body Focus Series)*, HeinemannLibrary (Oxford, 2003).

Rufus Bellamy, *How We Move (Body Science Series)*, Franklin Watts (London, 2003).

F. Chandler, *First Encyclopedia of the Human Body (First Encyclopedias)*, Usborne Publishing (London, 2004).

Luann Colombo, Craig Zuckerman (illustrator), and Jennifer Fairman (illustrator), *The Human Body*, Zondervan Publishing House (Michigan, 2003).

DK Guide to the Human Body, Dorling Kindersley, (London, 2004).

Wynn Kapit, Robert I. Macey, and Esmail Meisami, *The*

Physiology Colouring Book, Longman Publishing Group (Harlow, Essex, 1997).

Andrew Langley, *My Body (Oxford First Encyclopaedia)*, Oxford University Press (Oxford, 2002).

Steve Parker, *Human Body (Q & A Encyclopedia Series)*, Miles Kelly Publishing (Great Bardfield, Essex, 2004).

Steve Parker, *Digestion (Our Bodies Series)*, Hodder Wayland (London, 2004).

Peter D. Riley, *Checkpoint Biology*, John Murray Publishers (London, 2005).

Angela Royston, *My Amazing Body: Moving/Growing/ Breathing/Eating/Senses/ Staying Healthy (Raintree Perspectives)*, HeinemannLibrary (Oxford, 2004).

Ola Schaeffer, *It's My Body: Compilation Big Book (It's My Body Series)*, Raintree (2003).

Richard Walker, *How We Breathe (Body Science Series)*, Franklin Watts (London, 2003).

Allan Wolf and Greg Clarke (illustrator), *The Blood-hungry Spleen and Other Poems About Our Parts*, Walker Books (London, 2003).

WEB SITES

Biology in Motion
biologyinmotion.com
Interactive online activities and 3-D animations on body topics such as fat digestion, the thyroid gland, and the cardiovascular system.

BodyQuest
library.thinkquest.org/10348
Take a tour of the human body, with many graphics, experiments, and a quiz for each body system.

Brain Connection
www.brainconnection.com
A site with articles, brain-building activities, animations, library, gallery, and an anatomy section.

Cells Alive
www.cellsalive.com/toc.htm
Loads of information and visuals about cells, including animations and videos, microphotographs, and illustrations of cells.

Cells R Us
www.icnet.uk/kids/cellsrus/ cellsrus.html
The Imperial Cancer Research Fund's online slide show about cells.

DNA From the Beginning
www.dnaftb.org/dnaftb
An animated primer on the basics of DNA, genes, and

heredity, from the Dolan DNA Learning Center.

DNA Interactive
www.dnai.org/index.htm
See an interactive timeline, learn how the code was cracked, and find out how the discovery of the structure of DNA changed the field of biology.

DNA: Life's Instruction Manual
www.thetech.org/hyper/ genome/overview.html
The University of California's exhibit tells you everything you need to know about DNA.

Genetic Science Learning Center
gslc.genetics.utah.edu
Build your own DNA molecule, discover what makes a firefly glow, and get the recipe for extracting DNA out of any living thing using household items.

How Cells Work
science.howstuffworks.com/ cell.htm
Text and graphics that provide a sound introduction to cell biology.

How Stuff Works (human reproduction)
www.howstuffworks.com/hum an-reproduction.htm
With text, diagrams, and links to other articles.

Kidshealth
www.kidshealth.org/kid/body/ index.html
Illustrations, music, and lessons about your body at the "My Body" section. Learn how to stay healthy.

MicroAngela Cells
www.pbrc.hawaii.edu/bemf/ microangela/cells.htm
Browse false-color photos of cells taken with a scanning electron microscope at the University of Hawaii.

Neuroscience for Kids
faculty.washington.edu/ chudler/neurok.html
An excellent and fun introduction to how the brain works.

Organ Farm
www.pbs.org/wgbh/pages/ frontline/shows/organfarm
Frontline reports on the transplantation of genetically modified pig cells and whole organs into human beings.

Pregnancy calender
pregnancy.about.com/cs/preg nancycalendar/l/blwbw.htm
Designed for pregnant moms to follow the development of their baby from week to week; with pictures and scans.

Sighting the First Sense: Seeing is Believing
library.thinkquest.org/C00146 4/cgi-bin/view.cgi

A unique resource about the eye and sight, including nteractive demonstrations.

The Geee! in Genome
nature.ca/genome
More than 200 richly illustrated and interactive pages on genes, stem cells, genetically modified organisms, cloning, and the diversity of life. By the Canadian Museum of Nature.

The Heart Online
sln.fi.edu/biosci/index.html
Explore the heart, its development and structure. Follow blood through blood vessels, and learn how to have a healthy heart.

The Virtual Body
www.medtropolis.com/ VBody.asp
Interactive, animated tour of the human body with "build-your-own" features.

The Virtual Cell
www.ibiblio.org/virtualcell/ index.htm
Use a virtual textbook, print out worksheets, or take The Virtual Cell Tour, on which you can rotate and zoom in on organelles inside cells.

Way Cool Surgery
www.waycoolsurgery.com
Videos of heart surgery, case histories, and information about medical careers and heart-disease prevention.

INDEX